VISUAL QUICKSTART GUIDE

UNIX

Deborah S. Ray and Eric J. Ray

Peachpit Press

Visual QuickStart Guide

UNIX

Deborah S. Ray and Eric J. Ray

Peachpit Press
1249 Eighth Street
Berkeley, CA 94710
(800) 283-9444
(510) 524-2178
(510) 542-2221 (fax)

Find us on the World Wide Web at: `http://www.peachpit.com`

Peachpit Press is a division of Addison Wesley Longman

Editor: Simon Hayes
Copy editor: Bill Cassel
Production coordinator: Amy Changar
Compositor: David Van Ness
Cover design: The Visual Group
Indexer: Ann Longknife/Creative Studios

ISBN: 0-201-35395-4

0 9 8 7 6

Printed and bound in the United States of America

Acknowledgments:

This book came together with the help of many talented and supportive people. A special thanks to Simon Hayes for his confidence and enthusiasm as well as his careful and thorough editing and feedback. Bill Cassel did a marvelous job copy editing, Ann Longknife provided a great index, and Amy Changar and David Van Ness did a fantastic job in production.

A final thanks to Melissa (and Molly) for being there.

Dedication

To each other, Ashleigh, and Alex.

Table of Contents

INTRODUCTION

Greetings, and welcome to UNIX! In this book, you'll find the information you need to get started with the UNIX operating system, advance your skills, and make UNIX do the hard work for you. This book focuses on the most common UNIX commands, but it also gives you ideas for working smartly and efficiently.

How do you use this book?

We designed this book to be used as both a tutorial and a reference. If you're a UNIX newbie, you should start at the beginning and work forward through the first several chapters. As you progress through the chapters, you'll build on concepts and commands you learned in previous chapters. Then, as you become more proficient, you can start picking and choosing topics, depending on what you want to do. Be sure to reference the table of contents, index, and the appendix to find information.

Each chapter covers several topics, each of which is presented in its own section. Each section begins with a brief overview of the topic, often including examples or descriptions of how or when you'd use a command.

Next, you'll find a step-by-step list (or a couple of them) to show you how to complete a process. Note that the code you type appears as the numbered step, and a description follows it, like this:

1. `The code you type will appear like`
   `→ this.`

   An explanation will appear like this. Here, we often describe what you're typing, give alternatives, or provide cross-references to related information.

If a line of code in a numbered step is particularly long, the code might wrap to a second line. Just type the characters shown, without pressing Enter until the end of the command.

Also, in code listings throughout the book, a single line of code on screen might wrap to two lines in the book. In this happens, the continued line will start with a →, so it might look like:

```
The beginning of the code is here
→ and continues on this line.
```

Sometimes you'll have to press a special key or key combination—like Ctrl C, which means to hold down the Ctrl key and press C. We'll use this special keyboard font for these keys, but not for plain letters, numbers, or symbols you might type.

Finally, most sections end with a couple of handy tips. Look here for ways to combine UNIX commands, suggestions for using commands more efficiently, or ideas for finding out more information.

Who are you?

We assume that you've picked up this book because you already have a need for or an interest in learning to use UNIX. We assume that

- You want to know how to use UNIX to do things at work, school, or home.
- You may or may not already have experience with UNIX.
- You don't necessarily have other geeky—er, um, techie—computer skills or experience.
- You want to learn to use UNIX, but probably do not want to delve into all of the arcane details about the UNIX system.

In short, we assume you want to use UNIX to achieve your computing goals. You want to know what you can do, get an idea of the potential that a command offers, and learn how to work smart. Very smart.

You can do all of these things using this book. Basically, all you need is access to a UNIX account and a goal (or goals) that you want to achieve.

What do you need to know to get started?

As you get started learning UNIX, keep in mind the following UNIX conventions for typing in commands:

- UNIX terminology and commands are typically arcane, cryptic, and funny-looking. For example, the command to list files or directories is just `ls`—short and cryptic. We'll walk you through the commands one step at a time, so you know how to read them and apply them to your own uses. Just follow the steps in the order provided.
- UNIX is case-sensitive, so type commands following the capitalization used in the book.
- Whenever you type a command, you also have to press Enter. For example, if we say:

  1. `funny-looking command goes here`

  you'll type in the code, then press Enter, which sends the command along to the UNIX system.
- Some commands have *flags* associated with them that give you additional, optional control. For example, you might see the `ls` command used in variations like `ls -la` or `ls -l -a`. In either case, `ls` lists the files in a directory, the optional `-l` flag specifies that you want the long format, and the optional `-a` flag specifies all files, including hidden ones (don't worry, we'll go over this again!). Just keep in mind that flags are essentially options you can use with a given command.
- You can also put multiple commands on the same line. All you have to do is separate the commands with a semicolon (`;`), like this:

  ```
  ls ; pwd
  ```

  which would list the files in the current directory (`ls`) and find out what directory you're in (`pwd`)—all in one step!

So, with these things in mind, see you in Chapter 1!

Anything else you should know?

Yup! Feel free to contact us at `unixvqs@raycomm.com`. We welcome your input and suggestions as well as questions related to this book. Thanks, and we look forward to hearing from you!

INTRODUCTION

GETTING STARTED WITH UNIX

1

To start you on your journey through UNIX, we'll take a quick look at a few basic concepts and commands. In this chapter, we'll get you started with basic UNIX skills, such as logging in and listing and viewing files and directories. We'll also do a bit of exploring to give you the lay of the land.

This chapter is essential for all UNIX guru-wannabes. If you're a UNIX novice, you should start at the beginning of this chapter and work through each spread in sequence. With these basic skills mastered, you can then skip through this book and learn new skills that look useful or interesting to you. If you've used UNIX before, you might peruse this chapter to review the basics and dust off any cobwebs you might have.

The skills covered in this chapter apply to any version of UNIX you might be using, from Linux or SunOS through your ISP, to AIX or HP-UX at work, to any other *flavor* (that's the technical term) you can find. Keep in mind, though, that the exact output and prompts you see on the screen might differ slightly from what is illustrated in this book. The differences probably won't affect the steps you're completing, although you should be aware that differences could exist. (As much as possible, our examples will give you a sample of the diversity of UNIX systems.)

Chapter contents:

Connecting to the UNIX system

Your first step in using UNIX is to connect to the UNIX system. Exactly how you connect will vary depending on what kind of Internet connection you use, but the following steps should get you started:

1. To begin, have your connection information, such as an IP number or name, handy.

   Contact your system administrator if you don't yet have these. (Throughout this book, we'll use "system administrator" to refer to your help desk, ISP technical support line, or anyone else you can call on who runs your UNIX system and can help you.)

2. Connect to the Internet, if necessary.

   If you use a PPP connection to dial into an Internet service provider (ISP), fire it up now. If you're a lucky duck and use a full-time Internet connection at work or school, just ignore this step.

3. Start your telnet program and connect to the UNIX system.

   Using telnet, you can connect to a remote computer (such as your ISP's computer) and work as if the remote computer were sitting on your desk. Essentially, telnet brings a remote computer's capabilities to your fingertips, regardless of where you're physically located.

   Exactly how you telnet depends on the particular telnet program you're using. For example, most Macintosh users prefer a program called NCSA Telnet, but some are adopting Nifty Telnet as a newer and more reliable alternative. If you're using Windows, you might use Windows Telnet or any one of many shareware telnet programs. You can also

The Preferences Dialog Box

In the Preferences dialog box, you can fix some of the idiosyncrasies that are caused by how your telnet program talks to the UNIX system. You can't identify these idiosyncrasies until you actually start using your UNIX system, but you should remember that you can fix most problems here. For example:

- If your Backspace and Delete keys don't work, look for an option in your telnet program that defines these keyboard functions. You cannot control these options from the Windows Telnet client, although you can from other telnet programs that run under Windows.
- If you start typing and nothing shows up onscreen, set local echo to *on*.
- If you start typing and everything shows up twice, set local echo to *off*.
- If you want to be able to scroll up onscreen and see what's happened during your UNIX session, change the buffer size to a larger number.

Again here, exactly which options you'll have will vary from program to program, but these are ones that are commonly available. Click OK when you're done playing with the settings.

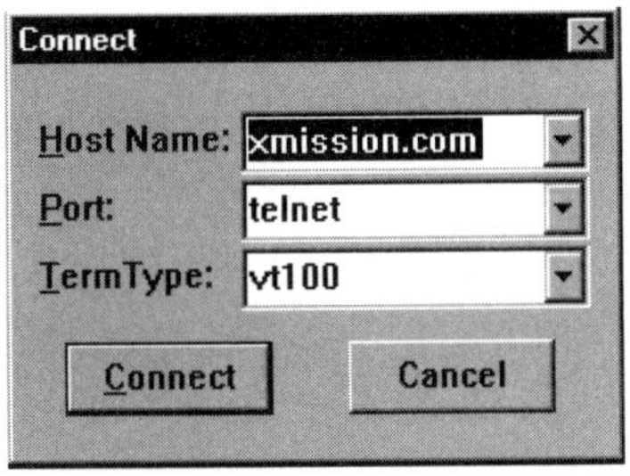

Figure 1.1 Here we're connecting to xmission.com using Windows Telnet. Other telnet programs might look slightly different, but this shows the general idea.

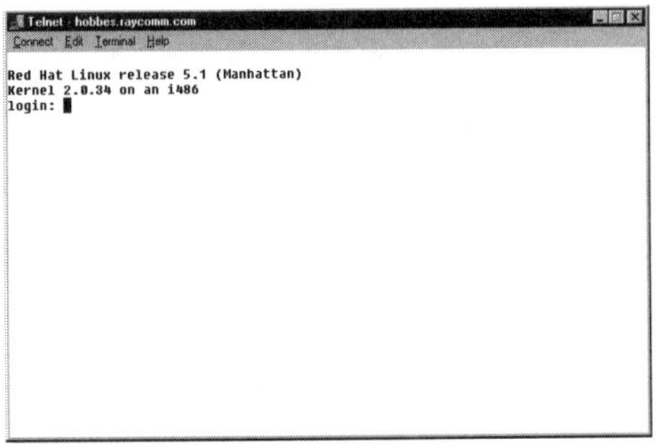

Figure 1.2 After you've connected to the UNIX system, you'll see the login: prompt waiting for you to, well, log in.

purchase telnet programs, such as Kermit or KoalaTerm (both of these Windows programs we like, by the way). And, of course, after you're logged into your UNIX system, you can use the UNIX `telnet` command to access other computers. Each program works a bit differently, and you'll have to refer to the specific documentation for details about using them.

In this example, we're connecting to a UNIX system using Windows Telnet software. **Figure 1.1** shows the Connection dialog box, in which we've filled in the host name (varies), the port (telnet), and the Term(inal) Type (vt100).

4. Visit the Preferences dialog box and become familiar with your options.

   In our case, we accessed the Preferences dialog box by going to Terminal>Preferences.

5. Marvel at the `login:` prompt, which is what you should see if you've connected properly (**Figure 1.2**), and move along to the next section.

✔ Tips

- If you've modified the telnet settings, you may need to disconnect from the telnet session, then reconnect again for the new settings to take effect. See your telnet documentation for specifics about disconnecting from your telnet session.
- In addition to viewing the buffer, as mentioned in the sidebar, you can also see commands that you've issued using a UNIX command. See page 51 and page 57 in Chapter 3, for details.

Logging in

After you've connected to the UNIX system, your next step is to *log in*, or identify yourself to the UNIX system. Logging in serves a few purposes, including giving you access to your e-mail, files, and configurations. It also, however, keeps you from inadvertently accessing someone else's files and settings, and it keeps you from making changes to the system itself.

To log in:

1. To begin, have your *userid* (user identification) and *password* ready.

   Contact your system administrator if you don't have these yet.

2. Type your userid at the `login:` prompt, then press Enter.

   Your userid is case-sensitive, so be sure you type it exactly as your system administrator instructed.

3. Type your password at the `password:` prompt, then press Enter.

   Yup. Your password is case-sensitive, too.

4. Read the information and messages that come up on the screen.

   The information that pops up—the message of the day—might be just a funny, like in **Figure 1.3**, or it might contain information about system policies, warnings about scheduled downtime, or useful tips, as shown in **Figure 1.4**, or both, or possibly neither, if your system administrators have nothing to say to you.

After you've logged in, you'll be located in your *home directory*, which is where your personal files and settings are stored. Your "location" in the UNIX system is a slightly unwieldy concept that we'll help you understand throughout this chapter.

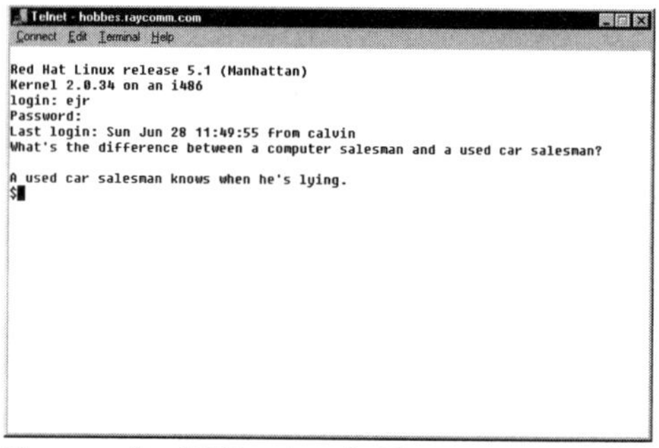

Figure 1.3 Our UNIX system (hobbes.raycomm.com) greets us with a thought for the day called a "fortune."

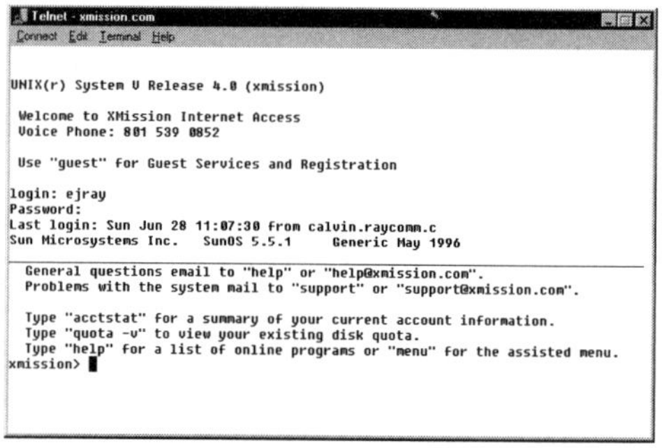

Figure 1.4 Some systems might greet you with system information or helpful tips.

✔ Tips

- If you get an error message after attempting to log in, press Enter and try again. You likely just mistyped your userid or password. Whoops!
- When you log in, you might see a message about failed login attempts. If you unsuccessfully tried to log in, then don't worry about it; the message just confirms that you attempted to log in but failed. If, however, all of your login attempts (with you sitting at the keyboard) have been successful or if the number of failed login attempts seems high—say, five or more—then you might also mention the message to your system administrator, who can check security and login attempts. This could be a warning that someone unauthorized is trying to log in as you.

Write down a few details about your specific login procedure:

As you go through your login procedure, take a minute to write down some of the details for your future reference.

Your userid (but *not* your password):

____

The name of the program you use to connect to your UNIX system and the process you use to get connected:

____

____

____

____

The name of your UNIX system (such as `hobbes.raycomm.com` or `xmission.com`):

____

The IP number of your UNIX system (such as `166.70.111.36` or `198.60.22.2`):

____

Changing your password with passwd

Virtually all UNIX systems require *passwords* to help ensure that your files and data remain your own and that the system itself is secure from vandals and hackers. **Code Listing 1.1** shows how you change your password.

Throughout your UNIX adventure, you'll likely change your password lots of times:

- You'll probably want to change the password provided by your system administrator after you log in for the first time. Hint, hint.
- You'll probably change your password at regular intervals, as many UNIX systems require that you change your password every so often—every 30 or 60 days or so is common.
- You might also change your password voluntarily if you think that someone might have learned it or if you tell anyone your password (although you really shouldn't do that anyway).

To change your password:

1. `passwd`

   To start, type `passwd`.

2. `youroldpassword`

   Enter your old password—the one you're currently using. (Of course, type in *your* old password, not the sample one we've used here!) Note that the password doesn't show up on the screen when you type it, in case someone is lurking over your shoulder, watching you type, and asking "whatcha doing?"

3. `yournewpassword`

   Type in your new password. Check out the sidebar called *The lowdown on*

Code Listing 1.1 Change your password regularly using the `passwd` command.

```
$ passwd
Changing password for ejr
(current) UNIX password:
New UNIX password:
Retype new UNIX password:
passwd: all authentication tokens updated
  → successfully
$
```

passwords for specifics about choosing a password.

4. `yournewpassword`

   Here, you're verifying the password by typing it again.

The system will report that your password was successfully changed (specific terminology depends on the system) after the changes take effect. This is also shown in **Code Listing 1.1**.

✔ Tip

- Consider double-checking your new password *before* you log out of the system by typing `su - yourid` at the prompt. Of course, substitute your real userid (or login name) for `yourid` here. This command (*switch user*) lets you log in again without having to log out, so if you made a mistake when changing your password and now get a failed login message, you can find out before you actually disconnect from the system. If you have problems, contact your system administrator *before* you log out to get the problem resolved.

The lowdown on passwords

In addition to following any password guidelines your system administrator mandates, you should choose a password that is:

- At least six characters long
- Easy for you to remember
- Not a word or name in any dictionary in any language
- A combination of capital and lowercase letters, numbers, and symbols
- Not similar to your userid
- Not identical or similar to one you've used recently
- Not your telephone number, birthdate, kid's birthdate, anniversary (even if you can remember it), mother's maiden name, or anything else that anyone might associate with you.

Listing directories and files with ls

Your UNIX system is made up of directories and files that store a variety of information, including setup information, configuration settings, programs, and options, as well as other files and directories. You might think of your UNIX system as being a tree (tree roots, actually), with subdirectories stemming from higher-level directories. As shown in **Figure 1.5**, all of these files and directories reside within the *root directory*, which contains everything in the system.

Using the `ls` command, you can find out exactly what's in your UNIX system and thereby find out what's available to you. You can list the files and directories of:

- A directory that you're currently in
- A directory that you specify

To list the files and directories of the directory you're in:

- `ls`

  At the shell prompt, type `ls` to list the files and directories in the current directory, which in this case is our home directory (**Code Listing 1.2**).

To list the files and directories of a specified directory:

- `ls /bin`

  Here, you type the `ls` command plus the name of a directory. As shown in **Code**

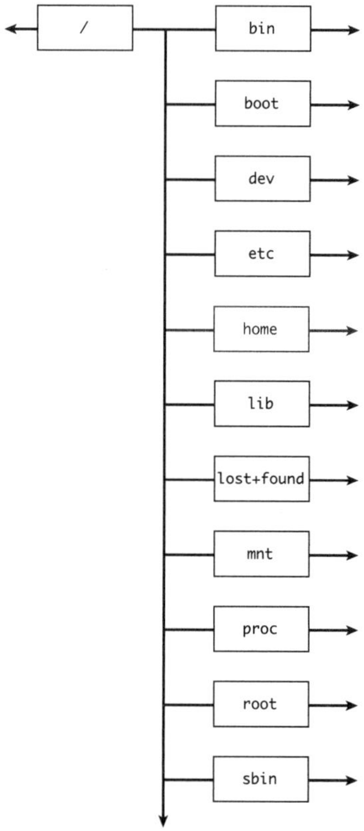

Figure 1.5 All files and directories are nested within the root directory, which serves to contain everything in the system.

Code Listing 1.2 Use `ls` by itself to list the files and directories of the directory you're in.

```
xmission> ls
Mail/          Project/       chat.conf/     mail/
NewProject/    access/        dead.letter    public_html/
News/          ch1info.txt    ftp@           temp/
xmission>
```

Listing 1.3, this command lists the files and directories in the /bin directory, in which you'll find system commands and programs.

✔ Tips

- You can list the files and directories of the root directory at any time and in any place by typing `ls /`.
- Can't remember that pesky file name? Just use `ls` to help jog your memory. Or, refer to page 37 in Chapter 2 for information about using the find command.
- Many other `ls` options are available to control the amount of information about your files that you see and the format in which they appear onscreen. See page 30, Chapter 2, *Listing files and directories with `ls` (more goodies)*, for details.

Code Listing 1.3 Use `ls` with the name of a directory to list the contents of that directory—/bin, in this case.

```
$ ls /bin
arch        dmesg           hostname    netconf        stty
ash         dnsdomainname   igawk       netstat        su
ash.static  doexec          ipcalc      nice           sync
awk         domainname      kill        nisdomainname  tar
basename    echo            linuxconf   ping           tcsh
bash        ed              ln          ps             touch
bsh         egrep           login       pwd            true
cat         ex              lpdconf     red            umount
chgrp       false           ls          remadmin       uname
chmod       fgrep           mail        rm             userconf
chown       fsconf          mkdir       rmdir          usleep
cp          gawk            mknod       rpm            vi
cpio        gawk-3.0.3      mktemp      sed            view
csh         gecko           more        setserial      vim
date        grep            mount       sh             xconf
dd          gunzip          mt          sleep          ypdomainname
df          gzip            mv          sort           zcat
$
```

Changing directories with cd

In order to explore UNIX and its capabilities, you'll need to move around among the directories. You do so using the `cd` command, which takes you from the directory you're currently in to one that you specify. **Code Listing 1.4** illustrates how you use `cd` to change directories.

To change directories:

- `cd Projects`

  To move to a specific directory, type `cd` plus the name of the directory. In this example, we move down in the directory tree to a subdirectory called `Projects`. See the sidebar called *Moving up and down* on page 11 for an explanation of what "up" and "down" mean in UNIX terms.

- `cd ..`

  Type `cd ..` to move up one level in the directory tree.

- `cd /etc`

  Here, `/etc` tells the system to look for the `etc` directory located at the system root.

✔ Tips

- If you don't remember the name of the directory you want to change to, you can use `ls` to list the directories and files in your current directory, then use `cd` as shown in step 1. See the previous section, *Listing directories and files with* `ls`, for more information.

- You can return to your home directory from anywhere in the UNIX system by entering `cd` without specifying a directory.

- On most UNIX systems, you can use a tilde (~) as a handy shortcut to your home directory. For example, if you want

Code Listing 1.4 Using cd, you can change directories and move around in the system. Note that the prompt in this code listing shows the name of the current directory, which can be handy.

```
[deb@hobbes deb]$ cd /home/ejr
[deb@hobbes ejr]$ cd Projects
[deb@hobbes Projects]$ cd ..
[deb@hobbes ejr]$ cd /etc
[deb@hobbes /etc]$
```

to change to the `Urgent` directory within the `Projects` directory in your home directory, you could use something like `cd /home/users/y/yourid/Projects/Urgent`, or just use the shortcut `cd ~/Projects/Urgent`.

- Visit Chapter 2 for much more about directories and files.
- Keep in mind that your home directory isn't the same as the system root directory. You might think of your home directory as "the very small section of the UNIX system that I can call my own." Every person using the UNIX system has his or her own little personal section.

Moving up and down

Throughout this book, we'll talk about moving "up" and "down" through the UNIX file system. Moving "up" means moving into the directory that *contains* the current directory, that is, closer to the root directory. Moving "down" means moving into subdirectories that *are contained by* the current directory, that is, farther from the root directory.

Finding yourself with pwd

As you begin using UNIX and start moving around in directories and files, you're likely to get a bit lost—that is, forget which directory or subdirectory you're in. You can use the pwd command to get a reminder of where you are, as shown in **Code Listing 1.5**.

You can request just the directory name, or you can get fancy and request the directory's name and its contents, courtesy of `ls`.

To find out the name of the current directory:

◆ pwd

This command displays the path and name of the directory you are currently in. The *path* names each of the directories "above" the current directory, giving you the full picture of where you are in relationship to the system root.

To find out the name of the current directory and its contents:

◆ `ls ; pwd`

By combining the `ls` and pwd commands, you can request the directory's name and contents, as shown in **Code Listing 1.5**.

✔ Tips

- Type in pwd immediately after you log in. You'll see where your home directory is in the overall system (aka the full path name for your home directory).
- On some UNIX systems, you won't need to use pwd to find out where you are. Some systems display the current directory at the shell prompt by default—something like `/home/ejr>`. If you'd like to add or get rid of this, or if you want more information about shells and customizing your shell, see Chapter 8, *Configuring your UNIX environment*.

Code Listing 1.5 pwd displays the name of the current directory, which is particularly handy if you've been exploring the system. By combining commands, you can request the directory's name and contents at one time.

```
xmission> pwd
/home/users/e/ejray
xmission> ls ; pwd
Mail/           Project/        chat.conf/      ftp@            temp/
NewProject/     access/         dead.letter     mail/
News/           ch1info.txt     files           public_html/
/home/users/e/ejray
xmission>
```

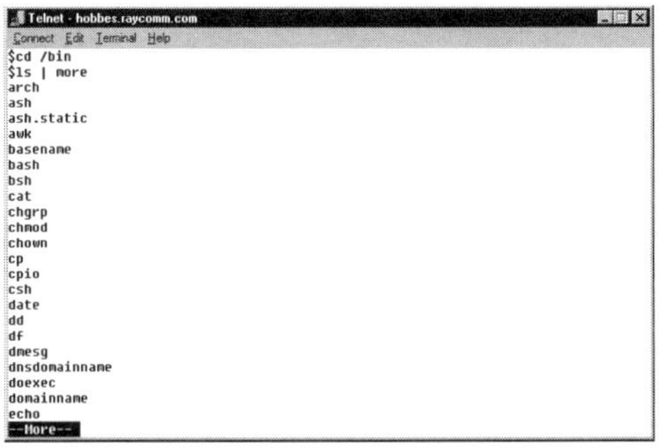

Figure 1.6 To execute multiple commands in sequence, pipe them together using the pipe symbol (|).

Piping input and output

In general, you can think of each UNIX command (`ls`, `cd`, and so on) as an individual program that UNIX executes. For example, if you type `ls /etc` at the prompt, UNIX will run the `ls` program on the `/etc` directory. Each program requires *input* (in this example, the contents of a directory or any other information that the program processed) and produces *output* (i.e., the displayed results).

Frequently, you'll want to run programs in sequence. For example, you could tell UNIX to read your resume and then spell-check it. In doing this, you connect two commands together and have them run in sequence. This process, in which you connect the output of one program to the input of another, is called *piping*. Depending on what you want to do, you can pipe together as many commands as you want—with the output of each acting as the input of the next.

As **Figure 1.6** shows, you pipe commands together using the pipe symbol, which is the | character. In the following example, we'll pipe the output of the `ls` command (which lists the contents of a directory) to the `more` command (which lets you read results one screen at a time). For details about `more`, see *Viewing file contents with* `more` on page 17 of this chapter.

To pipe commands:

- `ls | more`

  Here, all you do is include a pipe symbol between the two commands. This code produces a list of the files in the current directory, then pipes the results to `more`, which then lists the results one screen at a time (**Figure 1.6**).

✔ Tips

- If you want to pipe more than two commands, you can. Just keep adding the commands (with a pipe symbol for each) in the order you want them executed.
- Remember that the *output* of each command is piped to the next command. So a piped command, such as `ls | spell | sort`, could list files within a directory, then spell-check the list, then sort the misspelled words and display them onscreen. The correctly spelled file names would *not* appear.
- Venture to Chapter 15 to find out more about running a spell-checker and Chapter 6 to find out more about sorting.

Redirecting output

Suppose you've developed your resume and spell-checked it. As you learned in the previous section, the results you see onscreen will be the output of the last command—in this case, a list of misspelled words. A lot of times, you'll want to redirect the final output to another location, such as to a file or a printer (if a printer is an option for you), rather than viewing it onscreen. You can do this using *redirection*, which sends the final output to somewhere other than your screen.

As shown in **Code Listing 1.6**, you will often redirect output results to a file. Notice the greater-than symbol (>), which indicates that the output of the program is to be redirected to the location (or file name) you specify after the symbol.

In the following examples, we'll show you how to redirect output to a new file and how to redirect output to append it to an existing file.

To redirect output to a new file:

1. `ls /usr/local/bin >`
   `→ local.programs.txt`

   In this case, we start with the `ls` command and a specific directory, add a greater-than symbol (>), then specify a file name. This will redirect the output of `ls` to a file named `local.programs.txt`.

   Be careful with this! If the file already exists, it will be replaced with the output of the `ls` program here.

2. `ls local*`

   Here, we're just checking to see that the new `local.programs.txt` file has successfully been created. The asterisk wildcard (*) specifies that we want a list of all files that begin with the word `local`, such as `localize`, `localyokel`, or `localuno` (see **Code Listing 1.6**). See the next section, *Using wildcards*, for handy wildcard information.

Code Listing 1.6 In this case, the output of ls gets redirected to local.programs.txt, as indicated by the greater-than (>) symbol. The asterisk wildcard (*) acts as a placeholder for letters or numbers in ls. Finally, the listing of /usr/bin gets appended to the all.programs.txt file.

```
$ ls /usr/local/bin > local.programs.txt
$ ls local*
local.programs.txt   localize    localuno
  → localyokel
$ ls /usr/bin > all.programs.txt
$
```

To append output to an existing file:

- `ls /usr/bin >> all.programs.txt`

  Appending output to an existing file is similar to redirecting it to a new file; however, instead of creating a new file to hold the output (or replacing the contents of an existing file), you add content to the end of an existing file. Notice that you use *two* greater-than symbols here, rather than one.

✔ Tip

- You can pipe and redirect at the same time. For example, you might list a directory, pipe it to `wc` to count the entries, then append the results to a `directoryinfo` file, like this:
  `ls | wc -l >> directoryinfo`.
  You can learn more about `wc` on page 98 in Chapter 6.

Using wildcards

You might think of *wildcards* as being placeholders for omitted letters or numbers. For example, if you're looking for a file but aren't sure whether you named it `kidnews` or `kidupdate`, you can include a wildcard to stand for the part you're uncertain of. That is, you could list the files of a directory with `ls kid*`, (**Code Listing 1.7**), which would list all files starting with the characters "kid". In the resulting list, you'd find a file named `kid` if there were one, as well as files that begin with `kid` but have varying endings, such as `kidnews` (ah-ha, the lost file!), `kiddo`, or `kidneypie`.

You can use wildcards for just about any purpose in UNIX, although listing files and directories will likely be the most common use. Just follow these guidelines:

- You use ? as a placeholder for one character or number.
- You use * as a placeholder for zero or more characters or numbers. Zero characters, in case you're curious, specifies that the search results include all variants of `kid`, including the word itself with no suffix.
- You can include a wildcard at any place in a name: at the beginning (`*kid`), somewhere the middle (`k*d`), at the end (`ki*`), or even in multiple places (`*kid*`).

Code Listing 1.7 You use wildcards (? or *) to act as placeholders for missing characters.

```
[ejr@hobbes Projects]$ ls
keep        kept        kiddo       kidneypie
  → kidupdate
keeper.jpg  kidder.txt  kidnews     kids
[ejr@hobbes Projects]$ ls kid*
kidder.txt  kiddo       kidnews     kidneypie
  → kids        kidupdate
[ejr@hobbes Projects]$ ls k???
keep  kept  kids
[ejr@hobbes Projects]$ ls *date
kidupdate
[ejr@hobbes Projects]$ ls *up*
kidupdate
[ejr@hobbes Projects]$ ls k?d*
kidder.txt  kiddo       kidnews     kidneypie
  → kids        kidupdate
[ejr@hobbes Projects]$
```

USING WILDCARDS

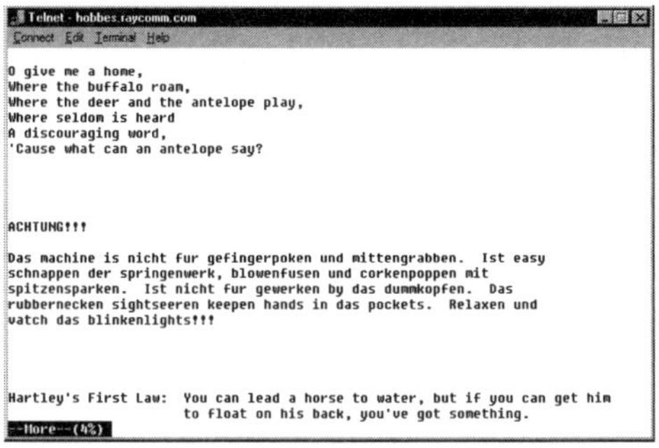
Telnet - hobbes.raycomm.com
Connect Edit Terminal Help
O give me a home,
Where the buffalo roam,
Where the deer and the antelope play,
Where seldom is heard
A discouraging word,
'Cause what can an antelope say?
ACHTUNG!!!
Das machine is nicht fur gefingerpoken und mittengrabben. Ist easy schnappen der springenwerk, blowenfusen und corkenpoppen mit spitzensparken. Ist nicht fur gewerken by das dummkopfen. Das rubbernecken sightseeren keepen hands in das pockets. Relaxen und vatch das blinkenlights!!!
Hartley's First Law: You can lead a horse to water, but if you can get him to float on his back, you've got something.
--More--(4%)

Figure 1.7 The more command lets you move through a file one screen at a time, providing a "More" indicator at the bottom of each screen.

Viewing file contents with more

As you become more familiar with UNIX, you'll want to start exploring the contents of files, including some program files and scripts as well as files you (eventually) create. One of the easiest ways to view file contents is to use the `more` command, which tells UNIX to display files onscreen, a page at a time. As shown in **Figure 1.7**, long files are displayed with "More" at the bottom of each screen so that you can move through the file one screen at a time using the Spacebar on your keyboard.

To view a file with more:

1. `more fortunes`

   At the prompt, type `more` plus the name of the file you want to view. You'll see the contents of the file you requested, starting at the top (**Figure 1.7**).

2. Spacebar

   Press the Spacebar to see the next screen of information. As you move through the file, you can press `b` to move back through previous screens.

3. `q`

   When you're done, press q to go back to the shell prompt.

✔ Tips

- If you want to view just an additional line (rather than an entire screen) when using `more`, press Enter instead of the Spacebar.
- You can also use `less` to view files. `less` is very similar to `more`, but more powerful and flexible.
- You can also view files using the `cat` command. See the next section, *Displaying file contents with* `cat`, for the full scoop.

Displaying file contents with cat

Instead of using more to display files, you can use cat (as in "concatenate"), which displays files but does not pause so you can read the information. Instead, it displays the file or files—which whizzzz by onscreen—and leaves you looking at the last several lines of the file (**Code Listing 1.8**).

The cat command also lets you redirect one or more files, offering a function that some versions of more do not.

To display file contents with cat:

1. `cat newest.programs`

   To begin, type cat plus the file name.

   The file contents will appear onscreen; however, if the file is longer than a single screen, the contents will whir by, and all you'll see is the bottom lines of the file—the 24 or so that fit on a single screen.

- `cat newer.programs newest.programs`

  You can also list multiple files for cat, with each file being displayed in the order specified. In this example the contents of newer.programs will zip by, then the contents of newest.programs will zip by.

- `cat newer.programs newest.programs → > all.programs.`

  In this example, we've added a redirection symbol (>) plus a new file name. This tells UNIX to print out both files; however, instead of displaying the files onscreen, it redirects them to the file called all.programs. Aha! Here's where cat does something better than more. See *Redirecting input and output* in this chapter for more information about redirecting commands.

Code Listing 1.8 With cat, long files whir by, and all you'll see is the bottom of the file. You can also redirect cat output to a file, as shown at the end of the listing.

```
$ cat newest.programs
...
xtermdos
xvminitoppm
xwdtopnm
xxd
yacc
ybmtopbm
yes
yuvsplittoppm
yuvtoppm
zcmp
zdiff
zeisstopnm
zforce
zgrep
zip
zipcloak
zipgrep
zipinfo
zipnote
zipsplit
zless
zmore
znew
$ cat newer.programs newest.programs >
  all.programs
$
```

✔ Tips

- If you inadvertently use cat with a binary file, you might end up with a whole screen of garbage. On some systems, you might try `stty sane` to fix it—more on this in *Fixing terminal settings with* `stty` in Chapter 3.
- You can also view file contents using the more command. See the previous section, *Viewing file contents with* more, for details.

Table 1.1

Common UNIX Directories and Their Contents

Directory	Contents
/bin	Essential programs and commands for use by all users
/etc	System configuration files and global settings
/home	Home directories for users
/sbin	Programs and commands needed for system boot
/tmp	Temporary files
/usr/bin	Commands and programs that are less central to basic UNIX system functionality than those in /bin but were installed with the system
/usr/local	Most files and data that were developed or customized on the system
/usr/local/bin	Locally developed or installed programs
/usr/local/man	Manual (help) pages for local programs
/usr/share/man	Manual (help) pages
/var	Changeable data, including system logs, temporary data from programs, and user mail storage

Exploring the system

With these few key skills in hand, you're ready to start exploring your UNIX system. In doing so, you can quickly get an idea of what's available and gain some useful experience in entering commands.

Think of your UNIX system as being a thoroughly kid-proofed house: You can look around and touch some stuff, but you can't do anything to hurt yourself or the system. So, don't worry! You can't hurt anything by looking around, and even if you tried to break something, most UNIX systems are well-configured enough that you couldn't.

Table 1.1 shows some of the directories you're likely to find most interesting or useful (Appendix B of this book provides a more comprehensive list of directories). You can use the following steps to get you started exploring.

To explore locally installed programs:

1. `cd /usr/bin`

   Change to `/usr/bin`, which is where most installed programs are.

2. `ls | more`

   List the files (which will be programs, in this example) and pipe the output to `more` so you can read the names one screen at a time.

3. `telnet`

   Type the name of any program you want to run; `telnet` (see page 220), in this case, allows you to connect to another system and use it just as you're using your UNIX system now.

✔ Tip

- You can type `man` followed by a file name to learn more about UNIX programs. See the next section, *Getting help with* man, for information about UNIX help.

Getting help with man

Occasionally, you may need a bit of help remembering what a particular command does. Using man (which is short for "manual"), you can look up information about commands and get pointers for using them efficiently. **Figure 1.8** shows a UNIX help page (also called a man page, for obvious reasons) for passwords. In the following steps, we'll show you how to look up specific UNIX commands and find related topics.

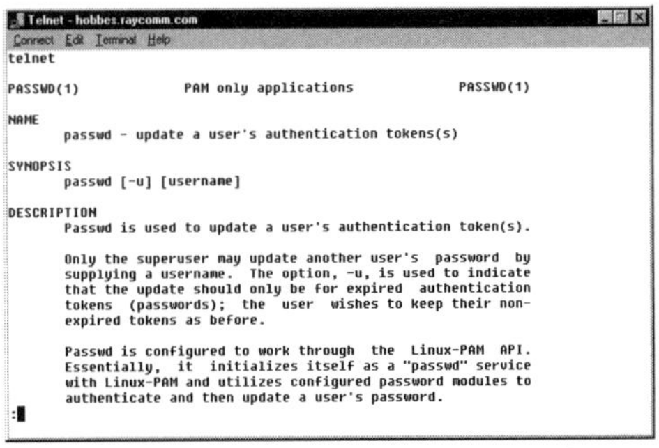

Figure 1.8 Using man passwd, you can access the standard man file about passwords.

To access a man page:

- `man passwd`

  At the prompt, type man plus the name of the command you want help with (in this case, passwd). You'll get the man page for that command. Use the Spacebar and b to navigate through the file, just as you do with more.

To find a specific man page:

1. `man -k passwd`

   Type man -k plus the name of the command or the topic you want help with (in this case, passwd). As **Code Listing 1.9** shows, you'll see a list of possible man pages, command names, man page names, and a description. Note the man page name (and number if more than one page with the same name exists) so you can reference it in the next step.

Code Listing 1.9 man -k passwd gives you these results, showing specific password-related man pages.

```
chpasswd (8)    - update password file in batch
gpasswd (1)     - administer the /etc/group file
mkpasswd (1)    - generate new password, optionally apply it to a user
mkpasswd (8)    - Update passwd and group database files
passwd (1)      - update a user's authentication tokens(s)
passwd (5)      - password file
userpasswd (1) - A graphical tool to allow users to change their passwords
$
```

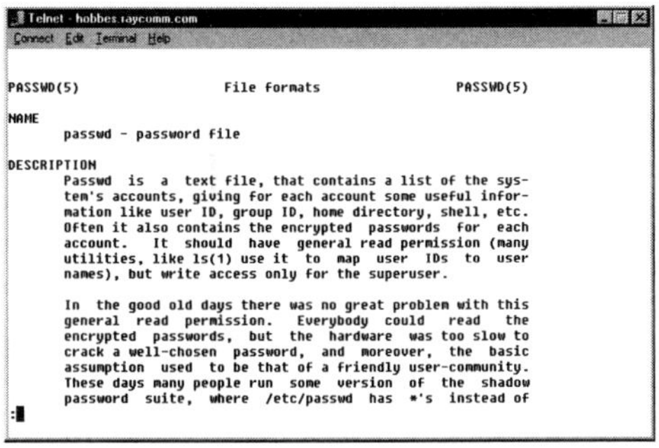

Telnet - hobbes.raycomm.com
Connect Edit Terminal Help
PASSWD(5) File Formats PASSWD(5)
NAME
passwd - password file
DESCRIPTION
Passwd is a text file, that contains a list of the system's accounts, giving for each account some useful information like user ID, group ID, home directory, shell, etc. Often it also contains the encrypted passwords for each account. It should have general read permission (many utilities, like ls(1) use it to map user IDs to user names), but write access only for the superuser.
In the good old days there was no great problem with this general read permission. Everybody could read the encrypted passwords, but the hardware was too slow to crack a well-chosen password, and moreover, the basic assumption used to be that of a friendly user-community. These days many people run some version of the shadow password suite, where /etc/passwd has *'s instead of
:

Figure 1.9 Using man 5 passwd, you can access a man file about a specific password topic from the list that you get from man -k passwd.

2. `man 5 passwd`

Here, you type `man`, the man page you want to view (indicated by 5 in this case to specify part 5—this is necessary because more than one man page with the name `passwd` was listed in the last step), and the command name (`passwd`). **Figure 1.9** shows the resulting `man` page.

✔ Tips

- You can make a copy of a man page so you can edit it or comment on it, adding additional notes for your information or deleting irrelevant (to you) stuff. Just type in `man - command name | col -b | → somefilename`. For example, use `man - passwd | col -b | ~/my.password. → command.notes` to make a copy of the `passwd` man page, sans formatting, in your home directory, under the name `my.password.command.notes`. Then you'll use an editor (from Chapter 4) to edit, add to, and tweak the important points. (The `col -b` command fixes some formatting oddities; without it, all of the underlined words show up as `_u_n_d_e_r_l_i_n_e`.)
- You can use `apropos` instead of the `man -k` flag. For example, your command might look like this: `apropos passwd`.
- Some UNIX systems might require a `-s` before the section number, as in `man -s 5 passwd`.

Logging out

When you finish your session, you need to log out of the system to ensure that nobody else accesses your files while masquerading as you.

To log out

- `logout`

  That's it! Just type `logout`, and the system will clean everything up and break the connection. **Figure 1.10** shows the final screen from Windows Telnet. Your telnet program might just close automatically or it might stay open and wait for you to do something—either quit the program or start a new telnet session (and move to Chapter 2).

✔ Tip

- On some UNIX systems, you can type `exit` or `quit` instead of `logout`, or press Ctrl D on your keyboard.

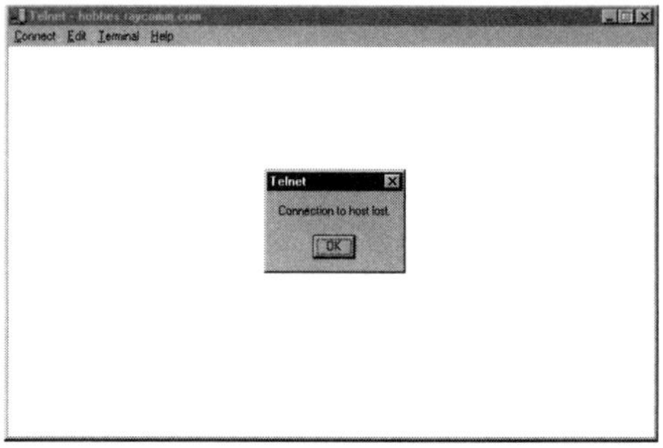

Figure 1.10 So long. Farewell. Auf Wiedersehen. Goodbye.

Using Directories and Files

2

As you learned in Chapter 1, directories and files are the heart of UNIX; they contain things like setup information, configuration settings, programs, and options, as well as anything that you create. You access directories and files every time you type in a UNIX command, and for this reason, you need to become familiar with the various things you can do with them.

Again in this chapter, the skills and commands we'll cover apply to any UNIX flavor. What you see onscreen (particularly system prompts and responses) may differ slightly from what's illustrated in this book; the general ideas and specific commands, however, will be the same on all UNIX systems.

Chapter contents:

- Creating directories
- Creating files
- Copying directories and files
- Listing directories and files
- Moving directories and files
- Removing files
- Removing directories
- Finding files
- Linking with hard links
- Linking with soft links

Creating directories with mkdir

You might think of directories as being drawers in a file cabinet; each drawer contains a bunch of files that are somehow related. For example, you might have a couple of file drawers for your unread magazines, one for your to-do lists, and maybe a drawer for your work projects.

Similarly, directories in your UNIX system act as containers for other directories and files; each subdirectory contains yet more related directories or files, and so on. You'll probably create a new directory each time you start a project or have related files you want to store at a single location. You create new directories using the `mkdir` command, as shown in **Code Listing 2.1**.

Code Listing 2.1 Typing `mkdir` plus a directory name creates a new directory. Listing the files, in long format, shows the new directory. The "d" at the left end of the line shows that it's a directory.

```
$ ls
Projects all.programs.txt   local.programs.txt schedule
Xrootenv.0        files     newer.programs     short.fortunes
all.programs      fortunes  newest.programs    temp
$ mkdir Newdirectory
$ ls -l
total 159
drwxrwxr-x   2 ejr     users       1024 Jun 29 11:40 Newdirectory
drwxrwxr-x   2 ejr     users       1024 Jun 28 12:48 Projects
-rw-rw-r--   1 ejr     users       7976 Jun 28 14:15 all.programs
-rw-rw-r--   1 ejr     users       7479 Jun 28 14:05 all.programs.txt
-rw-rw-r--   1 ejr     users        858 Jun 28 12:45 files
-rw-rw-r--   1 ejr     ejr       128886 Jun 27 09:05 fortunes
-rw-rw-r--   1 ejr     users          0 Jun 28 14:05 local.programs.txt
-rw-rw-r--   1 ejr     users        497 Jun 28 14:13 newer.programs
-rw-rw-r--   1 ejr     users       7479 Jun 28 14:13 newest.programs
lrwxrwxrwx   1 ejr     users         27 Jun 26 11:03 schedule -> /home/deb/Pre
-rw-rw-r--   1 ejr     ejr         1475 Jun 27 09:31 short.fortunes
drwxrwxr-x   2 ejr     users       1024 Jun 26 06:39 temp
$
```

Naming Directories (and Files)

As you start creating directories (and files), keep in mind the following guidelines:

- Directories and files must have unique names. For example, you cannot name a directory `Golf` and a file `Golf`. You can, however, have a directory called `Golf` and a file called `golf`. The difference in capitalization makes each name unique. By the way, directories are often named with an initial cap, and file names are usually all-lowercase.
- Directory and file names may *not* include the following characters: angle brackets (< >), braces (`{ }`), brackets (`[ ]`), parentheses (`( )`), double quotes (`" "`), single quotes (`' '`), asterisks (`*`), question marks (`?`), pipe symbols (`|`), slashes (`/ \`), carets (`^`), exclamation points (`!`), pound signs (`#`), dollar signs (`$`), ampersands (`&`), and tildes (`~`).
- Avoid names that include spaces and hyphens (`-`). You can use these, but they're more trouble than they're worth—that is, some programs don't deal with them correctly, so you have to use odd workarounds. Instead, stick to periods (`.`) and underscores (`_`) to separate words, characters, or numbers.
- Use names that describe the directory or file's contents so that you easily remember them.

To create a directory:

1. `ls`

   Start by listing existing directories to make sure that the planned name doesn't conflict with an existing directory or file name.

2. `mkdir Newdirectory`

   Type the `mkdir` command to make a new directory; in this case, it's called `Newdirectory`. Refer to the sidebar *Naming Directories (and Files)* for guidelines.

3. `ls -l`

   Now you can use `ls -l` (the `-l` flag specifies a *long* format) to look at the listing for your new directory (**Code Listing 2.1**). The `d` at the far left of the listing for `Newdirectory` indicates that it's a directory and not a file. Of course, after you trust UNIX to do as you say, you can skip this verification step.

✔ Tip

- If you attempt to create a directory with a file or directory name that already exists, UNIX will not overwrite the existing directory. Instead, you'll be told that a file by that name already exists. Try again with a different name.

Creating files with touch

Another skill you'll use frequently is creating files. You might think of creating files as getting an empty bucket that you can later fill with water...or sand...or rocks...or whatever. When you create a file, you designate an empty space that you can fill with programs, activity logs, your resume, or configurations—practically anything you want, or nothing at all.

Of course, you can always create a file by writing something in an editor and saving it, as described in Chapter 4, but you will likely encounter situations where you just need an empty file. You create empty files using the `touch` command, as shown in **Code Listing 2.2**.

To create a file:

1. `touch file.to.create`

   To create a file, type `touch` followed by the name of the file. This creates an empty file.

Code Listing 2.2 Use the touch command to create files, update their modification times, or both.

```
$ ls
$ touch file.to.create
$ ls -l file*
-rw-rw-r--   1 ejr      users         0 Jun 29 11:53 file.to.create
$ touch -t 12312359 oldfile
$ ls -l
total 0
-rw-rw-r--   1 ejr      users         0 Jun 29 11:53 file.to.create
-rw-rw-r--   1 ejr      users         0 Dec 31  1998 oldfile
$ touch -t 123123592001 new.years.eve
$ ls -l
total 0
-rw-rw-r--   1 ejr      users         0 Jun 29 11:53 file.to.create
-rw-rw-r--   1 ejr      users         0 Dec 31  2001 new.years.eve
-rw-rw-r--   1 ejr      users         0 Dec 31  1998 oldfile
$
```

2. `ls -l file*`

   Optionally, verify that the file was created by typing `ls –l` plus `file*`. As shown in **Code Listing 2.2**, you'll see the name of the new file as well as its length (0) and the date and time of its creation (likely seconds before the current time, if you're following along).

✔ Tips

- You can also use `touch` to update a file's date and time. For example, typing `touch -t 12312359 oldfile` at the prompt would update `oldfile` with a date of December 31, 23 hours, and 59 minutes in the current year. Or, typing `touch -t 123123592001 new.years.eve` would update the file called `new.years.eve` to the same time in the year 2001.
- Each time you save changes in a file, the system automatically updates the date and time. See Chapter 4 for details about editing and saving files.
- Refer to the sidebar called *Naming Directories (and Files)* on page 25 in this chapter for file-naming guidelines.

Copying directories and files with cp

When working in UNIX, you'll frequently want to make copies of directories and files. For example, you may want to copy a file you're working on to keep an original, unscathed version handy. Or, you might want to maintain duplicate copies of important directories and files in case you inadvertently delete them or save something over them. Accidents do happen, according to Murphy.

Whatever your reason, you copy directories and files using the `cp` command, as shown in **Code Listing 2.3**. When you copy directories and files, all you're doing is putting a duplicate in another location; you leave the original untouched.

To copy a directory:

1. `cp -r /home/ejr/Projects`
   `→ /home/shared/deb/Projects`

   At the shell prompt, type `cp -r`, followed by the old and new (to be created) directory names, to copy a complete directory. The `r` stands for "recursive," if that'll help you remember it.

2. `ls /home/shared/deb/Projects`

   You can use `ls` plus the new directory name to verify that the duplicate direc-

Code Listing 2.3 Use `cp -r` to copy directories.

```
$ cp -r /home/ejr/Projects
  → /home/shared/deb/Projects
$ ls /home/shared/deb/Projects
current    new.ideas  schedule
$
```

Code Listing 2.4 Just use `cp` to copy files and add `-i` to insist that the system prompt you before you overwrite an existing file.

```
$ cp existingfile newfile
$ ls -l
total 7
-rw-rw-r--   1 ejr      users        1475 Jun 29 12:18 existingfile
-rw-rw-r--   1 ejr      users        1475 Jun 29 12:37 newfile
-rw-rw-r--   1 ejr      users        2876 Jun 29 12:17 oldfile
$ cp -i existingfile oldfile
cp: overwrite 'oldfile'? n
$
```

access, then use the copying procedure described here.

- Rather than moving directories and files (using `mv`), consider copying directories and files (using `cp`) then deleting the original (using `rm`). This way you can ensure that you have a copy as you're reorganizing your directories and files. Stop by the sections called *Moving files with* `mv` and *Removing files with* `rm` in this chapter for details on these topics.
- Use `cp` with a `-i` flag to force the system to ask you before overwriting files. Then, if you like that, visit Chapter 8 to find out about using aliases with `cp` so that the system always prompts you before overwriting files.

tory and its contents are in the intended location (**Code Listing 2.3**).

To copy a file:

1. `cp existingfile newfile`

   At the prompt, type `cp`, followed by the old and new (to be created) file name.

2. `ls -l`

   Optionally, check out the results with `ls -l`. The `-l` (for long format) flag displays the file sizes and dates so you can see that the copied file is exactly the same as the new one (**Code Listing 2.4**).

3. `cp -i existingfile oldfile`

   If you use `cp` with the `-i` flag, it prompts you before overwriting an existing file, also shown in **Code Listing 2.4**.

✔ Tips

- When copying directories and files, you can use either *absolute* (complete) names, which are measured from the root directory (`/home/ejr/Projects`), or *relative* (partial) names, which specify files or directories in relationship to the current directory (`ejr/Projects`) and aren't meaningful from elsewhere in the UNIX filesystem. Using absolute names, you can manipulate directories and files anywhere in the UNIX system. Using relative names, you can manipulate files only with reference to your current location.
- You can compare the contents of two files or two directories using `cmp` and `dircmp`, respectively. For example, typing `cmp filename1 filename2` would compare the contents of the specified files. Breeze through Chapter 6 for more information.
- You can copy directories and files to or from someone else's directory. Skip to Chapter 5 to find out how to get

Listing files and directories with ls (more goodies)

If you've been following along, you're probably an expert at using `ls` to list directory contents and to verify that files and directories were copied as you intended. `ls`, though, has a couple more handy uses. In particular, you can also use it to

- List file names and information, which is handy for differentiating similar files (**Figure 2.1**).
- List all files in a directory, including hidden ones, such as `.profile` and `.login` configuration files (**Code Listing 2.5**). See Chapter 8 for more about configuration files.

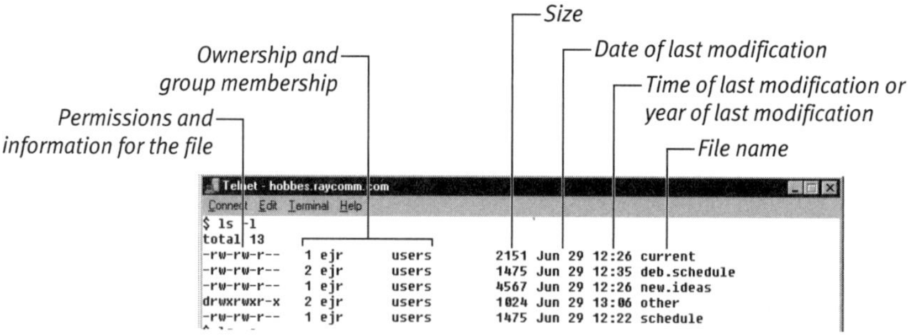

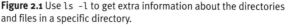

Figure 2.1 Use `ls -l` to get extra information about the directories and files in a specific directory.

Code Listing 2.5 Use `ls -l` to see a listing of the contents of a directory in long format.

```
$ ls -l
total 13
-rw-rw-r--   1 ejr     users       2151 Jun 29 12:26 current
-rw-rw-r--   2 ejr     users       1475 Jun 29 12:35 deb.schedule
-rw-rw-r--   1 ejr     users       4567 Jun 29 12:26 new.ideas
drwxrwxr-x   2 ejr     users       1024 Jun 29 13:06 other
-rw-rw-r--   1 ejr     users       1475 Jun 29 12:22 schedule
```

Code Listing 2.6 If you want to see hidden files, use `ls -a`.

```
$ ls -a
.          .stats        deb.schedule  other
..         current       new.ideas     schedule
```

Code Listing 2.7 If you want to see everything, use `ls -la`.

```
$ ls -la
total 22
drwxrwxr-x   3 ejr     users          1024 Jun 29
  → 13:07 .
drwxrwx---   7 ejr     users          1024 Jun 29
  → 12:16 ..
-rw-rw-r--   1 ejr     users          6718 Jun 29
  → 13:00 .stats
-rw-rw-r--   1 ejr     users          2151 Jun 29
  → 12:26 current
-rw-rw-r--   2 ejr     users          1475 Jun 29
  → 12:35 deb.schedule
-rw-rw-r--   1 ejr     users          4567 Jun 29
  → 12:26 new.ideas
drwxrwxr-x   2 ejr     users          1024 Jun 29
  → 13:06 other
-rw-rw-r--   1 ejr     users          1475 Jun 29
  → 12:22 schedule
$
```

To list file names and information:

- `ls -l`

  At the shell prompt, type `ls -l` (that's a lowercase "L", not a one). You'll see the list of files in your directory fly by with the following information about each file (**Code Listing 2.6**):

  - File name
  - File size
  - Date of last modification
  - Permissions information (find out more about permissions in Chapter 5)
  - Ownership and group membership (also covered in Chapter 5)
  - Time of last modification (if the file's been modified during the current year) or year of last modification (if the file was last modified in a previous year or later in the current year. Check out `touch` on page 26 to see how files might have modification dates in the future.)

To list all files in a directory:

- `ls -a`

  Enter `ls -a` at the shell prompt to list all the files in the directory, including hidden files, as shown in **Code Listing 2.7**.

✔ Tips

- You can hide files by giving them a name that starts with a dot (`.`) That is, `profile` would not be hidden, but `.profile` would be.
- Remember, you can combine any flags to specify multiple commands. For example, if you want to list all files (`-a`) in the long format (`-l`) you would use `ls -la`.

Moving files with mv

Moving directories and files means moving them from one location (think of location as an absolute file path, like `/home/ejr/aFile`) in your system to another location (say, `/temp/File` or `/home/ejr/AnotherFile`). Essentially, you have only one version of a file, and you change the location of that version. For example, you might move a directory when you're reorganizing your directories and files. Or, you might move a file to rename it—that is, move a file from one name to another name.

You move directories and files using `mv`, as shown in **Code Listing 2.8**.

To move a file or directory:

1. `ls`

   To begin, use `ls` to verify the name of the file you want to move. If you're changing the name of the file, you'll want to ensure that the new file name isn't yet in use. If you move a file to an existing file name, the contents of the old file will be replaced with contents of the new file.

2. `mv existingfile newfile`

   Type `mv` plus the existing file name and the new file name. Say goodbye to the old file and hello to the new one (**Code Listing 2.8**).

   You use the same process—exactly—to move directories; just include the directory names, as in `mv ExistingDirectory NewDirectory`.

3. `ls`

   Verify that the file is now located in the location you intended.

Code Listing 2.8 List files to see the current files, then use `mv` to rename one of the files.

```
$ ls
Completed     existingfile  oldfile
$ mv existingfile newfile
$ ls
Completed  newfile    oldfile
$
```

✔ Tips

- You can also use `mv` to move files into or out of directories. For example, `mv Projects/temp/testfile /home/deb/testfile` moves `testfile` from the `Projects` and `temp` subdirectories of the current directory to Deb's home directory, also using the name `testfile`.
- Use `mv -i oldfilename newfilename` to require the system to prompt you before overwriting (destroying) existing files. The `-i` is for "interactive," and it also works with the `cp` command.
- Visit Chapter 8 to find out about using aliases with `mv` so that the system always prompts you before overwriting files and you don't have to remember the `-i` flag.

Code Listing 2.9 Use `rm -i` to safely and carefully remove directories and files.

```
$ ls
Completed           oldfile
newfile             soon.to.be.gone.file
$ rm -i soon.to.be.gone.file
rm: remove 'soon.to.be.gone.file'? y
$ ls
Completed  newfile   oldfile
$
```

Removing files with rm

You can easily—perhaps too easily—remove (delete) files from your UNIX system. As Murphy will tell you, it's a good idea to think twice before doing this; once you remove a file, it's gone (unless, of course, you plead with your system administrator to restore it from a backup tape—but that's another story...). At any rate, it's permanent, unlike deletions in Windows 98 or the Macintosh OS, where the Recycle Bin or Trash Can give you a second chance.

You remove files using `rm`, as shown in **Code Listing 2.9**. And, as you'll see in the following steps, you can remove files one at a time or several at a time.

To remove a file:

1. `ls -l`

   List the files in the current folder to verify the name of the file you want to remove.

2. `rm -i soon.to.be.gone.file`

   At your shell prompt, type `rm -i` followed by the name of the file you want to remove. The `-i` tells the system to prompt you before removing the files (**Code Listing 2.9**).

3. `ls`

   It is gone, isn't it?

To remove multiple files:

1. `ls -l *.html`

   List the files to make sure that you know which files you want to remove (and not remove).

2. `rm -i *.html`

   Using the asterisk wildcard (*), you can remove multiple files at one time. In this example, we remove all files in the current directory that end with `.html`. (Refer to Chapter 1, specifically the section called *Using Wildcards* on page 16, for details about using wildcards.)

3. `rm -i dangerous`

   Here, `-i` specifies that you'll be prompted to verify the removal of a directory or file named `dangerous` before it's removed.

4. `rm -ir dan*`

   This risky command removes all of the directories or files that start with `dan` in the current directory and all of the files and subdirectories in the subdirectories starting with `dan`. If you're sure you're sure, don't use the `-i` flag to just have the files removed without prompting you for confirmation. (Remember that the flags `-ir` could also be written as `-i -r` or `-ri` or `-r -i`. UNIX is pretty flexible.)

✔ Tips

- If you have system administrator rights (and are logged in as *root*, rather than with your userid), be extremely careful when using `rm`. Rather than removing your personal directories or files, you could potentially remove system directories and files. Scope out the sidebar called *Can You Really Screw Up the System?*
- We suggest using `rm -i`, at least until you're sure you're comfortable with irrevocable deletions. The `-i` flag prompts you to verify your command before it's executed.
- Visit Chapter 8 to find out about using aliases with `rm` so that the system always prompts you before removing the directories or files even if you forget the `-i` flag.
- If you accidentally end up with a file that has a problematic filename (like one that includes `-i`, which looks to UNIX like a command flag, not a file name), use `rm -i *` to carefully delete it. You'll be prompted to delete each matching file (all of them) and can axe the offender that way.

Can You Really Screw Up the System?

In general, no. When you log into a UNIX system and use your personal userid, the worst you can do is remove your own directories and files. As long as you're logged in as yourself, commands you type won't affect anything critical to the UNIX system, only your own personal directories and files. Score one for UNIX—as an average user, you cannot really break the system. With Windows or Macintosh, though, it's a different story....

If you have system administrator rights, meaning that you can log in as *root* (giving you access to all the system directories and files), you can do a lot of damage if you're not extremely careful. For this reason, don't log in as root unless you absolutely have to.

See Chapter 3 for information about `su`, which can help reduce the risk of being logged in as root.

Removing directories with rmdir

Another handy thing you can do is remove directories using `rmdir`. Think of removing directories as trimming branches on a tree. That is, you can't be sitting on the branch you want to trim off. You have to sit on the next closest branch; otherwise you'll fall to the ground along with the branch you trim off. Ouch! Similarly, when you remove a directory, you must be located in the parent directory of the directory you want to remove.

You must remove a directory's contents (all subdirectories and files) before you remove the directory itself. In doing so, you can verify what you're removing and avoid accidentally removing important stuff. In the following steps (illustrated in **Code Listing 2.10**), we'll show you how to remove a directory's contents, then remove the directory itself.

To remove a directory:

1. `cd /home/ejr/Yourdirectory`

   To begin, type `cd` plus the name of the directory you want to remove to move to

Code Listing 2.10 Removing directories with `rmdir` can be a little tedious—but better safe than sorry.

```
$ cd /home/ejr/Yourdirectory
$ ls -la
total 7
drwxrwxr-x   2 ejr     users       1024 Jun 29 20:59 .
drwxrwx---   8 ejr     users       1024 Jun 29 20:59 ..
-rw-rw-r--   1 ejr     users       1475 Jun 29 20:59 cancelled.project.notes
-rw-rw-r--   1 ejr     users       2876 Jun 29 20:59 outdated.contact.info
$ rm *
$ cd ..
$ rmdir Yourdirectory
$ ls
Newdirectory        all.programs.txt    newer.programs     short.fortunes
Projects            files               newest.programs    temp
Xrootenv.0          fortunes            newstuff           touching
all.programs        local.programs.txt  schedule
$
```

that directory.

2. `ls -a`

   List all (`-a`) of the files, including any hidden files that might be present, in the directory, and make sure you don't need any of them. If you only see `.` and `..` (which indicate the current directory and its parent directory), you can skip ahead to step 4.

3. Do one or both of these:
   - If you only have files in the directory, type `rm *` to delete the files.
   - If you have subdirectories in the directory, type `cd` and the subdirectory name, essentially repeating the process starting with step 1. Repeat this process until you remove all subdirectories.

   When you finish this step, you should have a completely empty directory, ready to be removed.

4. `cd ..`

   Use the change directory command again to move up one level, to the parent of the directory that you want to remove.

5. `rmdir Yourdirectory`

   There it goes—wave goodbye to the directory! See **Code Listing 2.10** for the whole sequence.

✔ Tips

- You can remove multiple directories at one time. Assuming you're starting with empty directories, just list them like this: `rmdir Yourdirectory Yourotherdirectory OtherDirectory`.
- As an alternative to `rmdir`, you can remove a directory and all of its contents at once using `rm` with the `-r` flag; for example, `rm -r Directoryname`. Be careful, though! This method automatically removes the directory and everything in it, so you won't have the opportunity to examine everything you remove beforehand.
- If you're getting comfortable with long command strings, you can specify commands with a complete directory path as in `ls /home/ejr/DirectorytoGo` or `rm /home/ejr/DirectorytoGo/*`.

Code Listing 2.11 Use `find` to locate a missing file.

```
$ find . -name lostfile -print
./Projects/schedule/lostfile
$
```

Code Listing 2.12 By using wildcards and specifying multiple directories, you can make find yet more powerful.

```
$ find /home/deb -name pending* -print
/home/deb/Projects/schedule/pending.tasks
$ find /home/deb /home/ejr -name pending*
  → -print
/home/deb/Projects/schedule/pending.tasks
/home/ejr/pending.jobs.to.do.today.to.do
$
```

Finding forgotten files with find

Where, oh where, did that file go? Sometimes locating a file requires more than cursing at your computer or listing directory contents with `ls`. Instead, you can use the `find` command, which lets you search in dozens of ways, including through the entire directory tree (**Code Listing 2.11**) or through directories you specify (**Code Listing 2.12**).

To find a file:

- `find . -name lostfile -print`

  Along with the `find` command, this specifies to start in the current directory with a dot (`.`), provide the file name (`-name lostfile`), and specify that the results be printed onscreen (`-print`) (**Code Listing 2.11**).

To find files starting in a specific directory:

- `find /home/deb -name pending* -print`

  This command finds all of the files with names starting with `pending` under Deb's home directory.

Or, you can find files under multiple directories at one time, like this:

- `find /home/deb /home/ejr -name`
  `→ 'pending*' -print`

  This command finds files with names starting with `pending` in Deb and Eric's home directories or any subdirectories under them (**Code Listing 2.12**).

To find and act on files:

- `find ~/ -name '*.backup' -ok rm {}`
  `→ \;`

  Type `find` with a wildcard expression , followed by `-ok` (to execute the following command, with confirmation), `rm` (the command to issue) and {} \; to fill in each file found as an argument for the command. If you want to, say, compress matching files without confirmation, you might use `find ~/ -name '*.backup' -exec compress {} \;` to do the work for you.

✔ Tips

- On some UNIX systems, you may not need the `-print` flag. Try entering `find` without the `-print` flag. If you see the results onscreen, then you don't need to add the `-print` flag.
- Avoid starting the `find` command with the root directory, as in `find / -name the.missing.file -print`. In starting with the root directory (indicated by the /), you'll likely encounter a pesky error message for each directory you don't have access to. Of course, if you're logged in as root, this doesn't apply.
- If you know only part of the file name, you can use quoted wildcards with `find`, as in `find . -name 'info*' -print`.
- `find` offers many chapters worth of options. If you're looking for a specific file or files based on any characteristics, you can find them with `find`. For example, you can use `find /home/shared -mtime -3` to find all files under the shared directory that were modified within the last three days. See Appendix C for a substantial (but not comprehensive) listing of options.

Linking with ln (hard links)

Suppose your boss just hired an assistant for you. ('Bout time, right?) You'll need to make sure your new helper can access your files so that you can pawn off your work on him. And, you'll need to access the revised files just so you can keep up with what your helper's been doing—and perhaps take credit for his work at the next staff meeting.

A great way to give your helper easy access to your files is to create a *hard link* from your home directory. In making a hard link, all you're doing is starting with an existing file and creating a link, which (sort of) places the existing file in your helper's home directory. The link does not create a copy of the file; instead, you're creating a second pointer to the same physical file on the disk. Rather than the additional pointer being secondary (like an alias or shortcut in Macintosh or Windows computers), both of the pointers reference the same actual file, so from the perspective of the UNIX system, the file actually resides in two locations (**Code Listing 2.13**).

Because using hard links often requires that you have access to another user's home directory, you might venture to Chapter 5 for details about using chmod, chgrp, and chown to access another user's directories and files.

Code Listing 2.13 Hard links let two users easily share files.

```
$ ls /home/deb/Projects/schedule/our* /home/helper/our*
ls: /home/helper/our*: No such file or directory
/home/deb/Projects/schedule/our.projects.latest
/home/deb/Projects/schedule/our.projects.other
$ ln /home/deb/Projects/schedule/our.projects.latest /home/helper/our.projects
$ ls -l /home/helper/o*
-rw-r--r--   3 ejr      users       1055 Jun 26 11:00 /home/helper/our.projects
$
```

To make a hard link:

1. `ls -l /home/deb/Projects/schedule/`
   `→ our* /home/helper/our*`

   To begin, list the files in both directories to make sure that the file to link exists and that there's no other file with the intended name in the target directory. Here, we list the files that start with `our` in both `/home/deb/Projects/schedule` and in `/home/helper`. In this example, we're verifying that the file does exist in Deb's directory and that no matching files were found in the helper's directory (**Code Listing 2.13**).

2. `ln /home/deb/Projects/schedule/`
   `→ our.projects.latest`
   `→ /home/helper/our.projects`

   Here, `ln` creates a new file with a similar name in the helper's home directory and links the two files together, essentially making the same file exist in two different home directories.

3. `ls -l /home/helper/o*`

   With this code, your helper can verify that the file exists by listing files that begin with `o*`.

   Now the file exists in two places with exactly the same content. Either user can modify the file, and the content in both locations will change.

✔ Tips

- You can remove hard links just as you remove regular files, by using `rm` plus the file name. See the section called *Removing files with rm* on page 33 of this chapter.
- If one user removes the file, the other user can still access the file from his/her directory.
- Hard links work only from file to file within the same file system. To link directories or to link across file systems, you'll have to use soft links, which are up next in the section called *Linking with `ln -s` (soft links)*.
- If you're sneaky, you can use hard links to link directories, not just files. Make a new directory where you want the linked directory to be, then use `ln /home/` `→ whoever/existingdirectory/*` `→ /home/you/newdirectory/*` to hard link all of the files in the old directory to the new directory. New files won't be linked automatically, but you could use a `cron` job to refresh the links periodically—say, daily. See Chapter 9 for `cron` details.
- You can save time by using ~/ to represent your home directory. For example, rather than typing `/home/users/d/deb/Projects/` `→ schedule/our.projects.latest`, Deb could type `~/Projects/schedule/our.projects.` `→ latest`.

Linking with ln -s (soft links)

Now suppose you want to pawn off your entire workload on your new helper. Rather than just giving him access to a single file, you'll want to give him access to your entire directory. You can do this using *soft links* (created with `ln -s`), which essentially provide other users with a shortcut to the directory you specify.

Like hard links, soft links allow a file to be in more than one place at a time; however, with soft links, there's only one copy of it and, with soft links, you can link directories as well. The linked file or directory is dependent on the original one—that is, if the original file or directory is deleted, the linked file or directory will no longer be available.

Soft links are particularly handy because they work for directories as well as individual files, and they work across different file sys-

Code Listing 2.14 Use `ln -s` to make soft links and connect directories.

```
$ ls /home/deb /home/helper
/home/deb:
Projects

/home/helper:
our.projects
$ ln -s /home/deb/Projects /home/helper/Projects
$ ls -la /home/helper/
total 11
d-wxrwx---   2 helper   users      1024 Jun 29 21:18 .
drwxr-xr-x  11 root     root       1024 Jun 29 21:03 ..
-rw-rwxr--   1 helper   users      3768 Jun 29 21:03 .Xdefaults
-rw-rwxr--   1 helper   users        24 Jun 29 21:03 .bash_logout
-rw-rwxr--   1 helper   users       220 Jun 29 21:03 .bash_profile
-rw-rwxr--   1 helper   users       124 Jun 29 21:03 .bashrc
lrwxrwxrwx   1 ejr      users        18 Jun 29 21:18 Projects -> /home/deb/Prs
-rw-rwxr--   3 ejr      users      1055 Jun 26 11:00 our.projects
$
```

tems (that is, not just within /home, but anywhere on the UNIX system).

Like hard lines, soft links sometimes require that you have access to another user's directory and files. See Chapter 5 more on file permissions and ownership and Chapter 7 for the lowdown on file systems.

To make a soft link:

1. `ls -l /home/deb /home/helper`

   To begin, list the contents of both users' home directories. Here, we're verifying that the directory we want to link does exist in Deb's directory and that no matching directories or files exist in the helper's directory (so our link doesn't destroy an existing file or directory) (**Code Listing 2.14**).

2. `ln -s /home/deb/Projects`
   `→ /home/helper/Project`

   This command creates a soft link so that the contents of Deb's home directory can also be easily accessed from the helper's home directory.

3. `ls -la /home/helper`

   Listing the contents of `/home/helper` shows the existence of the soft link to the directory. Notice the arrows showing the link in **Code Listing 2.14**.

✔ Tip

- If you only need to create a link between two files within the same file system, consider using hard links, as discussed in the previous section, *Linking with `ln` (hard links)*.

3 Working with Your Shell

When you access UNIX, the first thing you see is the prompt, called the *shell prompt*, which is where you interact with the UNIX system. The shell determines how easily you can enter and reenter commands and how you can control your environment. What's cool about UNIX is that you're not stuck with one shell—that is, on most systems you can choose to use different shells that have different features and capabilities.

In this chapter, we'll look at your shell, show you how to change your shell, and get you started using a few of the more common shells.

Chapter contents

- Discovering what shell you're using
- Understanding shells and options
- Changing your shell
- Changing your shell temporarily
- Using command completion in the `bash` shell
- Viewing session history in the `bash` shell
- Using command completion in the `ksh` shell
- Viewing session history in the `ksh` shell
- Viewing session history in the `csh` shell
- Changing your identity
- Fixing terminal setting
- Exiting the shell

Discovering what shell you're using

When you first log in to your UNIX account, you'll be using the default shell on your system. The default shell, its features, and its options depend completely on what your system administrator specifies. **Code Listings 3.1** and **3.2** show examples of how default shell prompts differ on two different systems.

To discover what shell you're using:

◆ `echo $SHELL`

At your shell prompt, type `echo $SHELL` (capitalization counts!). This command tells UNIX to display (echo) information about shell settings. This information, by the way, is part of the *environment variables*, so the technical phrasing (which you might hear in UNIX circles) is to "echo your shell environment variable."

The system's response will be the full path to your shell—something like `/bin/csh`, `/bin/bash`, or `/bin/ksh`. **Code Listings 3.1** and **3.2** show you how two different UNIX systems respond.

✔ Tips

- You can also use `finger userid`, substituting your login name for `userid`, to find out more about your shell settings. You can substitute any other `userid` and see comparable information about the other account holders. See Chapter 7 for more about `finger`.
- You'll find more information about different shells and their capabilities throughout this chapter.

Code Listing 3.1 Our ISP account uses the `/bin/csh` shell by default.

```
xmission> echo $SHELL
/bin/csh
xmission> finger ejray
Login name: ejray
  → In real life: "RayComm
Directory: /home/users/e/ejray
  → Shell: /bin/csh
On since Jul 23 06:58:48 on pts/16 from
  calvin.raycomm.com
1 minute 28 seconds Idle Time
No unread mail
No Plan.
xmission>
```

Code Listing 3.2 On hobbes, a Linux system, the default shell is `/bin/bash`.

```
[ejr@hobbes ejr]$ echo $SHELL
/bin/bash
[ejr@hobbes ejr]$ finger ejr
Login: ejr
  → Name: Eric J. Ray
Directory: /home/ejr
  → Shell: /bin/bash
On since Wed Jul 22 07:42 (MDT) on tty1
  → 3 hours 15 minutes idle
On since Thu Jul 23 08:17 (MDT) on ttyp0 from
  → calvin
No mail.
Project:
Working on UNIX VQS.
Plan:
This is my plan--work all day, sleep all
  → night.
[ejr@hobbes ejr]$
```

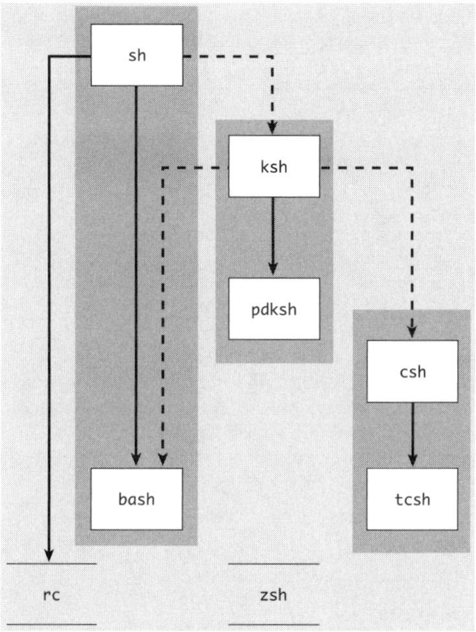

Figure 3.1 Shells fit neatly into a few "families" with the exception of a few stragglers. Each shell in a family shares many characteristics with the others in the same family.

Understanding shells and options

Depending on the particular UNIX system you're using, you may have several different shells available to you. **Table 3.1** describes a few of the more common ones. Each of these shells has slightly different capabilities and features. Keep in mind that the differences in shells do not affect what you can do in UNIX; rather, they affect how easily you can interact with the system.

You'll likely have `bash`, `ksh`, or `tcsh/csh` as your shell, but you can change to one of many other shells fairly easily. As **Code Listings 3.3** and **3.4** show, you can start by finding out which shells are available to you. **Figure 3.1** shows some shells and how they relate to each other.

To see which shells are available to you:

- `cat /etc/shells`
  At the shell prompt, type `cat /etc/shells` to find out which shells you have available to you. **Code Listings 3.3** and **3.4** show the results of this command on two different systems.

Table 3.1

Common UNIX Shells

Shell Name	Features
`sh`	This shell, which is the original UNIX shell (often called the Bourne shell), is great for scripting but lacks a lot of the flexibility and power for interactive use that you might want. For example, it doesn't have features like command completion, e-mail checking, or aliasing.
`csh` and `tcsh`	This family of shells adds great interactive uses but discards the popular scripting support that `sh` offers in favor of a C programming-ish syntax. Because of the C syntax, this shell is often just called the C shell.
`ksh`, `bash`, and `zsh`	These provide a good blend of scripting and interactive capabilities, but they stem from different sources (`bash` is most similar to `sh`, hence the Bourne Again SHell name).

✔ Tip

- Before you go leaping forward through the next sections and changing your shell, you might check with your system administrator or help desk folks to find out which shells they support and sanction.

Code Listing 3.3 A minimal listing of available shells on our UNIX system, including the basics but not too much in the way of choices

```
[ejr@hobbes]$ more /etc/shells
/bin/bash
/bin/sh
/bin/tcsh
/bin/csh
[ejr@hobbes]$
```

Code Listing 3.4 The following shells are available through our ISP. Notice the additional, custom shells that the ISP uses, including shells that provide special features such as not allowing logins.

```
xmission> cat /etc/shells
/usr/local/bin/tcsh
/bin/csh
/usr/bin/csh
/bin/ksh
/usr/bin/ksh
/sbin/sh
/usr/bin/sh
/usr/local/bin/zsh
/usr/local/bin/bash
/usr/local/bin/nologin
/usr/local/bin/terminated
/usr/local/bin/xmmenu.email
/usr/local/bin/xmmenu.noshell
/usr/lib/uucp/uucico
xmission>
```

Code Listing 3.5 You must remember the path to the shell to change shells on this system. Additionally, the password check helps ensure that only the account owner changes the shell.

```
[ejr@hobbes ejr]$ cat /etc/shells
/bin/bash
/bin/sh
/bin/tcsh
/bin/csh
[ejr@hobbes ejr]$ chsh
Changing shell for ejr.
Password:
New shell [/bin/bash]: /bin/csh
Shell changed.
[ejr@hobbes ejr]$
[ejr@hobbes ejr]$ su - ejr
Password:
[ejr@hobbes]$
```

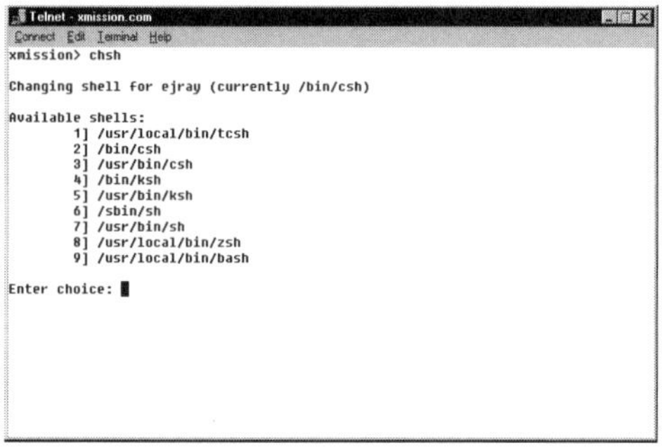

Figure 3.2 Our ISP provides a handy interface for changing shells that lets users pick their new shells from a menu.

Changing your shell with chsh

If you decide that you want to change your shell, you probably can, depending on how your system administrator has set things up. As **Code Listing 3.5** shows, you would do so using chsh. We usually change to bash.

To change your shell with chsh:

1. `cat /etc/shells`

   At the shell prompt, list the available shells on your system with `cat /etc/shells`.

2. `chsh`

   Enter chsh (for "change shell"). **Code Listing 3.5** shows the system response. Some systems prompt for a password, and some don't.

3. `/bin/bash`

   Type in the path and name of your new shell.

4. `su - yourid`

   Type in su - and your userid to re-log in to verify that everything works correctly. If it doesn't, then use chsh again and change back to the original shell or to a different one. If you can't change back, e-mail your system administrator for help.

✔ Tips

- Some systems don't let users use chsh to change shells. If this is the case, you'll need to e-mail your system administrator and ask for a change. You could also change your shell temporarily as described in the next section.
- After changing shells you might have problems running some commands or have a prompt or display that's not as good as the original. That's likely a result of your default shell being carefully customized by your system administrator. You're probably on your own to set up and configure your new shell, and Chapter 8 can help you do this.
- See *Changing your identity with* su later in this chapter for more about the su command.

Changing your shell temporarily

You can change your shell temporarily by creating a sub-shell and using that instead of the original shell. You can create a sub-shell using any shell available on your UNIX system. This means that you can look in the `/etc/shells` file and use a shell listed there, or you can use a shell installed elsewhere on the system (**Code Listing 3.6**).

To find out which temporary shells you can use:

1. `cat /etc/shells`

   At the shell prompt, type `cat /etc/shells` to find out which shells are listed in the shells file.

   If you don't find a shell you want to use in the shells file, look for other shells installed elsewhere on the system.

2. `ls /usr/local/bin *sh`

   At the shell prompt, type `ls /usr/local/bin *sh` to find additional shells in the `/usr/local/bin` directory. Note that not all programs that end with `sh` are shells, but most shells end with `sh` (**Code Listing 3.6**).

To create a temporary shell (sub-shell):

- `/usr/bin/csh`

  At the shell prompt, type the path and name of the temporary shell you want to use. In this case, we're using the `csh` shell, located at `/usr/bin/csh`. You might see a new prompt, perhaps something like the one shown in **Code Listing 3.7.**

Code Listing 3.6 Checking the list of shells from /etc/shells and looking for other programs that end with "sh" is a good way to find all of the shells on the system.

```
[ejr@hobbes]$ cat /etc/shells
/bin/bash
/bin/sh
/bin/tcsh
/bin/csh
[ejr@hobbes]$ ls /usr/local/bin/*sh
/usr/local/bin/pdksh
[ejr@hobbes]$
```

Code Listing 3.7 Type in the shell name (which is really just another UNIX command) to change shells.

```
[ejr@hobbes]$ /usr/bin/csh
ejr>
```

To exit a temporary shell (sub-shell):

- `exit`

  At the shell prompt, type `exit`. You'll be returned to the shell from which you started the sub-shell. If you created more than one sub-shell, you'll have to exit all of them.

✔ Tips

- Using temporary shells is a great way to experiment with other shells and their options. We'd recommend using a temporary shell to experiment with the shells covered in this chapter.
- You can also often use Ctrl D to exit from a sub-shell, but this depends on the system configuration. Try it out and see!
- See Chapter 1 and the listings of directories containing programs for other places to look for shells.

Using command completion in the bash shell

One of the cool features of the bash shell is command completion, with which you can type just part of a command, press [Tab], and have bash complete the command for you (**Code Listing 3.8**).

To use command completion in the bash shell:

1. `ls -l`

   Use `ls -l` to list the files in your current directory.

2. `cd pub`[Tab]

   Type in a partial command, then press the [Tab] key to complete the command. In this example, we typed the `cd` command and part of the `public_html` command (truncated to `pub` in the example), then pressed the Tab key to complete it (see **Code Listing 3.8**).

✔ Tip

- Command completion only works if there's only one possible match to the letters you type before you hit [Tab]. For example, if you type `cd pu` (for `public_html`) and there's another subdirectory called `puppy`, the shell will beep and wait for you to type in enough letters to distinguish the two subdirectories.

- You can use command completion to complete commands, directory names within commands, and nearly anything else you might enter that's sufficiently unambiguous.

Code Listing 3.8 In this example, we typed only the ls command followed by "cd pub" and pressed the [Tab] key; bash completed the command for us.

```
bash-2.00$ ls
Complete      NewProject    bogus2
  → ftp          puppy
Completed     News          dead.letter
  → mail         temp
Mail          access        files
  → public_html  testme
bash-2.00$ cd public_html/
bash-2.00$
```

Code Listing 3.9 In this example, we typed the first two commands, then pressed the Up Arrow to reuse the previous (ls) command. !40 recycled the 40th command from the listing.

```
[ejr@hobbes clean]$ ls
background.htm  info.htm        logo.gif
[ejr@hobbes clean]$ ls
background.htm  info.htm        logo.gif
[ejr@hobbes clean]$ history
    1  free
    2  id deb
    3  id ejr
    4  uname -a
    5  ls

...

   40  cd
   41  cp .bash_history oldhistory
   42  vi .bash_history
   43  elm
   44  ls -la
   45  ls -la .e*
   46  elm
   47  lynx
   48  history
   49  vi .bash*his*
   50  history
   51  cd clean
   52  ls
   53  ls
   54  history
[ejr@hobbes clean]$ !40
cd
[ejr@hobbes ejr]$
```

Viewing session history in the bash shell

Another cool feature of the bash shell is that it lets you easily reuse commands from your session history, which shows you the list of commands you've used during a session or in previous sessions (**Code Listing 3.9**). Viewing history is handy for reviewing your UNIX session, using previous commands again (rather than retyping them), and modifying (rather than completely retyping) complex commands.

To view session history in the bash shell:

1. Use the shell for a little while, changing directories, redirecting output, or doing other tasks.

   Take your time. We'll wait.

2. Press ↑ one time.

   Note that the last (previous) command you used appears on the command line, as shown in **Code Listing 3.9**. To reissue the command, just press Enter.

3. Continue to press ↑ or ↓ to scroll back or forward through your history. When you reach a command you want to use, press Enter.

   If you see a command that's close, but not exactly what you want to use, you can edit it. Just use the Left and Right Arrow keys to move across the line, insert text by typing it in, and use Backspace or Delete to delete text. When you've fixed the command, press Enter (you don't have to be at the end of the line to do so).

4. `history`

   Type `history` at the shell prompt to see a numbered list of previous commands you've entered.

✔ Tips

- Commands from the current session are kept in memory to scroll through, while commands from previous sessions are kept in the `~/.bash_history` file. You can edit `.bash_history` with any editor to delete unneeded commands, or simply delete the file to get rid of the whole history file, which will then be recreated with the next command you issue. (A history of commands is a great jumping off point to write a script to do the commands automatically. Chapter 10, *Writing Basic Scripts*, gives you the specifics.)
- When you're viewing the history, you can recycle commands by typing an exclamation point (`!`) and the line number of the command you want to run again. You'd type `!40`, for example, to rerun command 40.
- Use `history` followed by a number to specify the number of items to list. For example, `history 10` shows the last 10 commands.

Using command completion in the ksh shell

ksh is another shell that offers command completion. You type part of a command, press Esc *twice*, and ksh completes the command for you (see **Code Listing 3.10**). Using command completion in ksh isn't as easy as it is in bash, but the results are the same.

To use command completion in the ksh shell:

1. `set -o emacs`

   To begin, you must enable command completion by entering `set -o emacs`. This command enables command completion and sets it to use emacs commands. (emacs is an editor, but you do not need to use or be familiar with it to recycle ksh commands.)

2. `ls -l`

   Use `ls -l` to list the files in your current directory. You do this so you know which directory (`public_html`) you can change to in Step 3.

3. `cd pub` Esc Esc

   Type in a partial command.

   In this example, we typed the cd command and part of the `public_html`

Code Listing 3.10 After listing the files and directories, we set our options, then successfully completed a command. The ^[^[is how Esc appears on the screen when the shell doesn't know to use it to complete commands.

```
$ ls
Complete     NewProject   bogus2       files      public_html  testme
Completed    News         chat.conf    ftp        puppy
Mail         access       dead.letter  mail       temp
$ cd pub^[^[
ksh: pub:  not found
$ set -o emacs
$ cd public_html/
$
```

command (truncated to pub in the example).

Press Esc *two times* to complete the command.

Depending on your terminal emulation, you might need to use Ctrl[twice instead of Esc twice.

✔ Tips

- If you don't have ksh installed on your system, you might also look for pdksh, which is a freely distributable and nearly identical version of ksh.
- You can also type in `set -o vi` to use vi commands (instead of the command given in step 1). We've found, though, that this isn't as intuitive or effective, so we recommend the emacs mode.
- See Chapter 4 for more information about editors.
- If you use ksh, you'll probably want to add the `set -o emacs` command to your personal configuration files so you don't have to manually enter the command in each session. See Chapter 8 for the specifics of editing configuration files.

Viewing session history in the ksh shell

Using ksh, you can also view session history. In doing so, you can get a quickie reminder of what you've been doing (**Code Listing 3.11**), reuse commands, and modify commands you've already used.

Code Listing 3.11 Although it looks like we typed ls for both the first and second commands, we really just pressed Ctrl P to get the second ls command. The r 64 command recycles the command numbered 64 in the list.

```
$ ls
Complete     NewProject   bogus2       files        public_html  testme
Completed    News         chat.conf    ftp          puppy
Mail         access       dead.letter  mail         temp
$ ls
Complete     NewProject   bogus2       files        public_html  testme
Completed    News         chat.conf    ftp          puppy
Mail         access       dead.letter  mail         temp
$
$ history
56      cd ..
57      ls
58      lynx
59      ls temp
60      more Complete
61      ls
62      more testme
63      ls
64      ls
65      history
66      lynx
67      ftp ftp.raycomm.com
68      ls
69      ls
70      ls
71      history
$ r 64
ls
Complete     NewProject   bogus2       files        public_html  testme
Completed    News         chat.conf    ftp          puppy
Mail         access       dead.letter  mail         temp
$
```

To view session history in the ksh shell:

1. Use the shell for a little while, changing directories, redirecting output, or doing other tasks.
2. Ctrl P

   Recall the previous command with Ctrl P. **Table 3.2** shows you other keyboard combinations that you can use to navigate through the session history.

   After you've finished recalling and, optionally, editing the command, press Enter (you don't have to be at the end of the line to do so).
3. `history`

   Type `history` at the shell prompt to see the list of the most recent commands you've entered (**Code Listing 3.11**).

   Notice the command number by each command. You can type `r`, Spacebar, and the command's number to rerun it.

✔ Tip

- If you use `ksh`, you'll probably want to add the `set -o emacs` command to your personal configuration files so you don't have to manually enter the command in each session. See Chapter 8 for the specifics of editing configuration files.

Table 3.2

ksh History Navigation Commands

Command	Function
Ctrl P	Recalls the previous command
Ctrl N	Recalls the next command (only works after you've moved to a previous command)
Ctrl R *something*	Gets the previous command containing "something"
Ctrl B	Moves back one character within a command
Ctrl F	Moves forward one character within a command
Ctrl A	Goes to the beginning of the line within a command
Ctrl E	Goes to the end of the line within a command
Ctrl D	Deletes the current character

Code Listing 3.12 csh also lets you recycle commands by number, although other history functions are not available.

```
xmission> history
     1  ls
     2  vi temp.info
     3  ls
     4  cd pub*
     5  ls
     6  cp *.pdf ..
     7  cd ..
     8  rm *.pdf
     9  history
    10  lynx
    11  ftp ftp.wustl.edu
    12  ls
    13  vi .plan
    14  finger ejr@raycomm.com
    15  history
    16  finger ejr@hobbes.raycomm.com
    17  ls
    18  pine
    19  history
    20  lynx
    21  history
xmission>!10
```

Viewing session history in the csh shell

If you're a C programmer (or have C programmers to turn to for help), `csh` might be a good shell for you because the syntax is quite similar to the C programming language. `csh` doesn't offer command completion, but the history capabilities are fairly similar to those of `bash` or `ksh` (see Code Listing 3.12). In general, `csh` is a powerful scripting shell (and acceptable interactive shell) for those who take the time and effort to become familiar with it.

To view session history in the csh shell:

1. If you haven't already, use the shell for a little while, changing directories, redirecting output, or doing other tasks.
2. `history`

   Type `history` at the shell prompt to see the list of the most recent commands you've entered. Note the number of each command line (**Code Listing 3.12**).
3. `!10`

   Type `!` followed by the command number (no space in between) to rerun one of the commands. In this example, we're rerunning command 10.

✔ Tips

- See Chapter 8, *Setting aliases with* `alias`, to make `csh` easier and more productive, particularly if you don't have any other shell options available to you.
- You can edit commands in the session history. With `csh`, however, it's far easier to retype the commands than to edit them.

Changing your identity with su

Occasionally, you may need to log in with a userid other than your own or need to re-log in with your own userid. For example, you might want to check configuration settings that you've changed before logging out to make sure that they work. Or, if you change your shell, you might want to check it before you log out (and you should, by the way).

You can use the **su** (substitute user) command to either log in as another user (**Code Listing 3.13**) or to start a new login shell.

Code Listing 3.13 Changing back and forth from one user to another (and exiting from multiple shells) can get a little confusing, but the prompt often tells you who you are and what directory you're in.

```
[ejr@hobbes asr]$ ls
Projects  testing
[ejr@hobbes asr]$ su asr
Password:
[asr@hobbes asr]$ ls
Projects  testing
[asr@hobbes asr]$ su - ejr
Password:
[ejr@hobbes ejr]$ ls
Mail              editme            script2.sed
Projects          fortunes.copy     scriptextra.sed
Xrootenv.0        fortunes1.txt     sedtest
above.htm         fortunes2.txt     sorted.address.temp
address.book      groups            temp.htm
address.temp      history.txt       tempsort
axhome            html.htm          test
bogus             html.html         test2
chmod.txt         mail              testing.gif
clean             manipulate        testing.wp
compression       nsmail            typescript
[ejr@hobbes ejr]$ exit
[asr@hobbes asr]$ exit
[ejr@hobbes ejr]$ exit
```

To log in as a different user with su:

◆ `su asr`

At the shell prompt, type su plus the userid of the user you're logging in as. You'll be prompted for a password just as though you were logging in to the system for the first time (**Code Listing 3.13**).

If you're logged in as root to begin with, you won't be prompted to give a password.

You will now be logged in as the new user and be able to work just as though you were that user, though you'll be in the same directory with the same settings that you had before you issued the su command.

To start a new login shell with su:

◆ `su - yourid`

At the shell prompt, type `su - yourid` (of course, use your own userid or that of the user you want to change to). The addition of the hyphen (-) will force a new login shell and set all of the environment variables and defaults according to the settings for the user.

To return to the previous shell:

◆ `exit`

Type `exit` at the shell prompt to leave the current shell and return to the previous one. If you use `exit` from the original login shell, you'll log completely out of the UNIX system.

✔ Tips

■ If you have root access and you telnet to the system to administer it, you should use su to provide a little extra security. Rather than logging in directly as root and leaving the remote possibility of having your password stolen (or *sniffed*) over the network, log in as yourself, then use su (with no other information) to change to root.

■ If you su to another user with `su user` (no hyphen) and the new user doesn't have read and execute permissions for the current directory, you will see shell error messages. You can disregard these. See Chapter 5 for more about read and execute permissions.

Fixing terminal settings with stty

Another handy thing you can do with your shell is use it to fix those annoying problems that occur with `telnet`. Back in Chapter 1, we mentioned that you might encounter oddities such as your Backspace and Delete keys not working properly. You can fix these problems using `stty` (see **Code Listing 3.14**).

Fixing Backspace and Delete key oddities with stty:

◆ `stty erase '^?'`

If you're used to [Backspace] erasing characters to the left of the cursor and you just get a bunch of `^?` symbols on the screen when you try it, you need to educate the terminal about your preferences. Type `stty erase` [Backspace] to fix it (**Code Listing 3.14**).

In some cases, depending on your telnet program, you might need to set `stty erase '^H'` and then use [Ctrl][H] to backspace. To enter this command, type `stty erase` [Ctrl][V] [Ctrl][H] (**Code Listing 3.15**).

Fixing general terminal weirdness with stty:

◆ `stty sane`

Typing `stty sane` at the shell prompt will fix a lot of oddities. For example, if you accidentally issue a bad command and all of a sudden nothing shows up on the screen or if you have general gibberish showing up on the screen, `stty sane` will return your terminal session to sanity.

✔ Tips

■ If `stty sane` doesn't fix a messed up display, try logging out and logging back in or restarting your `telnet` program.

■ You can fix [Backspace] oddities permanently by adding the appropriate `stty` command to your configuration files or by making changes in your telnet client. See Chapter 8 for details about your configuration files. Refer to Chapter 1 for more helpful details about `telnet`.

Code Listing 3.14 You can often straighten out a confused telnet program or UNIX system by using a stty command. This one fixes the errant [Backspace] key.

```
xmission> ls ^?^?^?^?
  : No such file or directory
xmission> stty erase '^?'
xmission> ls
```

Code Listing 3.15 The stty command here fixes the [Delete] key to work like [Backspace].

```
xmission> jf^H^H
jf^H^H: Command not found
xmission> ls ^H^H
: No such file or directory
xmission> stty erase '^H'
xmission>
```

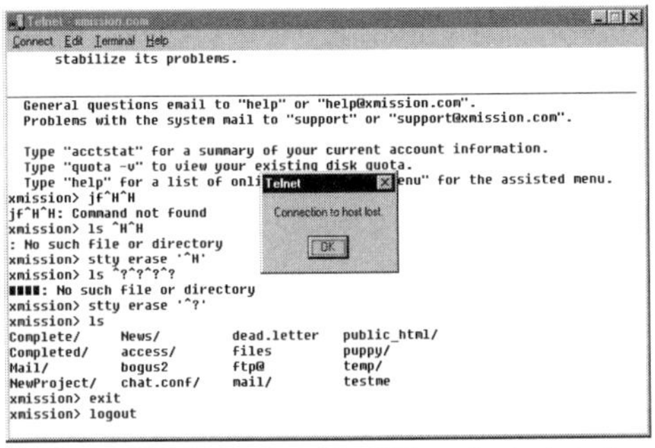

Figure 3.3 After we entered "exit" from the last shell, the system added "logout" and closed the connection.

Exiting the shell

When you're finished with your UNIX session, you need to exit the UNIX shell. If you've been playing with the `su` and shell commands, you might actually have shells within shells and need to exit from all of them. All you have to do is type `exit` once for each shell, as shown in **Figure 3.3**.

To exit from the shell:

- `exit`

  At the shell prompt, type `exit`, as shown in **Figure 3.3**. TaDaaaa!

✔ Tips

- If you're located at the login shell prompt, you could also type `logout`, rather than `exit`. At all other shells, though, you need to type `exit`. In some cases, you could also press Ctrl D, but that depends on your local system configuration.
- Be sure and log off rather than simply hanging up or breaking your telnet connection. It's possible, if the settings at your UNIX host are incorrect, that your session could remain open and someone else could pick up right where you left off with your session under your userid.

4

Creating and Editing Files

Creating and editing files are likely the most common tasks you'll perform in UNIX. If you're programming, developing Web pages, sending e-mail (uh-huh, really), or just writing a letter, you'll spend a lot of time in an editor.

In this chapter, we'll introduce you to two of the most common editors: `pico` and `vi`. We'll launch this chapter with a general overview of each, then we discuss some how-tos of using each one. With the information presented here, you'll be able to choose an editor based on your needs and get started using it (or using both of them).

Chapter contents

Choosing an editor

Basically, editors are all designed to do the same things: enable you to create, modify, and save text files. These files could include configuration files, e-mail messages, or shell scripts—essentially any text file you can create. Exactly which editor you choose is up to you, depending on your specific needs and how much you're willing to learn.

In this book, we'll stick to two biggies, `pico` and `vi`, which will likely give you all the capabilities you'll need. We chose these because `pico` is (arguably) the easiest UNIX editor to use, and `vi` is one of the most powerful and is available on almost every UNIX system.

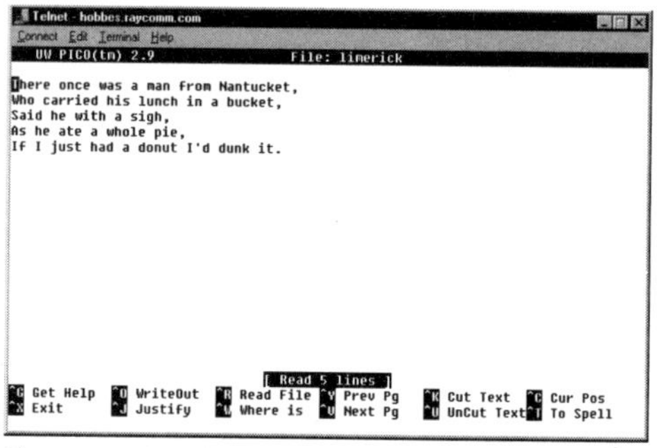

Figure 4.1 pico offers onscreen command reminders to make it easier to use.

About pico

`pico` is one of the newest UNIX editors and has become quite popular because it's extremely easy to use. In particular, as shown in **Figure 4.1**, it's menu-driven and intuitive. All of the commands are visible, and you can open, modify, and close files with little effort. `pico` is a great choice if you're just getting started with UNIX or if you won't be needing an editor able to leap tall files in a single bound.

`pico` is distributed with the `pine` e-mail program, so if you have `pine` available to you, you likely also have `pico`. (See Chapter 1 for a reminder on how to find out if `pine` and `pico` are available to you.) If it's not available to you, ask your system administrators to install it.

About vi

Although `vi` is likely responsible for much of UNIX's reputation for being complicated and confusing, it offers enormous power and flexibility—it *will* leap tall files in a single bound and do much, much more. Plus, `vi` is universally available (unlike `pico`), so for

Editors Abound

By the way, dozens of other editors exist, such as:

- `emacs`, which is infinitely customizable and loaded with bells and whistles, such as e-mail programs and Web browsing capabilities built right in
- `ed`, `ex`, and `red`, which are simple line-by-line editors
- `roff`, `nroff`, and `troff`, which are much fancier format-for-pretty-output editors

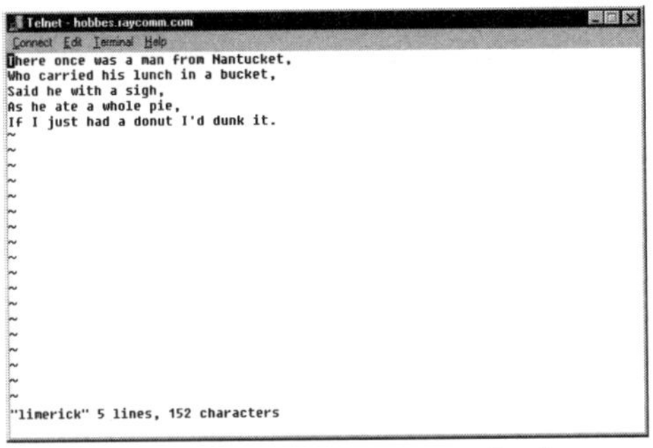
Telnet - hobbes.raycomm.com
Connect Edit Terminal Help
There once was a man from Nantucket,
Who carried his lunch in a bucket,
Said he with a sigh,
As he ate a whole pie,
If I just had a donut I'd dunk it.
"limerick" 5 lines, 152 characters

Figure 4.2 vi gives you a clean screen and makes you remember all of its cryptic commands.

these two reasons, you should consider taking the time to learn it. You might find `vi` cryptic, counterintuitive, and nitpicky, and for this reason, you might want to choose a different editor if you won't require `vi`'s capabilities. As **Figure 4.2** shows, if you use `vi`, you won't have menus at your disposal—you'll have to get used to using commands like [Esc] `:q` or [Esc] `:%s/vi is arcane/vi is powerful/`. Eesch.

✔ Tips

- You're not bound to one editor or another. You can use any editor at any time; we often use `pico` for e-mail or plain writing because you can type without thinking, switching to `vi` when we really need power or just want to make a quick edit without hassling with the menus—`pico` seems more cumbersome to us.

- You can specify a default editor that will start automatically in programs that start up an editor for you. Chapter 8 provides details about setting your editor environment variable.

- See Chapter 8 for more information about configuration files, Chapter 10 for more information about shell scripts, and Chapter 11 for more information about e-mail.

Starting pico and dabbling with it

You can start and dabble with `pico` using the following steps. Notice that the `pico` interface is intuitive and easy to navigate in, as shown in **Figure 4.3**.

To start pico and dabble with it:

1. `pico`

   To begin, type `pico` at the shell prompt. The program starts up and you'll see something like **Figure 4.3**, with the text area up at the top of the window and the command hints down at the bottom.

   If you know the name of the file you want to edit, type `pico` at the shell prompt followed by the path and name of the file you want to edit (`hairyspider`, for example).

2. `hairy spiders`

   Go ahead. Type in something—anything—just to try it out.

   - Use [Delete] and [Backspace] to help edit text.
   - Use the arrow keys move you up, down, right, or left.
   - Press [Page Up] and [Page Down] to navigate—well—up and down.

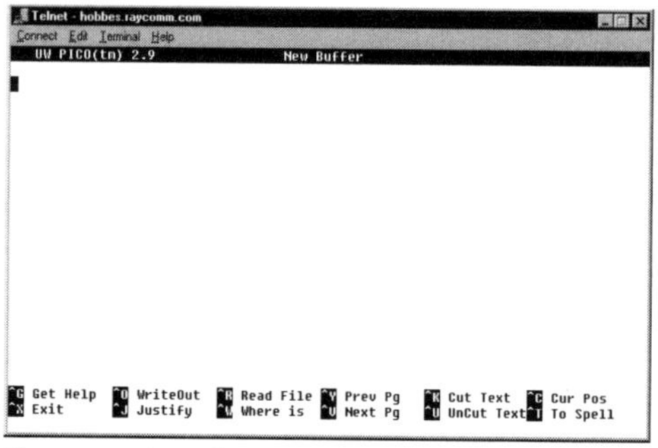

Figure 4.3 pico offers an intuitive interface for editing text.

STARTING pico AND DABBLING WITH IT

✔ Tips

- Start `pico` with the `-w` option (e.g., `pico -w filename`) to disable word wrapping. You'll find this particularly useful when editing configuration files, as covered in Chapter 8.
- Throughout `pico`, you'll see `^C`, `^J`, and dozens of other `^something` characters hanging out in the menu at the bottom. The `^` stands for `Ctrl`, so `^C` is Ctrl C, `^J` is Ctrl J, and so on.
- If you type `pico` and get an error message telling you that the command is not found, use `find`, `whereis`, or `ls` tosearch through the likely directories (`/usr/bin` or `/usr/local/bin`) to see whether the program is available but not located where your shell can find it. See Chapter 1 for a quickie review.
- After you establish a file and start adding content, save your changes using the instructions in the next section, *Saving in `pico`*.
- You can get helpful information about `pico`'s features by accessing `pico` help. See the section called *Getting help in `pico`* later in this chapter.

Saving in pico

You'll generally save your files frequently whenever you're editing them—and you should. Remember, Murphy is watching you....

To save in pico:

1. Ctrl O

   Use Ctrl O periodically to save (write Out) the text you're editing.

2. `hairyspiders`

   Specify the file name for your file (**Figure 4.4**).

✔ Tips

- After you save a file for the first time and want to save new changes, just press Ctrl O then press Enter to confirm the current file name and save it.
- When you exit `pico`, you'll get a last chance to save your changes. See *Exiting Pico* in this chapter for the specifics.

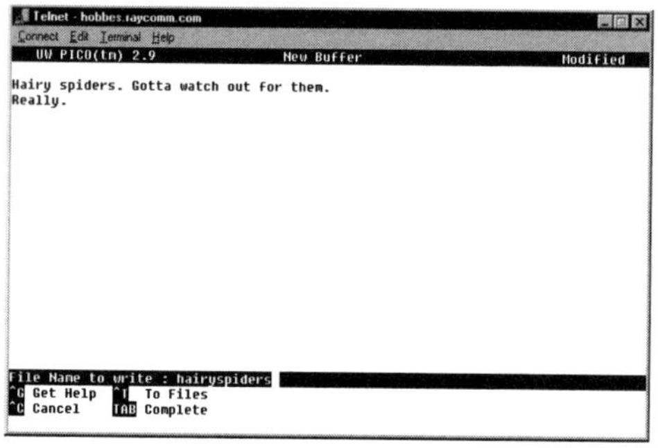

Figure 4.4 In pico lingo, "writing out" just means "saving."

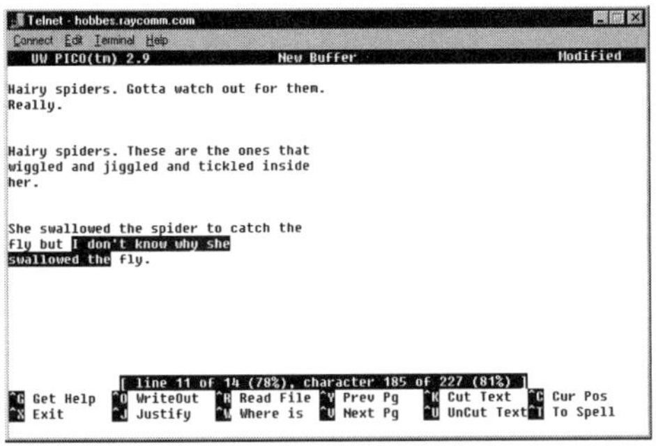

Figure 4.5 Marking, cutting, and pasting text in pico can be very handy.

Cutting and pasting text blocks in pico

As you're typing along in `pico`, you'll probably need to cut and paste blocks of text, as shown in **Figure 4.5**.

To cut and paste text in pico:

1. `pico hairyspider`

   At the shell prompt, type `pico` followed by the name of the file to edit.

2. Move the cursor to the first line of the text you want to cut.

3. Ctrl ^

   Press Ctrl ^ to mark the beginning of the text you want to cut. (Note that Ctrl ^ is really Ctrl Shift 6—it might work without Shift, but it might not. Try it out with your telnet program and see what happens.)

4. Use the arrow keys to move the cursor to the end of the text you want to cut.

   Note that the text gets highlighted as you select it (**Figure 4.5**).

5. Ctrl K

   This "kuts" the text.

6. Using the arrow keys, move the cursor to where you want to insert the cut text.

7. Ctrl U

   Use this key combination to paste the cut text into the file at the new location.

✔ Tips

- You can select and cut blocks of text without also pasting them back into a file. Just skip steps 6 and 7.
- You can paste text blocks as many times as you want. After you select and cut text, just press Ctrl U at each place where you want to insert the cut text.
- If you don't select text, Ctrl K just cuts a single line.

Checking spelling in pico

Another handy thing you can do in `pico` is chek yoor speling, as shown in **Figures 4.6** and **4.7**.

To spell-check in pico:

1. `pico hairyspider`

   At the shell prompt, type `pico` and the file name of the file to edit.

2. Ctrl T

   Pressing this command starts spell-checking the file. `pico` will stop at each misspelled word (**Figure 4.6**).

3. `correctspelling`

   Type in the correct spelling for any words flagged as misspelled, or press Enter to accept the current spelling and move along to the next word.

✔ Tips

- You can press Ctrl C to cancel spell-checking at any time.
- When the entire document has been spell-checked, `pico` will tell you that it's done checking spelling, and you can continue editing the file (**Figure 4.7**).

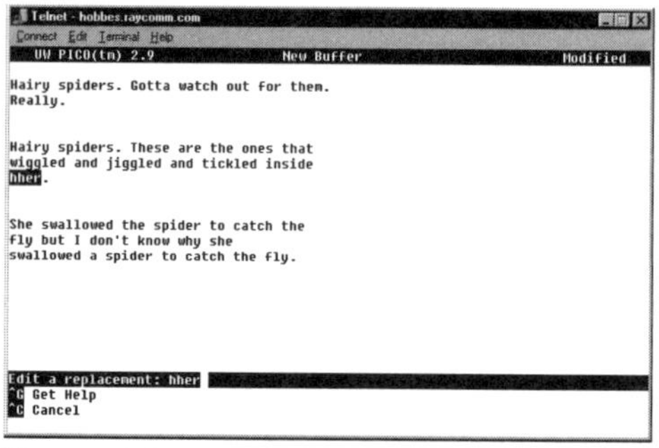

Figure 4.6 pico prompts you to correct the spelling of misspelled words.

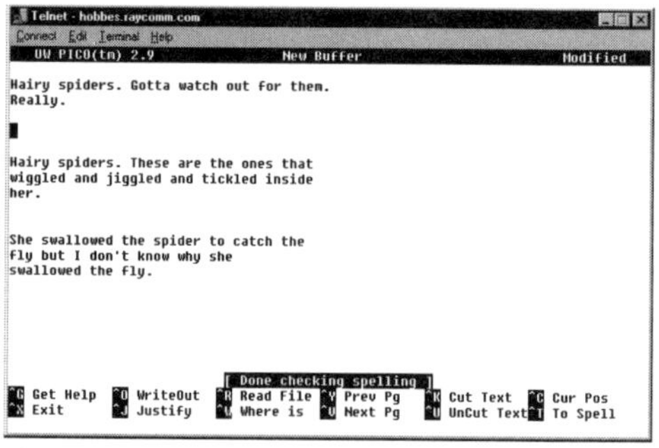

Figure 4.7 pico informs you when the procedure is complete.

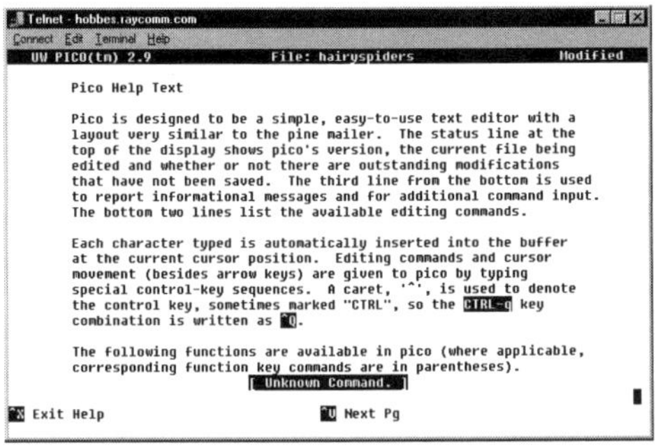

Figure 4.8 pico gives you all the information you need. The error message in the status line (resulting from a typo) is a bonus in this figure.

Getting help in pico

A great way to find out more about `pico` is to access `pico` help. In addition to finding answers to your questions, you can also find out about `pico` features and capabilities that you may have been unaware of (**Figure 4.8**).

To get help in pico:

1. Ctrl G

   In `pico`, type `Ctrl+g` to access help.

2. Move through the help pages:
   - Ctrl V moves you down through the help page.
   - Ctrl Y moves you up through the help page.

3. Ctrl X

   Use this combination to exit help.

To get help with pico startup options:

- `man pico`

  At the shell prompt, type `man pico` to learn more about startup options, including a variety of options that control how `pico` works.

✔ Tips

- Keep your eyes on the `pico` status line for current information, error messages, and occasional hints about using `pico`. The status line is the third line from the bottom of the screen, just above the menu, as shown in **Figure 4.8**.

- Keep in mind that `pico` really is a basic program. If you're looking for a command or function that isn't readily available, it's probably not there. You might check out `vi` instead.

Exiting pico

When you're done editing in `pico`, you'll exit it using the following steps.

To exit pico:

1. Ctrl X

   Within `pico`, press Ctrl X. If you haven't made any changes to the text since you last saved the file, you'll find yourself immediately back at the shell prompt. If you have made changes, you'll be prompted to "Save modified buffer" (**Figure 4.9**).

2. `Y`

   At the "Save modified buffer" prompt:
   - Type `Y` if you want to save your changes. Proceed to step 3.
   - Type `N` if you don't want to save your changes. You'll end up back at the shell prompt.

3. `bighairyspider`

   Specify the file name for your file if it's the first time you've saved it. If you've saved it before, press Enter to confirm the current file name or change the name to save a copy and not change the original file.

✔ Tip

- A buffer is what the computer uses to temporarily store information, and if it's modified, that means that it's temporarily storing something that you haven't saved to disk.

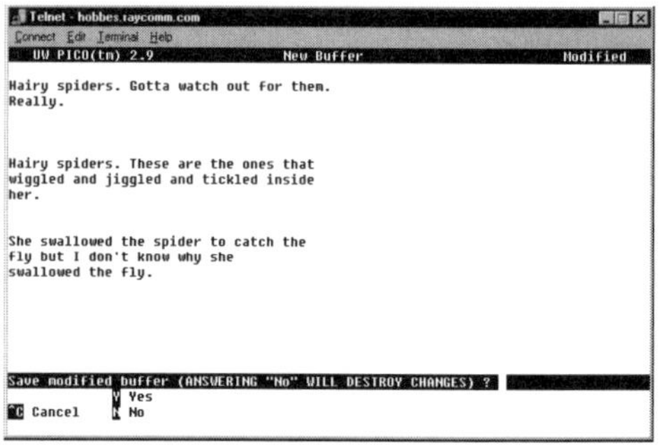

Figure 4.9 pico gives you the opportunity to "Save modified buffer." Without the technobabble, this means to save the text you just wrote or edited before you exit.

EXITING pico

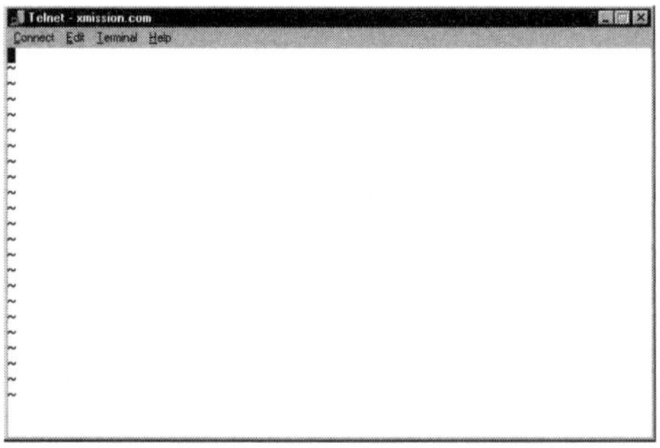

Figure 4.10 The vi editor innundates you with tons of onscreen help and advice, as shown here. Well, documentation is available, but the vi interface itself isn't really helpful at all!

Starting vi and dabbling with it

Before you go running off to use `vi`, understand that it has two modes (both of which look pretty much like **Figure 4.10**):

- An *input mode* (sometimes called *insert mode*), in which the keys you press actually show up in the file that you're editing. You use this mode to add or change text.
- A *command mode*, in which every keystroke is interpreted as a command. You use this mode to do everything except enter text.

What's confusing about `vi` is that it starts you in command mode, meaning that if you just start typing, you'll see some blank spaces, characters, and bits of words that you type—essentially, a bunch of garbage that does not exactly represent what you're typing—and you'll hear a lot of beeping. So, as we'll show you in the following steps, you'll need to access the input mode as soon as you start `vi`.

To start vi:

1. `vi`

   At the shell prompt, type `vi`. The program starts up and you'll see something like **Figure 4.10**. The ~ symbols show blank lines below the end of the file.

2. `i`

   Type `i` to get into input mode. This itself is a command issued in command mode, so it won't show up on the screen.

3. `hairy spiders lurk`

   In input mode, type anything you want.

   Everything you type will show up on the screen until you return to command mode by pressing Esc. You can use the arrow keys to navigate up and down in the file line by line and Ctrl U and Ctrl D to scroll up and down, respectively.

✓ Tips:

- To get help in `vi`, type `man vi`. See Chapter 1 for more about `man` pages.
- If you're not sure what mode you're in, press Esc to go into command mode. If you're already in command mode, you'll hear a beep. If you're in input mode, you'll change to command mode.
- You can open specific files or even multiple files when you access `vi`. At the shell prompt, type `vi filetoedit` (or whatever) to open a specific file. Or, for example, type `vi *.html` to open all of the HTML documents in a directory, then use Esc `:n` (for next) to move to each subsequent file.
- See *Adding and deleting text with* `vi` later in this chapter for more details about editing in `vi`.

Figure 4.11 Save early, save often. That's the safe rule for vi.

Saving in vi

You'll want to save changes to your documents frequently, especially as you're learning to use `vi` (**Figure 4.11**). Until you're accustomed to switching between command and input mode, you may accidentally type in commands when you think you're typing text, with unpredictable results. To save files, just follow these steps.

To save text in vi:

- Esc `:w limerick`

  Press Esc to get out of input mode and into command mode, then type `:w` (for write, as in write to the disk) followed by the file name (`limerick`, in this example) you want to use for the file, then press Enter. If you've already saved the file once, just type Esc `:w` and press Enter.

✔ Tips

- If you've already saved your file at least once, you can save changes and exit `vi` in one swell foop. In command mode, type `:wq` (for write quit). For more information about quitting `vi`, see the section called *Exiting* `vi` later in this chapter.
- If you want to save a file over an existing file (obliterating the original as you do), use `:w! existingfilename` in command mode. The `!` forces `vi` to overwrite the original.

Adding and deleting text in vi

Adding and deleting text in `vi` is a bit more complicated than doing the same in `pico`. Whereas in `pico`, you basically just place your cursor where you want to make changes, `vi` has a whole slew of commands that you use to specify where the changes should occur. (**Tables 4.1**, **4.2**, and **4.3** list your options.) Plus, to issue the commands, you have to switch between input mode and command mode.

To add or delete text in vi:

1. `vi`

   To begin, type `vi` at the shell prompt.

2. `i`

   Change into input mode.

3. `There once was a man from Nantucket`

   Type in some text that you'll want to add to.

4. Esc

   Press Esc to enter command mode before you issue the commands.

5. Choose a command, based on what you want to do to the text.

   Table 4.1 lists commands to add text.

   Table 4.2 lists commands to delete text.

   Table 4.3 lists miscellaneous editing commands.

6. Esc dd

   Type the command. Here, we're deleting the current line of text.

✔ Tip

- We recommend that you take a few minutes and try out some of the commands, which you'll use throughout your `vi` experience. If you don't think you'll be needing this range of commands, consider using `pico` rather than `vi`.

Table 4.1

vi Commands to Add Text

Command	Function
a	Adds text after the cursor
A	Adds text on the next line
i	Inserts text before the cursor
I	Inserts text at the beginning of the current line
o	Inserts a blank line after the current line
O	Inserts a blank line before the current line

Table 4.2

vi Commands to Delete Text

Command	Function
x	Deletes one character (under the cursor)
X	Deletes one character (behind the cursor)
dd	Deletes the current line
5dd	Deletes five lines starting with the current line (obviously, any number would work here)
r	Replaces the character under the cursor with the next character you type
R	Replaces the existing text with the text you type (like overtype mode in most word processors)

Table 4.3

Other Handy vi Editing Commands

Command	Function
y	Copies the current line
p	Pastes the copied line at the cursor
J	Joins the current and following lines
u	Undoes the last change
U	Undoes all changes on the current line

Figure 4.12 Reading an additional file into the current one can make your editing tasks much easier.

Importing files into vi

You can also merge multiple files in `vi` by reading additional files into the current one, as shown in **Figure 4.12**. Basically, all this means is that you insert one file into the file you're currently editing.

To import files in vi:

1. `vi hairyspider`

   At the shell prompt, type `vi` followed by the file name to start `vi` with—in this case, the `hairyspider` file.

2. [Esc] `:r filename`

   At the point in the file where you want to import text, press [Esc], then type `:r` and the file name you want to read into the file.

✔ Tip

- `vi` also lets you read the output of commands into the file. For example, if you want to read the list of files in a specific directory into the file, use [Esc]`:r! ls` in command mode.

IMPORTING FILES INTO VI

Searching and replacing in vi

One of vi's better features is that it allows you to search and replace throughout entire files. As shown in the next sections, you can just find a specific string of text (a *regular expression*, in UNIX lingo) or you can find the text and replace it with other text, as in **Figure 4.13**.

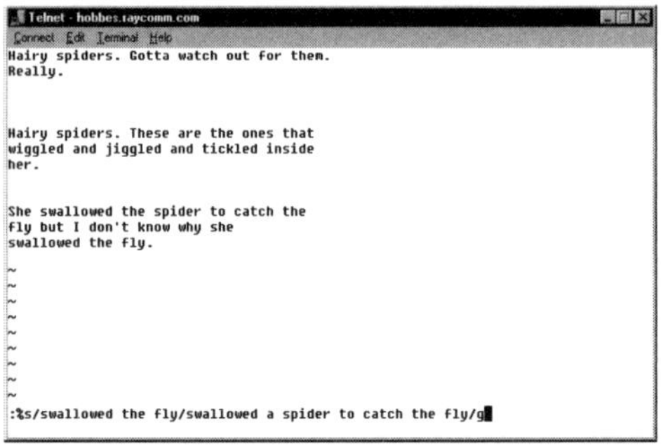

Figure 4.13 Searching for and replacing text in vi is quick and reliable.

To find a string of text in vi:

1. `vi hairyspiders`

   For starters, access `vi` and a specific file.

2. [Esc]`/spider`

   Enter command mode, then type / followed by the text you're looking for. Here, we're looking for "spider", but you may be looking for "the fly" or "wiggled and jiggled and tickled inside her". Or whatever.

3. [Enter]

   Press this to find the first occurrence of the term. Press [N] to find the next one?

To search and replace in vi:

1. `vi hairyspiders`

   For starters, access `vi` and a specific file.

2. [Esc]`:%s/swallowed the fly/swallowed` ➝ `a spider to catch the fly/`

   Enter [Esc]`:%s/` plus the text to find, followed by the replacement text. Here, we replace "swallowed a fly" with "swallowed a spider to catch the fly", but perhaps you might forego the spider and simply go for some antacid.

✔ Tips

- A great use for the search-and-replace feature is if you end up with DOS text files in your UNIX account (through uploading a text file from a DOS or Windows machine as a binary file, most likely). If you view DOS files through a UNIX shell, all the lines within the file will end with `^M`. But if you try to type `^M` when you're doing a search and replace, the `^M` won't show up. What to do? Press Ctrl V, then Ctrl M. Just search and replace with `:%s/` Ctrl V Ctrl M`//g`. The Ctrl V command "escapes" the following character, so you can type it without actually doing what the command would otherwise do. If you don't escape the Ctrl M, `vi` thinks you just pressed Enter and tries to execute the unfinished command.
- See the section on `grep` in Chapter 6 for information about searching with expressions.
- Add a `g` at the end of the command to make it apply to all occurances in the file.

Exiting (quitting) vi

Whew! Time to exit vi (**Figure 4.14**). Don't let the door hit you on the butt!

To exit vi:

- Esc :q

  Enter command mode with Esc, then type :q to quit vi. If you haven't saved your latest changes, vi will not quit and will tell you to use ! to override. To quit without saving your changes, use :q!, as shown in **Figure 4.14**.

✔ Tip

- If you don't really want to quit but want to edit a different file instead, type :e filename to open a new file to edit.

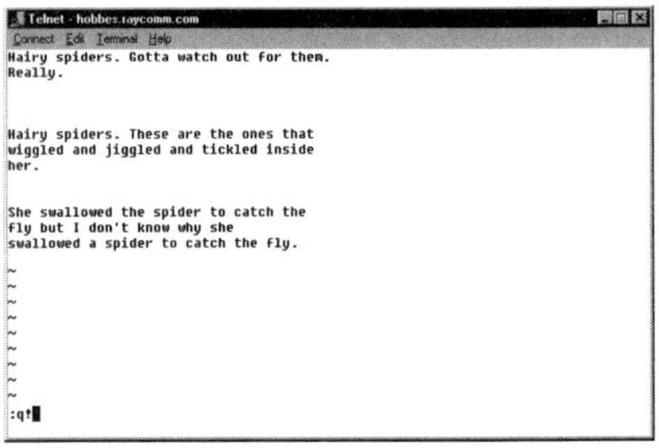

Figure 4.14 Use Esc:q! to quit vi without saving changes.

Controlling Ownership & Permissions

5

UNIX is a multi-user system in which your files are separate from Jane's files, which are separate from Joe's files, and so on. Any file you create is separate from other users' files and usually cannot be directly accessed by Jane, Joe, or any other user.

Occasionally, though, you will need to share files. For example, you might be collaborating on a project with Jane where sharing files (rather than creating and maintaining separate ones) is essential.

Chapter contents:

- Understanding file ownership and permissions
- Finding out who owns what
- Finding out which group you're in
- Changing the group association of files and directories
- Changing ownership of files and directories
- Changing permissions
- Translating mnemonic permissions to numeric permissions
- Changing permission defaults

Understanding file ownership and permissions

UNIX provides three levels of file ownership:

- **User:** Refers to the single userid that's primarily in charge of the file. You have this level of ownership for the files you create.
- **Group:** Refers to the group (of users) associated with a specific file. All users within a group have the same permissions for interacting with a file.
- **Other:** Refers to any users not identified with either the group or user for a file.

Within these groups, you can specify permissions for file access and rights in three categories:

- **Read:** Users with read permission can only view a file; they cannot make changes to it.
- **Write:** Users with write permission can make changes to or delete a file.
- **Execute:** Users with execute permission can run files (programs or scripts) and view directories.

In this chapter, we'll show you some of the commands you can use to set ownership and permissions. Keep in mind that you can set or change any permissions for files you create and possibly for files created by others; however, exactly which permissions and ownerships you can change depends on how your system administrator set up the system. Even if you don't currently need to change file ownerships or permissions, you should take a quick read through this chapter to see what options might be available to you.

✔ Tip

- An interesting twist on this whole ownership issue is that not all "owners" are people. Programs or processes (discussed in Chapter 9) run as a specific user, and if they create files, those files have permissions reflecting the individual and group membership of the program. See Chapter 9 for more information.

Finding out who owns what

Your first step in changing ownership and permissions is to find out who owns which files. You'll need this information to find out whether you can make changes to the permissions.

To find out who owns what:

1. `cd`

   At the shell prompt, type `cd` to return to your home directory.

2. `ls -l`

   Enter `ls -l` to see the long listing of the files in the current directory (see **Code Listing 5.1**).

   The left column contains nine characters that specify permissions for each file:

Code Listing 5.1 Many systems use only a few group names to allow easy file sharing and collaboration.

```
xmission> cd
/home/users/e/ejray
xmission> ls -l
total 60
drwx--x--x   2 ejray    users       512 Jul 21 13:32 Complete/
drwx--x--x   2 ejray    users       512 Jun 24 09:23 Completed/
drwx--x--x   2 ejray    users       512 Sep 15  1997 Mail/
drwx--x--x   2 ejray    users       512 Jun 24 09:35 NewProject/
drwx--x--x   2 ejray    users       512 Sep 15  1997 News/
drwx--x--x   2 ejray    users       512 Sep 15  1997 access/
-rw-------   1 ejray    users       163 Jul 22 07:28 bogus2
drwxrwx--x   2 ejray    www         512 Jul 24 04:44 chat.conf/
-rw-------   1 ejray    users       853 Sep 13  1997 dead.letter
-rw-------   1 ejray    users     14286 Jun 28 12:40 files
lrwxrwxrwx   1 ejray    users        27 Sep 15  1997 ftp -> /home/ftp/pub/users
-rw-------   1 ejray    users        36 Jul 24 12:09 limerick
drwx--x--x   2 ejray    users       512 Jun  8 13:32 mail/
drwxr-s--x  15 ejray    www        2560 Jul 10 10:30 public_html/
drwx--x--x   2 ejray    users       512 Jul 22 08:23 puppy/
drwx--x--x   2 ejray    users       512 Jul 24 04:44 temp/
-rw-------   1 ejray    users         0 Jul 19 13:24 testme
```

- r means read permission, w means write permission, and x means execute permission.
- The first set of rwx is for the user, the second set is for the group, and the last set is for other.
- A dash (-) instead of a letter indicates that the user/group/other does not have that level of permission. For example, `rwx------` would mean that the user has read, write, and execute permission, while group and other have no permissions at all.

The two columns in the middle indicate the file's owner (in all likelihood your userid, for this example) and the group membership for the file. In **Code Listing 5.1**, `ejray` is the owner of all of the files. Most of the files are associated with the `users` group, while just a few directories are associated with the www group.

On this system, files that individual users create are associated with the user's group, while files destined for the Web have www group associations. On other systems, the default group for files might be a group with the same name as the userid, as shown in **Code Listing 5.2**.

3. `ls -l /etc`

You can also use the `ls -l` command on a system directory, such as `/etc`. Here, you'll see that most of the files are owned by `root`, possibly with a variety of different group memberships (see **Figure 5.1**).

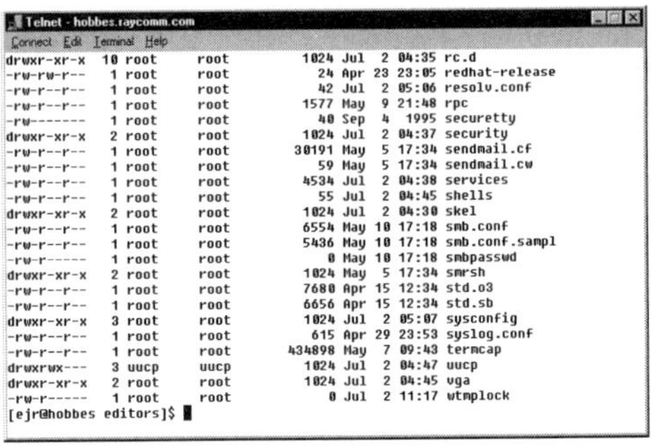

```
Telnet - hobbes.raycomm.com
Connect Edit Terminal Help
drwxr-xr-x  10 root     root         1024 Jul  2 04:35 rc.d
-rw-rw-r--   1 root     root           24 Apr 23 23:05 redhat-release
-rw-r--r--   1 root     root           42 Jul  2 05:06 resolv.conf
-rw-r--r--   1 root     root         1577 May  9 21:48 rpc
-rw-------   1 root     root           40 Sep  4  1995 securetty
drwxr-xr-x   2 root     root         1024 Jul  2 04:37 security
-rw-r--r--   1 root     root        30191 May  5 17:34 sendmail.cf
-rw-r--r--   1 root     root           59 May  5 17:34 sendmail.cw
-rw-r--r--   1 root     root         4534 Jul  2 04:38 services
-rw-r--r--   1 root     root           55 Jul  2 04:45 shells
drwxr-xr-x   2 root     root         1024 Jul  2 04:30 skel
-rw-r--r--   1 root     root         6554 May 10 17:18 smb.conf
-rw-r--r--   1 root     root         5436 May 10 17:18 smb.conf.sampl
-rw-r-----   1 root     root            0 May 10 17:18 smbpasswd
drwxr-xr-x   2 root     root         1024 May  5 17:34 smrsh
-rw-r--r--   1 root     root         7680 Apr 15 12:34 std.o3
-rw-r--r--   1 root     root         6656 Apr 15 12:34 std.sb
drwxr-xr-x   3 root     root         1024 Jul  2 05:07 sysconfig
-rw-r--r--   1 root     root          615 Apr 29 23:53 syslog.conf
-rw-r--r--   1 root     root       434898 May  7 09:43 termcap
drwxrwx---   3 uucp     uucp         1024 Jul  2 04:47 uucp
drwxr-xr-x   2 root     root         1024 Jul  2 04:45 vga
-rw-r-----   1 root     root            0 Jul  2 11:17 wtmplock
[ejr@hobbes editors]$
```

Figure 5.1 Most of the files in /etc are owned by root.

✔ Tips

- Sometimes you'll see references to world-readable or world permissions. This is the same as `other`. "Other" just refers to not you, not the group, but anyone else.
- Note that the ftp directory line shown in **Code Listing 5.1** is a little unusual. It's a link, as discussed in Chapter 2.

Code Listing 5.2 Sometimes the group name and user name are the same, depending on how the system was set up.

```
[ejr@hobbes permissions]$ ls -l
total 152
-rw-rw-r--   1 ejr      ejr       128889 Jul 24 14:33 sage.sayings
-rw-rw-r--   1 ejr      ejr        23890 Jul 24 14:33 sayings
[ejr@hobbes permissions]$
```

Code Listing 5.3 You'll find tons of information in /etc/passwd, including your default group number.

```
[ejr@hobbes permissions]$ grep ejr
  → /etc/passwd
ejr:aag2.UyC7yJWE:500:500:Eric J.
  → Ray:/home/ejr:/bin/bash
[ejr@hobbes permissions]$
```

Code Listing 5.4 The group file lists groups and additional members (as shown in the users group).

```
[ejr@hobbes permissions]$ cat /etc/group
kmem::9:
wheel::10:root,ejr
mail::12:mail
news::13:news
uucp::14:uucp
man::15:
games::20:
gopher::30:
dip::40:
ftp::50:
nobody::99:
users::100:ejr,deb,asr,awr
floppy:x:19:
pppusers:x:230:
popusers:x:231:
slipusers:x:232:
postgres:x:233:
ejr:x:500:
bash:x:501:
csh:x:502:
asr:x:503:
awr:x:504:
deb:x:505:
[ejr@hobbes permissions]$
```

Finding out which group you're in

If you want to collaborate on a project and share files, for example, you'll need to be in the same group with the other people on the team. Your first step is to find out which group you're in, as shown in **Code Listing 5.3**.

To find out which group you're in:

1. `grep yourid /etc/passwd`

   Here, `grep yourid` pulls your userid out of the `/etc/passwd` file (which is where user information is stored) and displays it as shown in **Code Listing 5.3**. From left to right, you see:

   - Your userid
   - The encoded password
   - The number of your userid (each userid has a unique number in the system)
   - The number of your group (each group has a unique number in the system, too)

2. Note the number of the group.

   You'll need the number to match it up with a group name in step 3. In this case, our group number is 500.

3. `more /etc/group`

   Here, we're exploring the contents of the `/etc/group` file using `more` to see which groups are currently defined on the system. As shown in **Code Listing 5.4**, the first column contains the name of the group, the second contains the group number, and the last column contains extra names the system administrator added to the group. Users can belong to multiple additional groups, and this is how the additional group membership is indicated.

4. Match up the group number for your ID with the group name.

   Our number was 500, which corresponds to the `ejr` group name here.

✔ Tips

- If you're collaborating on a project, ask your system administrator to create a special group just for the project. That way, you and your teammates can easily share files.
- You can also use the `id` command, which offers a quicker way of finding out about group membership. It gives you essential details about userids, but it doesn't flood you with these other most interesting and potentially useful details about the system. Wander to Chapter 7 for more information.
- Check out Chapter 1, page 17, for more on `more`.
- See Chapter 6 for the full scoop on `grep`.

Changing the group association of files and directories with chgrp

Suppose you have a file called `black` that is currently being used by the `pot` group and you want to change the file's permissions so that it can be accessed by the `kettle` group. To do this, you'll need to change which group the file is associated with—in this case, change the association from the `pot` group to the `kettle` group. You can change which group a file or directory is associated with using `chgrp`, as shown in **Code Listing 5.5**.

To change group association with chgrp:

1. `ls -l`

   To begin, type `ls -l` at the shell prompt to verify the file's name and the group it's associated with, as in **Code Listing 5.5**. Remember that the second column in the middle of the listing, immediately before the file sizes, lists the group membership.

2. `chgrp kettle black`

   Type `chgrp` followed by the name of the new group you want to the file to be associated with and the file name. Here, the `chgrp` command changes the group asso-

Code Listing 5.5 Pots and kettles can both be black, but only one at a time.

```
[ejr@hobbes permissions]$ ls -l
total 178
-rw-rw-r--   1 ejr      pot        24850 Jul 24 14:59 black
-rw-rw-r--   1 ejr      ejr       128889 Jul 24 14:33 sage.sayings
-rw-rw-r--   1 ejr      ejr        23890 Jul 24 14:33 sayings
[ejr@hobbes permissions]$ chgrp kettle black
[ejr@hobbes permissions]$ ls -l
total 178
-rw-rw-r--   1 ejr      kettle     24850 Jul 24 14:59 black
-rw-rw-r--   1 ejr      ejr       128889 Jul 24 14:33 sage.sayings
-rw-rw-r--   1 ejr      ejr        23890 Jul 24 14:33 sayings
```

ciation for the file called `black` to the `kettle` group.

You can also change the association of a directory and all of the contents using `chgrp -R`, like this: `chgrp -R kettle blackdirectory`.

✔ Tips

- If you try to change group ownership and get an error message like "Not owner" or something similarly obscure, your userid doesn't have the necessary authority to make the change. You'll have to ask your system administrator for help.
- Only change group association if you have a specific need to do so; you don't want to make your files available to other people unnecessarily. Unless you are the system administrator, you won't be able to control exactly who belongs to the group to which you've given access to your files.
- If you change the group association of a specific directory, you also need to check permissions for the directory containing it. Users will not be able to change into the specific directory (regardless of their group membership) unless they also have read and execute permission for the directory containing it.
- Just as with the `cp` and `mv` commands, covered in Chapter 1, you can use a `-R` flag with `chgrp` to recursively apply changes to a directory and all of the subdirectories and files in it. For example, to change the group association of the `LatestProject` directory and all its contents to the `project` group, use `chgrp -R project LatestProject` from the directory above `LatestProject`.

Changing ownership of files and directories with chown

Suppose you've been working on a file called rowyourboat, and your boss decides to let a coworker, Merrilee, take over the project. In this case, to fully pawn off the project to your coworker, you need to change ownership of the file from you to her. Depending on how your system administrator set up the system, you can usually change ownership of files using chown (**Code Listing 5.6**).

To change ownership with chown:

1. `ls -l`

   For starters, type `ls -l` at the shell prompt to verify the file's name and ownership, as in **Code Listing 5.6**. Remember that the ownership information is located after the permissions and linking information.

2. `chown merrilee rowyourboat`

   Type chown followed by the userid of the person you want to transfer ownership to and the file name. In this case, the chown command changes the ownership for rowyourboat to merrilee. rowyourboat

Code Listing 5.6 Changing ownership of files transfers complete control.

```
[ejr@hobbes merrilee]$ ls -l
total 26
-rw-rw-r--   1 ejr      users       24850 Jul 24 15:17 rowtheboat
[ejr@hobbes merrilee]$ chown merrilee rowtheboat
[ejr@hobbes merrilee]$ ls -l
total 26
-rw-rw-r--   1 merrilee users       24850 Jul 24 15:17 rowtheboat
[ejr@hobbes merrilee]$
```

and its associated problems will now be hers, and life will be but a dream.

✔ Tips

- After you change a file's ownership, what you can do with the file depends on the group and other permissions and memberships. The new owner, however, will be able to do anything with the file.
- You can add the `-R` flag to `chown` to make it apply to subdirectories.
- If your system administrator is particularly security-conscious and set up the system so that you cannot use `chown`, consider using `cp` to make your own copy of a file to accomplish the same thing. If you copy someone else's file (that you have permission to read) to another name or location, the copy is fully yours. (In this giving-the-file-away example, the recipient should use `cp`.)
- Even if your system administrator has set up the system so you can't use `chown`, you could still be able to request that he or she change file ownership for you: "Could you please change the ownership of my `rowyourboat` file to Merrilee, with `chown merrilee /home/shared/me/rowyour` → `boat`. Thanks!"

Changing permissions with chmod

Suppose that you've been working on a file called rowyourboat and you want to have your coworkers down the stream review it. To do so, you'll need to give other people permission to access the document. You can either give people in specific groups access, or you can give everybody on the UNIX system access. In particular, you can specify permissions for u(ser—that's you), g(roup), o(thers), and a(ll).

In addition to specifying permissions, you can also specify how much access a person or group can have to your file. For example, you can specify r(ead), w(rite), and (e)x(ecute) access, depending on how much you trust them not to ruin your rowyourboat masterpiece.

As shown in **Code Listing 5.7**, your first step is to check out what the current permissions are. Then, you can set permissions, add to them, or remove them as necessary.

To check current permissions:

- `ls -l r*`

  To begin, type `ls -l r*` to get a long listing of rowyourboat in the current directory. **Code Listing 5.7** shows that the permissions are -rwxr-x---. This is actually three sets of permissions:
  - For the user (rwx, in this example)
  - For the group (r-x, here)
  - For the world (---, here)

  In this example, the user has read, write, and execute permissions; the group has only read and execute permissions; and the other has no permissions.

Code Listing 5.7 Use ls -l to see the permissions on files.

```
[ejr@hobbes permissions]$ ls -l r*
-rwxr-x---   1 ejr     users     152779 Jul 24 15:10 rowyourboat
[ejr@hobbes permissions]$
```

To set permissions:

- `chmod u=rwx,g=rx,o=r row*`

  Type chmod and specify who has access. In this case users have read, write, and execute permissions, the group has read and execute permissions, and others have read permission for all files in the directory (**Code Listing 5.8**).

  The equals sign (=) specifies that the permissions granted in the command are the only permissions that apply. Any previous permissions will be removed.

  The wildcard expression here (row*) specifies that the command applies to all files and directories that start with "row" in the current directory.

To add permissions:

- `chmod g+w rowyourboat`

  At the shell prompt, enter chmod, followed by:

  - The category. In this case, we've used g, for group, but you could also use o for others, ...or, of course u for user, but you already have that access. You could also use a for all users (which includes u, g and o).

Code Listing 5.8 You can set permissions to ensure that all files have equivalent permissions.

```
[ejr@hobbes permissions]$ ls -l
total 332
-rw-rw-r--   1 ejr      users       24850 Jul 24 14:59 black
-rwxr-x---   1 ejr      users      152779 Jul 24 15:10 rowyourboat
-rw-rw-r--   1 ejr      users      128889 Jul 24 14:33 sage.sayings
-rw-rw-r--   1 ejr      users       23890 Jul 24 14:33 sayings
[ejr@hobbes permissions]$ chmod u=rwx,g=rx,o=r row*
[ejr@hobbes permissions]$ ls -l
total 329
-rwxr-xr--   1 ejr      users       24850 Jul 24 14:59 black
-rwxr-xr--   1 ejr      users      152779 Jul 24 15:10 rowyourboat
-rwxr-xr--   1 ejr      users      128889 Jul 24 14:33 sage.sayings
-rwxr-xr--   1 ejr      users       23890 Jul 24 14:33 sayings
[ejr@hobbes permissions]$
```

- A plus sign indicates that you're adding the permission to the existing permissions, rather than setting absolute permissions.
- The permissions to grant. Here, we've used `w`, for write permission, but you could also use `r` for read or `x` for execute permissions, as your needs dictate.
- The file name (`rowyourboat`)

Removing permissions:

- `chmod go-w rowyourboat`

  At the shell prompt, use `chmod go-w` plus the file name to remove write permissions for everyone except you, the file's owner. Note that we handled both `group` and `other` in a single command this time, although we could have used `chmod g-w` → `rowyourboat` and `chmod o-w rowyour` → `boat` to accomplish the same thing.

✔ Tips

- You can also use the `-R` flag with `chmod` to recursively apply the changes you make to permissions to all subdirectories in a directory. For example, `chmod -R go-rwx *` revokes all permissions from everyone except the user for all files in the current directory, all subdirectories in the current directory, and all files in all subdirectories.
- There are approximately a million and one ways to express permissions. For example, you could use `chmod ugo= *` (note the space before the `*`) or `chmod u-rwx,g-rwx,` → `o-rwx *` to revoke all permissions from all files in the directory. (Note that you'll have to add your own permissions back to the files before you can do anything with them, if you try this out.)
- If you want to change permissions for multiple files, either use a wildcard expression or separate the file names with commas (but no spaces).

Translating mnemonic permissions to numeric permissions

The permissions for a file, as you've seen throughout this chapter, come in sets of three—rwx, for read, write, and execute permissions. And, as we showed you, you set these permissions by specifying that each one is either "on" or "off." For example, ugo+rwx sets read, write, and execute permission to on for user, group, and other, while a+rw sets read and write to on for everyone and a-x sets execute to off (indicated in directory listings with the -).

Rather than setting permissions with letters and hyphens, however, you can translate them into numeric values, using 1 for on and 0 for off. So, rw-, with read and write on and execute off, would translate into the numbers 110. You could think of this as counting in binary—000, 001, 010, 011, 100, 101, 110, 111, with a 1 in each place that the permission is set to "on."

Each of these combinations of on/off permissions (or binary numbers) can be expressed as a unique decimal digit between 0 and 7, as shown in Table 5.1. It is these decimal digits that you use to set permissions.

To set permissions using numeric equivalents:

- `chmod 777 rowyourboat`

  Type chmod followed by the desired permissions for user, group, and other using the numeric equivalents listed in **Table 5.1**, followed by the file name. In this example, we've used 777 to set read, write, and execute permissions to on for the user, group, and other.

  Or, for example, 724 would give the user full read, write, and execute permissions, the group only write permissions, and other only read permissions.

Table 5.1

Numeric Equivalents for Mnemonic Permissions

MNEMONIC (RWX) PERMISSIONS	BINARY EQUIVALENT	NUMERIC EQUIVALENT
---	000	0
--x	001	1
-w-	010	2
-wx	011	3
r--	100	4
r-x	101	5
rw-	110	6
rwx	111	7

✔ Tips

- Setting permissions with numeric equivalents sets permissions absolutely, rather than adding to or subtracting from existing permissions.
- Numeric equivalents don't give you any more control than you have with ugo+rwx; however, you will need to use the numeric system to set default permissions that apply when you create new files. See the next section, *Changing permission defaults with umask*, for the full scoop.

Changing permission defaults with umask

Every time you create a file, the UNIX system applies default permissions for you. This is great because, for many uses, the default permissions will be just what you want. In other cases, though, you'll want to specify different default permissions.

You can change the default permissions using `umask`. The `umask` command uses a numeric representation for permissions (as discussed in the previous section), but the numeric value you specify here is not the same as the one you'd use with `chmod`. (Don't ask why. We assume that Batman and Robin got together and made this command only usable by the Wonder Twins when their Powers were Activated.) So you have to figure out the `umask` value for the permissions you want, then use that value to set the new default permissions (**Code Listing 5.9**). The new defaults will apply to all files that you create in your current session.

To figure the umask value:

1. 666

   Start with 666. Again, don't ask why; it's just what you're supposed to start with.

2. Figure out which numeric values you'd use to set your desired permissions with the `chmod` command.

   You might review the previous section, *Translating mnemonic permissions to numeric permissions*, and peek at Table 5.1 in that section.

3. Subtract that numeric value from 666.

   For example, if the numeric value you'd use with `chmod` is 644, subtract that value from 666: 666–644=022. 022 is the number you'll use with `umask`.

To set default file-creation permissions with umask:

- `umask 022`

  Enter umask plus the number you calculated in the previous steps in this section (**Code Listing 5.9**).

✔ Tips

- Any changes made with umask apply only to the current shell session. If you want to revert to the default permissions but don't remember what they were, just log out and log back in and you'll be back to normal.
- If you want to change permission defaults permanently—or at least beyond the current shell session—change them in the configuration files as discussed in Chapter 8.
- You cannot set the default permissions to include execute permission; it's a security *feature*, not an omission in UNIX's capabilities. For example, suppose you make a new file and copy your favorite commands (or the ones you often forget) into it. If you accidentally type the file name and the file is executable, you'll run that list of commands and the consequences could be unfortunate. Therefore you have to explicitly grant execute permission for all files.
- Yes, 666 is considered the Number of the Beast. We think that it's just a coincidence, but given the potential for confusion in this section, we're not sure.

Code Listing 5.9 Use umask to set default permissions for future files.

```
[ejr@hobbes permissions]$ umask 022
[ejr@hobbes permissions]$ touch tryit
[ejr@hobbes permissions]$ ls -l try*
-rw-r--r--   1 ejr      users          0 Jul 26 16:35 tryit
[ejr@hobbes permissions]$
```

6

MANIPULATING FILES

As you learned back in Chapter 4, you can fairly easily work with text by opening up an editor and making the changes you want. But you can do more than just copy, paste, cut, or move text in files. As we'll discuss in this chapter, you can manipulate entire files and look at specific parts of them, get information about the files, find text in files, compare files, and sort files. All kinds of neat stuff!

In this chapter, we'll use a lot of flags to augment commands. You'll find a full list of the most common commands and their flags in Appendix C if you need further explanation or a quickie reminder.

Chapter contents

Counting files and their contents with wc

One of UNIX's handiest capabilities lets you count files and their contents. For example, you can count the number of files in a directory, or you can count the number of words or lines in a file. You do this counting with the wc command, as shown in **Code Listing 6.1**.

To count words using wc:

◆ `wc -w honeydo`

At the shell prompt, type `wc -w` (for words) and the name of the file you want to count the words in. wc will oblige, as shown in **Code Listing 6.1**.

To count lines with wc:

◆ `wc -l honeydo`

Use `wc -l` followed by the file name to count the lines in the file (**Code Listing 6.2**). This is useful for poetry or for things like lists (e.g., our "honey-do" list always has a minimum of 73 items on it).

✔ Tips

- You can find out how many files you have in a directory by using `ls | wc -l` to count the regular files, or `ls -A | wc -l -2` to count all files and directories (except for the . and .. directories).
- You can also find out how many bytes a specific file takes up using `wc -b`. Or, you can use wc with no flags at all to get the lines, words, and bytes.

Code Listing 6.1 Use wc -w to count the words in a file. The "honey-do" list in this example is quite a way from being the length of a novel.

```
[ejr@hobbes manipulate]$ wc -w honeydo
    235 honeydo
```

Code Listing 6.2 With 85 separate items in the list, however, it's plenty long enough.

```
[ejr@hobbes manipulate]$ wc -l honeydo
     85 honeydo
```

Code Listing 6.3 Use head to look at just the top of a file, which gives you a manageable view of the file.

```
[ejr@hobbes manipulate]$ head honeydo
Take garbage out
Clean litter box
Clean diaper pails
Clean litter box
Mow lawn
Edge lawn
Clean litter box
Polish swamp cooler
Buff garage floor
Clean litter box
[ejr@hobbes manipulate]$
```

Code Listing 6.4 head, with the help of more, lets you see the beginnings of several files in sequence.

```
[ejr@hobbes manipulate]$ head honey* | more
==> honeyconsider <==
Mother-in-law visits next week
Cat mess in hall to clean up
Cat mess in entry to clean up
Cat mess in living room to clean up
Toddler mess in family room to clean up
Cat and toddler mess in den to clean up
IRS called again today
Neighbors on both sides looking for donations
        for the annual fund drive

Boss called last Friday and said it's urgent

==> honeydo <==
Take garbage out
Clean litter box
Clean diaper pails
Clean litter box
Mo: lawn
Edge lawn
Clean litter box
Polish swamp cooler
Buff garage floor
--More--
```

Viewing file beginnings with head

You can find out in a jiffy what's in a file just by viewing the top few lines. This is particularly handy when you're browsing file listings or trying to find a specific file among several others with similar content. Using head, you can view the first several lines or so of a file and find out what's in it, as shown in **Code Listing 6.3**.

To view file beginnings with head:

◆ `head honeydo`

  At the shell prompt, type head followed by the file name. As **Code Listing 6.3** shows, you'll see the first ten lines on the screen. Notice that "lines" are defined by hard returns, so a line could, in some cases, wrap to many screen lines.

To view a specified number of lines:

◆ `head -20 honeydo`

  Add `-20` (or whatever number of lines you want to view) to view a specific number of lines.

To view the beginnings of multiple files:

◆ `head honey* | more`

  You can view the tops of multiple files by piping head (plus the file names) to more. Note that head conveniently tells you the file name of each file, as shown in **Code Listing 6.4**.

✔ Tip

■ head and its counterpart, `tail`, are great for splitting long files. Use `wc -l` to count the lines. If the file has 50 lines, then type `head -25 filename > newfilename` to put the first 25 lines of the file into a new file. Then do the same with `tail` to put the last 25 lines of the file into another new file.

Viewing file endings with tail

Occasionally, you might also need to use `tail`, which displays the last lines of a file. `tail` is particularly handy for checking footers or for updating information in a footer (see **Code Listing 6.5**). Just as with head (described in the previous pages), `tail` offers several options for viewing files.

To view file endings with tail:

- `tail honeydo`

  At the shell prompt, type `tail` followed by the file name. As **Code Listing 6.5** shows, you'll see the last ten lines on the screen.

To view a specified number of lines:

- `tail -15 honeydo`

  Here, all you do is add a specific number of lines you want to view (-15).

To view the endings of multiple files:

- `tail honey* | more`

  Pipe the `tail` command and the files (multiple files indicated with `*`) to more (**Code Listing 6.6**).

Code Listing 6.5 tail lets you check out just the end of files.

```
[ejr@hobbes manipulate]$ tail honeydo
Empty diaper pails
Take garbage out.
--End of today's list--




Buy more garbage bags
Get cleaning supplies at store
Take cat to vet
Fix lawnmower


[ejr@hobbes manipulate]$
```

Code Listing 6.6 Use tail with more to see the ends of multiple files.

```
[ejr@hobbes manipulate]$ tail honey* | more
==> honeyconsider <==
Cat mess in entry to clean up
Cat mess in living room to clean up
Toddler mess in family room to clean up
Cat and toddler mess in den to clean up
IRS called again today
Neighbors on both sides looking for donations
        for the annual fund drive
Boss called last Friday and said it's urgent
--End of today's list--



==> honeydo <==
Empty diaper pails
Take garbage out
--End of today's list--

Buy more garbage bags
Get cleaning supplies at store
Take cat to vet
Fix lawnmower

--More--
```

Finding text with grep

You can search through multiple files for specific strings of characters and then view the resulting list of matching files onscreen. You do this using the `grep` command (which stands for "global regular expression print"), as shown in **Code Listing 6.7**. As we'll show you in the following steps, you can add several flags to `grep` to get slightly different results.

To find text strings with grep:

1. `grep bucket limericks`

   At the shell prompt, type `grep`, the text you're trying to locate (in this case, `bucket`), and the file you're searching in (here, `limericks`). `grep` will return all lines in the file that contain the specified string, as shown in **Code Listing 6.7**.

2. `grep -5 bucket limericks`

   You can specify that a number of lines (for example, `-5`) on either side of the found text string should also be displayed. Sometimes you can't tell exactly what you need to know with just the line that contains your search string, and adding lines around it can help give you a context (see **Code Listing 6.8**).

3. `grep -c Nantucket limericks`

   By adding the `-c` flag, you can find out how many times a text string appears in a file.

4. `grep -v Nantucket limericks`

   Or, with the `-v` flag, you can find all of the lines that do *not* contain the specified string.

5. `grep -i nantucket limericks`

   With the `-i` flag, you can search without case-sensitivity. Here any line with `nantucket` or `Nantucket` would be found.

Code Listing 6.7 Use grep to see all occurrences of a specific string in a file.

```
[ejr@hobbes manipulate]$ grep bucket
  → limericks
Who carried his lunch in a bucket,
[ejr@hobbes manipulate]$
```

Code Listing 6.8 grep can show the context around instances of the string as well.

```
[ejr@hobbes manipulate]$ grep -5 bucket
  → limerick
he strummed and he hummed,
and sang dumdeedum,
But him a musician...whoda thunk it?

There once was a man from Nantucket,
Who carried his lunch in a bucket,
Said he with a sigh,
As he ate a whole pie,
If I just had a donut I'd dunk it.

A nice young lady named Debbie,

[ejr@hobbes manipulate]$
```

✔ Tips

- Use the `-n` flag (for example, `grep -n string file`) to print each found line with a line number.
- You can use `grep` in conjunction with multiple file names, such as in `grep Nantucket lim*`, or `grep` → `Nantucket lim* poetry humor`.
- If you want to get creative, you can look for spaces as well, but need to use quotes, like `grep "from Nantucket" limerick*`.

Using regular expressions with grep

In addition to using `grep` to search for simple text strings, you can also use `grep` to search for regular expressions. *Regular expressions* are kind of like fancy wildcards, where you use a symbol to represent a character, number, or other symbol. With regular expressions, you can search for different parts of files, such as the end of a line or a text string next to another specified text string. **Table 6.1** lists some of the more common regular expressions.

To use regular expressions with grep:

- `grep .logan limerick`

  Type `grep` followed by the regular expression and the file name. Here, we've used the regular expression `.logan` to find all instances of "logan" or "slogan" (**Code Listing 6.9**). Note that this usage of a `.` closely resembles the ? wildcard used with `ls`.

  - You could also use multiple periods for specific numbers of characters. For example, to find "Dogbert" and "Dilbert," you might use `grep D..bert plagiarized.sayings`.
  - In some cases, you may need to structure the code slightly differently, depending on the expression you're using and the information you're looking for. Check out the additional examples in **Table 6.1** for more information.

Code Listing 6.9 Use grep with regular expressions to create fancy wildcard commands.

```
[ejr@hobbes manipulate]$ grep .logan limerick
Worked hard all day on a slogan,
You see, the slogan's still brogan.
[ejr@hobbes manipulate]$
```

✔ Tips

- "Regular expression" is often abbreviated as "regexp" in UNIX documentation and Internet discussions.
- The command **egrep** is closely related to **grep**, adding a little more flexibility for extended regular expressions, but it fundamentally works the same. On many systems the **grep** command is really **egrep**—when you type in either one, you're really running **egrep**.
- See Chapter 1 for details about wildcards

Table 6.1

Regular Expressions, Examples, and Explanations

Regular Expression	Function	Example	Explanation
.	Matches any character	b.rry	This finds all instances of "berry" or "barry".
*	Matches 0 or more instances of the preceding character, so a*b would find b as well as ab, aaab, but not acb.	grep s*day /home/ejr/schedule	Here, the * matches 0 or more of the character that immediately *precedes* the *.
^	Matches only instances of the string at the beginning of a line	grep ^Some sayings	With the ^, you specify that the search string must appear at the beginning of a line. The example would find a line beginning with "Some", but not one beginning with "Read Some".
$	Matches only instances of the string at the end of a line	grep ach$ sayings	With grep ach$ sayings, you could find all lines in the file sayings that end with "ach".
\	Escapes (quotes) the following character—so you can search for characters like * or $ that are also operators	grep * sayings	grep * sayings searches for all instances of * in the sayings file. The \ tells UNIX to interpret the * literally, as an asterisk character, rather than as a wildcard.
[]	Matches any member of the set	grep [32,64]-bit specifications	Use square brackets ([ ]) to enclose a set of options. Here, grep [32,64]-bit specifications would look for all lines that mention 32-bit or 64-bit in the file called specifications.

Using other examples of regular expressions

In the previous section, we showed you how to use the `grep` command to search with regular expressions. You can, though, do other neat finding things tasks, as we'll discuss in this section.

To review files and spell check them:

- `cat limerick[1256].htm | spell`

  In this example, we use the regular expression `[1256]` to find `limerick1.htm`, `limerick2.htm`, and so on. Then, we pipe the four files to `spell` for a quick spell check.

To find lines with specific characteristics:

1. `grep ^Nantucket limerick*`

   Here, we use `grep` to find all of the lines in the limericks that start with `Nantucket`, if there are any.

2. `grep Nantucket$ limerick*`

   Similarly, you can find the lines that end with Nantucket.

3. `grep ^[A-Z] limerick`

   Or, you can find the lines that start with a capital letter by including the `[A-Z]` regular expression.

4. `grep ^[A-Z,a-z] limerick`

   Here, you can find all the lines that start with any letter, but not a number or symbol. Fancy, huh?

✔ Tip

- You can also use regular expressions with `awk` and `sed`. See *Making global changes with `sed`* and *Changing files with `awk`* in this chapter for details.

Code Listing 6.10 You can use sed to make changes throughout files, such as the address change here.

```
[ejr@hobbes manipulate]$ sed
  → s/oldaddr@raycomm.com/newaddr@raycomm.com
  → /g address.htm > address.htm
[ejr@hobbes manipulate]$ head address.htm

<BODY BACKGROUND="/images/background.gif"
  BGCOLOR="#FFFFFF" TEXT="#000000" LINK=
"#009900" VLINK="#000000" ALINK="#ff0000">

<P>
Please send all comments to <A
  HREF="mailto:newaddr@raycomm.com">newaddr@r
  aycomm
.com</A>.
</P>

<TABLE BORDER=0>
<TR>
<TD WIDTH="150" VALIGN=TOP>
[ejr@hobbes manipulate]$
```

- Because sed commands can be long and unwieldy, it might be helpful to save the commands in a separate text file (so you don't have to retype them). For example, if you saved the command `s/oldaddr@raycomm.com/newaddr@ray` → `comm.com/g` in a file called `script.sed`, you could issue `sed -f script.sed address.htm > address.htm` to run the sed commands from the `script.sed` file.

Making global changes with sed

Another handy command you can use is **sed**, which lets you make multiple changes to files, without ever opening an editor. For example, as a new Webmaster, you might use **sed** to change all occurrences of the previous Webmaster's e-mail address to your own, as shown in our example below. As we'll show in this section, you can use **sed** to make global changes within documents.

To make global changes with sed:

- `sed /oldaddr@raycomm.com` → `/newaddr@raycomm.com/g address.htm` → `> address.htm`

  Type **sed**, followed by

  - /the text you want to replace (`/oldaddr@raycomm.com`)
  - A slash (/)
  - The replacement text (`newaddr@raycomm.com`)
  - Another /
  - `g`, which tells UNIX to apply the change globally. (If you omit the g, only the first occurrence on each line will be changed.)
  - The name of the file in which the changes should be made (`address.htm`).

  You can redirect the output to the same file name (as we did here; see **Code Listing 6.10**), redirect it to a new one, or pipe it to another command entirely.

✔ Tips

- You can have **sed** zip through multiple documents. See Chapter 10 for information on how to make a shell script with a loop.

MAKING GLOBAL CHANGES WITH sed

Changing files with awk

While sed is line-oriented and lets you fiddle and diddle to your heart's content, awk is field-oriented and is ideal for manipulating database or comma-delimited files. For example, if you have an address book file, you can use awk to find and change information in fields you specify, as in **Code Listing 6.11**. In the following steps, we'll show you a sampling of the things you can do using awk to modify an address book file.

To change files with awk:

1. `awk '{ print $1 }' address.book`

   At the shell prompt, use `awk '{ print $1 }' address.book` to look at the address.book file and select (and send to standard output) the first field in each record (line). More specifically, starting from the inside out:

   - $1 references the first field in each line. Unless you specify otherwise, awk assumes that a space separates the fields, so the first field starts at the beginning of the line and continues to the first space.
   - {} contain the awk command, and the quotes are necessary to tie the awk command together (so the first space within the command isn't interpreted as the end of the command). (**Code Listing 6.11**)

2. `awk -F, '{ print $1 }' address.book`

   The -F flag tells awk to use the character following it—in this case, a comma (,)—as the field separator. This change makes the output of the command a little cleaner and more accurate. If you were working with /etc/passwd, you'd use -F: to specify that the : is the field separator.

Code Listing 6.11 awk lets you access individual fields in a file.

```
[ejr@hobbes manipulate]$ awk '{ print $1 }'
  → address.book
Schmidt,
Feldman,
Brown,
Smith,
Jones,
[ejr@hobbes manipulate]$
```

De-what?

A *delimited file* uses a specific character to show where one bit of information ends and another begins. Each piece of information is a separate *field*. For example, a file that contains "John, Doe, Logan, Utah" is comma-delimited, a comma between every two fields. Other files, such as the /etc/passwd file, use a colon (:) to separate the fields. Just about any symbol could be used as a delimiter.

CHANGING FILES WITH awk

Code Listing 6.12 With a little more tweaking, awk lets you do a lot of processing on the files to get just the information you need.

```
[ejr@hobbes manipulate]$ awk -F, '{print $2 "
  → " $1 " " $7 }' address.book > phone.list
[ejr@hobbes manipulate]$ more phone.list
 Sven Schmidt  555-555-8382
 Fester Feldman
 John Brown  918-555-1234
 Sally Smith  801-555-8982
 Kelly Jones  408-555-7253
[ejr@hobbes manipulate]$
```

3. `awk -F, '{ print $2 " " $1 " " $7 }'`
`→ address.book > phone.list`

With this code, you can pull specific fields, in an arbitrary order, from your database. Although it looks complex, it's just one additional step from the previous example.Rather than printing a single field from the address book, we're printing field 2, then a space, then field 1, then a space, then field 7. The final bit just redirects the output into a new file. This example would produce a list of names and phone numbers, as shown in **Code Listing 6.12**. See the previous section, *Making global changes with* `sed`, for a reminder about `$`.

4. `awk -F, /CA/'{ print $2 $1 $7 }'`
`→ address.book > phone.list`

You can also specify a matching pattern. Here, we added `/CA/` to search and act on only the lines that contain `CA`, so only those lines will be in the `phone.list` file.

✔ Tips

- You can load `awk` scripts from a file with `awk -f script.awk filename`. Just as with `sed`, this keeps the retyping to a minimum, which is helpful with these long and convoluted commands. Refer to Chapter 10 for more details about scripting.
- Take a glance at *Sorting files with* `sort` later in this chapter and consider piping your `awk` output to `sort`. Let UNIX do the tedious work for you!

Comparing files with cmp

Suppose you've been working on the `dear` → `liza` file and you want to know how it differs from the `dearhenry` file. Using `cmp`, you can compare the two files as shown in **Code Listing 6.13**.

To compare files with cmp:

- `cmp dearliza dearhenry`

  At the shell prompt, type `cmp` followed by both file names. As **Code Listing 6.13** shows, these two files are not the same.

  If the files are identical, you'll find yourself back at the shell prompt with no comment from UNIX. If both files are identical until one of them ends—that is, say, the first 100 lines are the same, but one continues and the other ends—then you'll see an EOF (end of file) message, as in **Code Listing 6.14**.

✔ Tip

- You can find out other ways that files differ using `diff`, as described in the next section, *Finding differences in files with* `diff`.

Code Listing 6.13 cmp gives just the facts about the first difference between two files.

```
[ejr@hobbes manipulate]$ cmp dearliza
  → dearhenry
dearliza dearhenry differ: char 20, line 2
[ejr@hobbes manipulate]$
```

Code Listing 6.14 cmp also tells you if the files matched until one ended (EOF stands for "end of file").

```
[ejr@hobbes manipulate]$ cmp limerick
  → limericks
cmp: EOF on limerick
[ejr@hobbes manipulate]$
```

Code Listing 6.15 diff tells you all you ever wanted to know about the differences between two files, but not in an easily readable manner.

```
[ejr@hobbes manipulate]$ diff dearliza
  → dearhenry
2,3c2,3
< Dear Liza,
< There's a hole in my bucket, dear Liza, dear
  → Liza, dear Liza.
---
> Dear Henry,
> Please fix it dear Henry, dear Henry, dear
  → Henry.
5,6c5,6
< Henry
<
---
> Liza
> PS, you forgot your toolbox last time.
[ejr@hobbes manipulate]$
```

Finding differences in files with diff

In addition to using `cmp` to find out how files differ, you can also use `diff`. This command tells you specifically where two files differ, not just that they differ and at which point the differences start (see **Code Listing 6.15**).

Finding differences with diff:

- `diff dearliza dearhenry`

  Type `diff`, followed by both file names. The `diff` output, as in **Code Listing 6.15**, shows lines that appear only in one file or the other. The lines from file 1 are indicated with a <, while the lines from file 2 are indicated with >.

  Above each line is its line number in the first file, then `d`, `a`, or `c`, then the corresponding line number from the second file:

  - `d` means that the line would have to be deleted from file 1 to make it match file 2.
  - `a` means that text would have to be added to file 1 to match file 2.
  - `c` means that changes would have to be made to the line for the two files to match.

✔ Tips

- You can also use `diff` to find out which files are in one directory but not another. Just type `diff` followed by the names of the two directories; for example, `diff /home/ejr/Directory → /home/ejr/Newdirectory`.
- If you're comparing e-mail messages or other less-structured documents, you might consider adding the flags `-i` (case insensitive) `-b` (ignore blank lines) or even `-w` (ignore spaces and tabs) to avoid cluttering your results with unimportant differences. For example, you could use `diff -ibw file1 file2` to find all differences between two files except those involving blank lines, spaces, tabs, or lowercase/uppercase letters.
- You might also check out the next section, *Finding differences in files with `sdiff`*, for yet another way to compare files.

Finding differences in files with sdiff

Yet another way to compare files is to use `sdiff`, which presents the two files onscreen so that you can visually compare them (see **Code Listing 6.16**).

To compare files with sdiff:

- `sdiff dearliza dearhenry`

  At the shell prompt, type `sdiff` and the file names to compare the two files. The output, as shown in **Code Listing 6.16**, presents each line of the two files side by side, separating them with

  - (Nothing) if the lines are identical
  - < if the line exists only in the first file
  - > if the line exists only in the second file
  - | if they are different

✔ Tips

- If most of the lines are the same, consider using the `-s` flag so the identical lines are not shown. For example, type `sdiff -s dearliza dearhenry`.
- If the output scoots by too fast to read, remember that you can pipe the entire command to `more`, as in `sdiff dearliza dearhenry | more`.

Code Listing 6.16 sdiff puts the files side by side, so you can easily see the differences.

```
[ejr@hobbes manipulate]$ sdiff dearliza dearhenry
July 25, 1998                                          July 25, 1998
Dear Liza,                                           | Dear Henry,
There's a hole in my bucket, dear Liza, dear Liza.   | Please fix it dear Henry, dear Henry.
Yours,                                                 Yours,
Henry                                                | Liza
                                                     | PS, you forgot your toolbox last time.

[ejr@hobbes manipulate]$
```

Sorting files with sort

If you want to be really lazy—er, um, *smart*—let UNIX sort files for you. You can use `sort` to, for example, sort your address book alphabetically—as opposed to the random order you might have entered addresses in (see **Code Listing 6.17**).

To sort files with sort:

◆ `sort address.book >`
`→ sorted.address.book`

To begin, type `sort`, followed by the name of the file you want to sort. UNIX will sort the lines in the file alphabetically and present the sorted results in the file you specify (here, `sorted.address.book`), as shown in **Code Listing 6.17**.

✔ Tips

■ If you have multiple files to sort, you can use `sort file1 file2 file3 > com-`

Code Listing 6.17 An unsorted address book springs to order with the help of sort.

```
[ejr@hobbes manipulate]$ more address.book
Schmidt, Sven, 1 Circle Drive, Denver, CO, 80221, 555-555-8382
Feldman, Fester, RR1, Billings, MT 62832, 285-555-0281
Brown, John, 1453 South Street, Tulsa, OK, 74114, 918-555-1234
Smith, Sally, 452 Center Ave., Salt Lake City, UT, 84000, 801-555-8982
Jones, Kelly, 14 Main Street, Santa Clara, CA, 95051, 408-555-7253
[ejr@hobbes manipulate]$ sort address.book
Brown, John, 1453 South Street, Tulsa, OK, 74114, 918-555-1234
Feldman, Fester, RR1, Billings, MT 62832, 285-555-0281
Jones, Kelly, 14 Main Street, Santa Clara, CA, 95051, 408-555-7253
Schmidt, Sven, 1 Circle Drive, Denver, CO, 80221, 555-555-8382
Smith, Sally, 452 Center Ave., Salt Lake City, UT, 84000, 801-555-8982
[ejr@hobbes manipulate]$ sort address.book > sorted.address.book
[ejr@hobbes manipulate]$ cat sorted.address.book
Brown, John, 1453 South Street, Tulsa, OK, 74114, 918-555-1234
Feldman, Fester, RR1, Billings, MT 62832, 285-555-0281
Jones, Kelly, 14 Main Street, Santa Clara, CA, 95051, 408-555-7253
Schmidt, Sven, 1 Circle Drive, Denver, CO, 80221, 555-555-8382
Smith, Sally, 452 Center Ave., Salt Lake City, UT, 84000, 801-555-8982
[ejr@hobbes manipulate]$
```

`plete.sorted.file`, and the output will contain the contents of all three files, sorted, of course.

- You can sort fields in comma-delimited files by adding `-t` to the code. For example, `sort -t, +1 address.book tells UNIX to sort by the second field.` The `-t` and following character (`,`) indicate what character separates the fields—the comma in this case. If a character isn't given, `sort` thinks that white space marks the boundaries between fields. The `+1` says to skip the first field and sort on the second one.
- You can sort numerically too, with `sort -n filename`. If you don't use the `-n` flag, the output will be ordered based on the leftmost digits in the numbers—for example "1, 203, 50"—because the alphabetic sort starts at the left of the field.

Eliminating duplicates with uniq

If you've sorted files using the handy-dandy `sort` command, you might end up with results that have duplicates in them. Heck, you might have files with duplicates anyway. At any rate, here's how to find and work with them. As **Code Listing 6.18** shows, you can get rid of duplicate lines by using the `uniq` command (short for "unique") in conjunction with `sort`.

To eliminate duplicates with uniq:

- `sort address.book | uniq`

  At the shell prompt, type `sort` and the file name, then type `| uniq` to pipe the output to `uniq`. The output of `uniq` will not contain any duplicated entries (**Code Listing 6.18**).

✔ Tips

- `uniq` only finds identical, adjacent (sorted) lines. For example, if you have both `Jones` and `jones` in your address book, `uniq` won't identify either entry because they differ in capitalization.
- You can also use the `-d` flag to specify that you want to see only the duplicate lines. For example, say you want to see all of the people who are in both your `carpool` file and your `nightout` file. You'd just use `sort carpool nightout | uniq -d`.

Code Listing 6.18 Use sort with uniq to eliminate duplicates.

```
[ejr@hobbes manipulate]$ more long.address.book
Schmidt, Sven, 1 Circle Drive, Denver, CO, 80221, 555-555-8382
Feldman, Fester, RR1, Billings, MT 62832, 285-555-0281
Brown, John, 1453 South Street, Tulsa, OK, 74114, 918-555-1234
Smith, Sally, 452 Center Ave., Salt Lake City, UT, 84000, 801-555-8982
Jones, Kelly, 14 Main Street, Santa Clara, CA, 95051, 408-555-7253
Schmidt, Swen, 1 Circle Drive, Denver, CO, 80221, 555-555-8382
Feldman, Fester, RR1, Billings, MT 62832, 285-555-0281
Brown, Jonathon, 1453 South Street, Tulsa, OK, 74114, 918-555-1234
Smith, Sally, 452 Center Ave., Salt Lake City, UT, 84000, 801-555-8982
Jones, Kelly, 14 Main Street, Santa Clara, CA, 95051, 408-555-7253
[ejr@hobbes manipulate]$ sort long.address.book | uniq
Brown, John, 1453 South Street, Tulsa, OK, 74114, 918-555-1234
Brown, Jonathon, 1453 South Street, Tulsa, OK, 74114, 918-555-1234
Feldman, Fester, RR1, Billings, MT 62832, 285-555-0281
Jones, Kelly, 14 Main Street, Santa Clara, CA, 95051, 408-555-7253
Schmidt, Sven, 1 Circle Drive, Denver, CO, 80221, 555-555-8382
Schmidt, Swen, 1 Circle Drive, Denver, CO, 80221, 555-555-8382
Smith, Sally, 452 Center Ave., Salt Lake City, UT, 84000, 801-555-8982
[ejr@hobbes manipulate]$
```

Redirecting to multiple locations with tee

Suppose you just updated your address book file and want to send it to your boss in addition to putting it in your own files. You can, using `tee`, which redirects output to two different places (see **Code Listing 6.19**).

To redirect output to two locations with tee:

◆

```
sort address.book new.addresses
→ | tee sorted.all
→ | mail boss@raycomm.com -s
→ "Here's the address book, boss" -
```

At the shell prompt, use the `tee` command plus a file name in the middle of the pipeline to send the sorted information to that file name as well as to the standard output (which could, of course, be redirected to another file name). Here, we send the results of the sort to the `sorted.all` file and to standard output, where `mail` will take over and send the file to the boss (see Chapter 11 for more on fancy mail tricks).

Tee time?

You might think of the `tee` command as being similar to a plumber's pipe joint—that is, it takes stuff from one location and sends it out to two different places.

Code Listing 6.19 Use tee to send output to two different places at once.

```
[ejr@hobbes manipulate]$ sort address.book new.addresses | tee sorted.all | mail boss@raycomm.com
  → -s "Here's the address book, boss" -
[ejr@hobbes manipulate]$
```

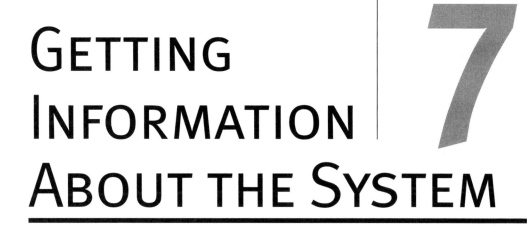

Getting Information About the System

7

Now is your chance to nose around in everyone else's business! In this chapter, we'll show you how to get information about the system, about other users, and about your own userid.

Chapter contents

- Finding out system information
- Viewing file systems
- Determining disk usage
- Finding out file types
- Finding out about other users
- Learning who else is logged in (two methods)
- Getting information about your userid

Getting system information with uname

Information about your UNIX system might come in handy if you're planning to try some new software or need to figure out system idiosyncrasies. Some systems tell you this information when you log in. Sometimes, however, especially if you're using an ISP, you may not have been told any particulars about the UNIX system. You can easily find out what kind of UNIX system you're using with `uname`, as shown in **Code Listings 7.1** and **7.2**.

To find out about the system using uname:

1. `uname`

   To begin, type `uname` to find out what kind of a system you're on. The UNIX system in **Code Listings 7.1** and **7.2** is SunOS. Other common systems (not an exhaustive list, by any means) are Linux, AIX, BSD, and HP/UX.

2. `uname -sr`

   Add the `-sr` flags to the command, yielding `uname -sr`, to find out both the system type and the release level. This is useful to find out whether specific software is compatible with the operating system.

3. `uname -a`

   For the whole nine yards, use `uname -a` to print all information, including the operating system type, host name, version, and hardware. The specifics you get here will vary a bit from system to system.

Code Listing 7.1 Variants on the uname command provide all kinds of interesting or useful information about the system.

```
xmission> uname
SunOS
xmission> uname -sr
SunOS 5.5.1
xmission> uname -a
SunOS xmission 5.5.1 Generic_103640-19 sun4m
  → sparc SUNW,SPARCstation-10
xmission>
```

Code Listing 7.2 On a different system, the same commands provide slightly different details, although the basic information remains the same.

```
Red Hat Linux release 5.1 (Manhattan)
Kernel 2.0.34 on an i486
login: ejr
Password:
Last login: Fri Jul 24 12:14:37 from calvin
[ejr@hobbes ejr]$ uname
Linux
[ejr@hobbes ejr]$ uname -sr
Linux 2.0.34
[ejr@hobbes ejr]$ uname -a
Linux hobbes.raycomm.com 2.0.34 #1 Fri May 8
  → 16:05:57 EDT 1998 i486 unknown
[ejr@hobbes ejr]$
```

Viewing file systems with df

If you're used to Windows or Macintosh operating systems, you're probably accustomed to having separate hard drives (C:, D:, E:, for Windows users, or real names for Macs) which are just different storage spaces. In UNIX systems, different storage spaces are grafted onto the overall tree structure—tacked on to what's already existing, and without any clear distinction indicating where actual disk drives are located. For example, if you have a folder on a Mac or Windows computer, you know that all of the subfolders and files within it are located on the same hard drive. In UNIX, everything resides within the root directory, but any different directory could be located on a different physical hard drive. You might think of it as tacking a new branch onto your artificial Christmas tree.

These tacked-on storage spaces are called *file systems*. Particularly if you're running a UNIX system (as opposed to just using one), you might need to find out what file systems are in use (or *mounted* in the system, in technical terms), how much space they have, and where they attach to the UNIX system (or where their *mountpoints* are). You can find out this information using `df`, as shown in **Code Listings 7.3** and **7.4**.

To find out about file systems with df:

- `df`

  At the shell prompt, type `df`. You'll get output showing you

  - The name of the *device*, which refers to the physical part that stores the data, such as a hard drive, CD-ROM, or whatever. In **Figure 7.3** the first one is /dev/hda, indicating the first hard drive in the system.

- The number of blocks, which are 1K-sized storage units. (1K-sized in this case, although some systems report them as 512 bytes).
- The number of used and available blocks on the device.
- The percentage of the space on the device that is being used.
- The name of the file system, which is the full path name from the UNIX system. This is also known as the mountpoint.

Code Listings 7.3 and **7.4** on the next page show the output of df on two different systems.

If you're a system administrator, you can use this information to help diagnose problems occurring in the system. If you're an average user (of above-average curiosity), you can use this information to satisfy your inquisitive inclinations or to tip off a system administrator to problems. For example, if you're getting odd errors or unpredictable results with a specific program, using df might reveal that the /home file system is full or maybe that you don't have the /dev/cdrom file system that you thought was installed and mounted. Hmmm!

Code Listing 7.3 This small Linux system has relatively simple file systems.

```
[ejr@hobbes ejr]$ df
Filesystem         1024-blocks  Used Available Capacity Mounted on
/dev/hda1             515161  316297   172255     65%   /
/dev/hdb4              66365    4916    58022      8%   /home
/dev/hdb1             416656  324633    70504     82%   /usr/local
/dev/sbpcd            596704  596704        0    100%   /mnt/cdrom
[ejr@hobbes ejr]$
```

✔ Tips

- You can use `df` with a specific directory to get a report on the status of the file system containing that directory. For example, you might use `df /usr/local/src` to find out where that directory is mounted and how much space is available on it.
- Use `df -k /home` to make sure that the usage is reported in 1K blocks, not in 512 byte blocks.

Code Listing 7.4 This large ISP's file systems are considerably more complex.

```
xmission> df
/               (/dev/dsk/c0t3d0s0 ):  154632 blocks    71721 files
/usr            (/dev/dsk/c0t3d0s6 ):  225886 blocks   144820 files
/proc           (/proc             ):       0 blocks     7830 files
/dev/fd         (fd                ):       0 blocks        0 files
/var            (/dev/dsk/c0t1d0s0 ): 1001142 blocks   962598 files
/tmp            (swap              ): 1236032 blocks    95277 files
/usr/local      (/dev/dsk/c0t1d0s5 ):  630636 blocks   457211 files
/archive        (/dev/dsk/c0t1d0s3 ): 1180362 blocks  1789487 files
/var/mail       (mail.xmission.com:/var/mail): 2776576 blocks  1438385 files
/home           (krunk1.xmission.com:/home):20091072 blocks 13066932 files
/var/spool/newslib (news.xmission.com:/var/spool/newslib):19327664 blocks  1248s
/.web           (krunk1.xmission.com:/.web): 1019408 blocks   470095 files
/var/maillists   (lists.xmission.com:/var/maillists):  293744 blocks    89732s
xmission>
```

VIEWING FILE SYSTEMS WITH df

Determining disk usage with du

Another piece of information that you can access is how much disk space within the UNIX system is in use. You can do so using du, as shown in **Code Listing 7.5**.

To determine disk usage with du:

- du

  At the shell prompt, enter du. As **Code Listing 7.5** shows, you'll get information about disk usage in the current directory as well as in all subdirectories. The numbers are usually measured in 1K blocks (as with `df`). You can make sure by using `du -k`.

✔ Tips

- If you're on a system that enforces disk-space quotas (like most ISPs do), you can find out what your quota is and how close you are to reaching it. Just type `quota -v` at the shell prompt.
- You can use du with a path name to check the disk usage in just a single directory or subdirectory (see **Code Listing 7.6**). du summarizes the usage by subdirectory as it prints the results..

Code Listing 7.5 The du command reports—exhaustively—about the disk usage in the current directory and in its subdirectories.

```
[ejr@hobbes ejr]$ du
2       ./Mail
1       ./nsmail
1       ./.netscape/cache/0F
3       ./.netscape/cache/1A
22      ./.netscape/cache
1       ./.netscape/archive
172     ./.netscape
1       ./Projects
28      ./.wprc
3       ./axhome
5       ./groups
1       ./manipulate/empty
154     ./manipulate
1       ./mail
1       ./unixvqs/ch6
2       ./unixvqs
6       ./dupgroups
255     ./compression/Folder
670     ./compression/temp/BackupFolder
1921    ./compression/temp
670     ./compression/BackupFolder
4657    ./compression
5       ./clean
1       ./.elm
15      ./editors
5619    .
[ejr@hobbes ejr]$
```

Code Listing 7.6 Using du with a specific directory name gives you focused results.

```
[ejr@hobbes ejr]$ du /home/ejr/compression
255     /home/ejr/compression/Folder
670     /home/ejr/compression/temp/
  → BackupFolder
1921    /home/ejr/compression/temp
670     /home/ejr/compression/BackupFolder
4657    /home/ejr/compression
[ejr@hobbes ejr]$
```

Code Listing 7.7 The file command provides useful information about what kind of data is in specific files.

```
[ejr@hobbes ejr]$ file /usr/bin/pico
/usr/bin/pico: ELF 32-bit LSB executable,
  → Intel 80386, version 1, dynamically ld
[ejr@hobbes ejr]$ file temp.htm
temp.htm: ASCII text
[ejr@hobbes ejr]$
```

Finding out file types with file

If you come from a Windows, Macintosh, or DOS background, you're probably used to accessing files and being able to see what type of files they are—HTML files, GIFs, documents, or whatever. In UNIX, though, you often can't tell the file type just by listing files or displaying directory contents. That's where `file` comes in handy, as shown in **Code Listing 7.7**.

To identify file types with file:

- `file /usr/bin/pico`

  At the shell prompt, type `file`, followed by the path (if necessary) and file name. You'll see output similar to that in **Code Listing 7.7**.

✔ Tip

- Not all files have the "magic" information that makes `file` work associated with them, but most do. Where they don't, you get a best-guess response, like the second response in **Code Listing 7.7**. Unfortunately, you can't tell by looking if it's definitive information or a guess, but if it's terse (as in the second response), take it with a grain of salt.

Finding out about users with finger

Using the `finger` command, you can find out who is currently logged into the UNIX system as well as what they're doing, how long they've been logged in, and other snoopy, not-necessarily-your-business information (**Code Listing 7.8**).

To find out who is logged in using finger:

1. `finger`

   At the shell prompt, type `finger` to see who else is logged into the system and to get a little information about them (**Code Listing 7.8**).

2. `finger @stc.org`

   Type `finger`, `@`, and a host name (in this case `stc.org`) to find out who is logged into another host.

   Fingering a different host doesn't always work, depending on security settings on the other host computer(s). If the host

Code Listing 7.8 The finger command often provides interesting information about who is logged onto different systems.

```
[ejr@hobbes ejr]$ finger
Login     Name         Tty  Idle  Login Time   Office     Office Phone
asr                    *4      1  Jul 24 13:32
deb                     5      1  Jul 24 13:32
ejr       Eric J. Ray   1   3:20  Jul 22 07:42
ejr       Eric J. Ray   p1  1:12  Jul 24 12:14 (calvin)
ejr       Eric J. Ray   p0        Jul 24 13:02 (calvin)
root      root         *2     1d  Jul 22 15:13
[ejr@hobbes ejr]$ finger @stc.org
[stc.org]
No one logged on
 [ejr@hobbes ejr]$ finger @osuunx.ucc.okstate.edu
[osuunx.ucc.okstate.edu]
finger: connect: Connection refused
[ejr@hobbes ejr]$
```

doesn't allow it, you'll get an error message like the one in **Code Listing 7.8**.

To find out about users using finger:

1. `finger ejr`

   At the shell prompt, type `finger` followed by the userid of the person you want to know about. You'll get a ton of information, including some or all of the following: the user's name, home directory, and default shell; when, from where, and for how long they've been logged on; and whatever other information they choose to provide. **Code Listing 7.9** shows two users with varying activity. `deb` has apparently been loafing, and `ejr` has been working his buns off.

Code Listing 7.9 The finger command can also provide in-depth information about specific users.

```
[ejr@hobbes ejr]$ finger deb
Login: deb                             Name:
Directory: /home/deb                   Shell: /bin/bash
Never logged in.
No mail.
No Plan.
[ejr@hobbes ejr]$ finger ejr
Login: ejr                             Name:
Directory: /home/ejr                   Shell: /bin/bash
On since Wed Jul 22 07:42 (MDT) on tty1    2 hours 32 minutes idle
On since Wed Jul 22 06:58 (MDT) on ttyp1 from calvin
No mail.
Project:
Working on UNIX VQS.
Plan:
This is my plan--work all day, sleep all night.
[ejr@hobbes ejr]$
[ejr@hobbes ejr]$ finger ejray@xmission.com
[xmission.com]
Login       Name              TTY        Idle    When     Where
ejray    "RayComm             pts/57       <Jul 22 09:39> calvin.raycomm.c
[ejr@hobbes ejr]$
```

2. `finger ejray@xmission.com`

   Using `finger` plus a specific user address, you can find out about users on other systems. As with generic `finger` requests, sometimes they're blocked for security reasons.

✔ Tips

- You can also sniff out user information using `who`. See the next section, *Learning who else is logged in with* `who`.
- You can provide extra information to anyone who gets your user information with `finger` by creating files that describe your "plan" and "project" (as `ejr` has done in **Code Listing 7.9**). Use your favorite editor to create `.plan` and `.project` files in your home directory. Then, change the protection so that the files are both world readable (`chmod go+r .plan ; chmod go+r .project`) and so the directory is accessible (`chmod go+x .`). See Chapter 5 for specifics about `chmod`.
- Information you obtain through `finger` can be handy when diagnosing connection difficulties. In particular, system administrators or help desk personnel are likely to ask where you're connected, (`pts57`, for `ejray@xmission.com`) and what kind of software you're using.

Code Listing 7.10 Use who to find out who else is currently logged into the system.

```
[ejr@hobbes ejr]$ who
ejr      tty1     Jul 22 07:42
root     tty2     Jul 22 15:13
asr      tty4     Jul 24 13:32
deb      tty5     Jul 24 13:32
ejr      ttyp1    Jul 24 12:14
  → (calvin.raycomm.com)
ejr      ttyp0    Jul 24 13:02
  → (calvin.raycomm.com)
[ejr@hobbes ejr]$
```

Learning who else is logged in with who

If you're not interested all the gory details you get about users when you `finger` them, you can instead use `who` to get just the basics. With `who` you get just the users' names, connection information, login times, and host names, as shown in **Code Listing 7.10**.

To snoop with who:

- `who`

  At the shell prompt, type `who`. You'll get user information like that shown in **Code Listing 7.10**. Optionally, you could pipe the output of `who` to `more`, as in `who | more`, which would give you a long list of results one screen at a time.

✔ Tips

- If you're a system administrator or use several different userids, you might occasionally need to use a special case of `who`, called `whoami`. Just type `whoami` at the shell prompt, and it'll tell you which userid you're currently logged in as.
- See Chapter 1 for more on `more` and on piping commands.

Learning who else is logged in with w

Another way to find out about other people logged into the UNIX system is to use w, which tells you who is logged in, what they're doing, and a few other details (**Code Listing 7.11**).

To find out who is logged in with w:

- w

  At the shell prompt, type w. You'll see output like that in **Code Listing 7.11**. The top line shows
  - The time
  - System uptime in days, hours, and minutes (*uptime* is how long it's been since the system was restarted, and is usually measured in weeks or months for UNIX systems, as opposed to hours or days for personal computers).
  - The number of users
  - System load averages (the numbers indicate jobs (programs or scripts to execute) lined up to run in the last 1, 5, and 15 minutes)

  The following lines, one per logged-in user, show
  - The login name
  - The tty name (the connection to the UNIX host)
  - The remote host name

Code Listing 7.11 The w command provides tons of information about the system and its users.

```
[ejr@hobbes ejr]$ w
  1:49pm  up 6 days,  4:21,  6 users,  load average: 0.08, 0.02, 0.01
USER     TTY      FROM              LOGIN@   IDLE   JCPU   PCPU  WHAT
ejr      tty1                      Wed 7am  3:36m  7.07s  6.01s  -bash
root     tty2                      Wed 3pm 28:46m  1.22s  0.32s  -bash
asr      tty4                       1:32pm 17:22   1.04s  0.30s  pine
deb      tty5                       1:32pm  3.00s  1.22s  0.42s  lynx
ejr      ttyp1    calvin           12:14pm  1:28m  1.33s  0.57s  vi hairyspiders
ejr      ttyp0    calvin            1:02pm  1.00s  1.70s  0.24s  w
[ejr@hobbes ejr]$
```

- The login time
- Current idle time (that is, the time since a key on the keyboard was touched)
- JCPU (*job CPU time*, or the total processing time for jobs on the current connection, which is the `tty`, for those into the jargon)
- PCPU (*process CPU time*, or the processing time for the current process)
- The command line of the current process

Whew! As you can see from **Code Listings 7.11** and **7.12**, different systems' `w` commands produce slightly different (but similar) output.

✔ Tip

- Use `w` with `grep` to find information (slightly more abbreviated) about a specific user. For example, `w | grep ejr` gives limited information, but just about a specific user. See Chapter 1 for more information about piping commands.

Code Listing 7.12 w yields different information on different systems.

```
xmission> w
  1:47pm  up 38 day(s), 23:35,  36 users,  load average: 1.58, 1.78, 1.75
...
ejray    pts/16      Thu 6am        1:14         -csh
...
```

Getting information about your userid with id

Occasionally, you may need to find out information about your userid, such as what your userid's numeric value is and what groups you belong to. This information is essential when you're sharing files (as discussed in Chapter 5) because you'll need it to let people access your files and to access theirs. You can easily get information about your userid with `id`, as shown in **Code Listing 7.13**.

To check userid information using id:

◆ `id`

At the shell prompt, type `id` to find out what the numeric value of your userid is and what groups (by name and numeric userid value) you belong to (see **Code Listing 7.13**). See Chapter 5, page 85 for more about the `/etc/`group file.

✔ Tip

- You can also check someone else's status with `id` to find out what groups they're in. Just use `id userid` (substituting the other person's userid for `userid`, of course).

Code Listing 7.13 Use id to get information about userids and group memberships.

```
[ejr@hobbes ejr]$ id
uid=500(ejr) gid=500(ejr)
  → groups=500(ejr),10(wheel),100(users)
[ejr@hobbes ejr]$ id deb
uid=505(deb) gid=505(deb) groups=100(users)
[ejr@hobbes ejr]$
```

CONFIGURING YOUR UNIX ENVIRONMENT

8

Chapter contents

- Understanding your UNIX environment
- Discovering your current environment variables
- Adding or changing environment variables
- Looking at your bash configuration files
- Changing your bash path
- Changing your bash prompt
- Looking at your ksh configuration files
- Changing your ksh path
- Changing your ksh prompt
- Looking at your csh configuration files
- Changing your csh path
- Changing your csh prompt
- Setting aliases

Back in Chapter 3, we introduced you to UNIX shells—what they are and what you can do with them. In this chapter, we'll take you a bit further and look at configuring your environment using the `bash`, `csh`, and `ksh` shells. By configuring your environment (through changing environment variables), you can make the UNIX system adapt to your needs, rather than adapting to an existing environment that may not work for you.

These configuration tips differ (slightly) for different shells, so make sure you're following along with the instructions appropriate for the shell you use.

Understanding your UNIX environment

Environment variables are settings in the UNIX system that specify how you, your shell, and the UNIX system interact. When you log into the UNIX system, it sets up your standard environment variables—the shell prompt you want to use, the default search path, and other information to help programs run, among other things. You might think of your environment variables as being similar to having a standing order with a deli to deliver the same thing to you every day. You set up your "standing environment variables" and the UNIX system delivers them to you session after session unless you specify otherwise.

Basically, just like with the lunch deli, you can configure your environment in one of two ways:

- Changing the variables for the current session—kind of like calling in a special order for the day (as in ordering onion and extra cheese on the day's sandwich). You do this from the shell prompt, as discussed in *Adding or changing environment variables* in this chapter.
- Changing the variables for all subsequent sessions—kind of like changing your standard order (say, when the doctor tells you to cut back on mayonnaise and suggests mustard for your long-term deli order). You do this within the configuration files, as discussed in sections following *Adding or changing environment variables* in this chapter.

If you want to change your environment variables, you might first try changing them from the shell prompt for the current session. This way, you can try out the change before you make it permanant in your configuration files.

If you'd rather change your environment in the configuration files, keep in mind that configuration files are run in a specific order:

1. System-wide configuration files (such as `/etc/profile`) run first upon login. These system-wide configuration files in `/etc` help set up your environment, but you cannot change them.
2. Configuration files specific to your UNIX account (such as `~/.profile` and `~/.kshrc`) run next if they're available. If you want to change environment variables originally set in the system-wide files, you can reset the values in your own personal files.

What this order means to you is that your own personal configurations override system ones. So, in making changes to your configuration files, make sure that you make changes to the configuration file that runs last. We'll tell you which specific files to look for in the relevant sections of this chapter.

✔ Tips

- Find out about discovering your current environment variables and adding or changing environment variables manually in the next two sections in this chapter.
- You can use `echo $SHELL` to remind yourself of what shell you're using. Visit Chapter 3 for more details.
- Find out about changing environment variables in your system configuration files in other sections of this chapter, according to which shell you're using.

Discovering your current environment variables

A good first step in changing your environment is determining what environment variables you have. Using the steps in this section, you can discover which environment variables are currently set—including ones set in the configuration files as well as ones you've set for the current session (**Code Listings 8.1** and **8.2**).

As you're going through these steps, you might check out the sidebar called *Environment variables you shouldn't touch* in this section for a list of variables you should leave alone. Then, in the next section, check out *Environment variables you can mess with* to find ones you can change.

To find current environment variables in bash or ksh:

- `set`

  At the shell prompt, type `set`. You'll see a list of the current environment variables, as shown in **Code Listing 8.1**.

  Some of the variables might look familiar to you (such as the ones showing your shell or user name), while others are likely to be more cryptic (such as the line showing the last command you ran, in this case, `_=cd`).

To find current environment variables in csh:

- `setenv`

  At the shell prompt, type `setenv`. As **Code Listing 8.2** shows, the preconfigured variables will closely resemble the environment variables that `bash` or `ksh` offer.

Code Listing 8.1 You can find out which variables exist in the bash or ksh shells with set.

```
[ejr@hobbes ejr]$ set
BASH=/bin/bash
BASH_VERSION=1.14.7(1)
COLUMNS=80
ENV=/home/ejr/.bashrc
EUID=500
HISTFILE=/home/ejr/.bash_history
HISTFILESIZE=1000
HISTSIZE=1000
HOME=/home/ejr
HOSTNAME=hobbes.raycomm.com
HOSTTYPE=i386
IFS=
LINES=24
LOGNAME=ejr
MAIL=/var/spool/mail/ejr
MAILCHECK=60
OLDPWD=/home/ejr/src/rpm-2.5.1
OPTERR=1
OPTIND=1
OSTYPE=Linux
PATH=/usr/local/bin:/bin:/usr/bin:/usr/X11R6/
  bin:/home/ejr/bin
PPID=1943
PS1=[\u@\h \W]\$
PS2=>
PS4=+
PWD=/home/ejr
SHELL=/bin/bash
SHLVL=3
TERM=vt220
UID=500
USER=ejr
USERNAME=
_=cd
[ejr@hobbes ejr]$
```

Code Listing 8.2 Or, use setenv find out the which variables exist in the csh shell at the c-shore.

```
xmission> setenv
HOME=/home/users/e/ejray
PATH=/usr/local/bin:/usr/local/bin/X11:/usr/
  → openwin/bin:/usr/bin:/usr/ucb:/usr/.
LOGNAME=ejray
HZ=100
TERM=vt100
TZ=MST7MDT
SHELL=/usr/bin/csh
MAIL=/var/mail/ejray
PWD=/home/users/e/ejray
USER=ejray
EDITOR=pico -t
OPENWINHOME=/usr/openwin
MANPATH=/usr/man:/usr/local/man:/usr/openwin/
  → man
LD_LIBRARY_PATH=/usr/local/lib:/usr/openwin/
  → lib
PAGER=more
xmission>
```

✔ Tips

- If you do as we often do and try to use `show` to show the environment variables ("showing" the variables seems logical, right?), you'll likely get a weird question about the standard mail directories and the MH mailer. Just press Ctrl C to return to your shell prompt.
- If the list of environment variables is long, you can pipe `set` or `setenv` to `more` so that you can read the variables one screen at a time. Try `set | more` or `setenv | more`. See Chapter 1 for a reminder about piping commands.

Environment variables you shouldn't touch

Before you go running off and changing your environment variables, note that there are some that you should really leave alone. These variables that the shell automatically sets which affect how your UNIX system works (or doesn't work, if you try to change some of these variables!). See the sidebar called *Environment variables you can mess with* in the following section for a list of environment variables you can change.

Bash and ksh	csh	Description
HISTCMD		Keeps track of the number of the current command from the history.
HOSTTYPE		Holds a string describing the type of hardware bash is running on.
IFS		Specifies the characters that indicate the beginning or end of words. Don't reset this.
LINENO		Contains the number of the current line within the shell or a shell script.
OLDPWD		Contains the previous working directory.
OSTYPE		Holds a string describing the operating system the shell is running on.
PPID		Contains the process ID of the shell's parent.
PWD	cwd	Contains the current working directory.
RANDOM		Contains a special value to generate random numbers.
SECONDS		Contains the number of seconds since the shell was started.
SHELL	shell	Contains the name of the current shell.
SHLVL		Contains a number indicating the subshell level (if SHLVL is 3, two parent shells exist and you'll have to exit from three total shells to completely log out).
UID		Contains the userid of the current user.

Adding or changing environment variables

After you've poked around in your environment variables, you might determine that you want to set one that's currently not available or change one to make it better meet your needs. In general, you won't randomly specify environment variables; you'll do it because a certain program requires a specific variable in order to run.

Environment variables you can mess with

The following table includes environment variables you can safely change. Keep in mind that the shell itself might not use a specific variable, like NNTPSERVER, while programs running under the shell might. Sometimes shells assign default variables, while in other cases, you'll have to manually set the value.

Bash and ksh	csh	Description
CDPATH	cdpath	Specifies the search path for directories specified by cd. This is similar to PATH.
COLUMNS		Specifies width of the edit window in characters.
EDITOR		Specifies the default editor.
ENV		Specifies where to look for configuration files.
HISTFILE		Specifies the name of the file containing the command history.
HISTFILESIZE	savehist	Specifies the maximum number of lines to keep in the history file.
HISTSIZE	History	Specifies the number of commands to keep in the command history.
HOSTFILE		Specifies the name of the file containing hostname aliases for expansion.
IGNOREEOF	ignoreeof	Specifies that Ctrl D should not log out of the shell. Use IGNOREEOF=.
LINES		Specifies the number of lines on the screen.
MAIL	mail	Specifies the location of incoming mail so bash can notify you of mail arrival.
MAILCHECK	mail	Specifies how often (in seconds) bash checks for mail.
MAIL_WARNING		Specifies the message to be displayed if you have read mail but not unread mail.
noclobber	noclobber	Specifies that the shell should not overwrite an existing file when redirecting output.
PATH	path	Specifies the search path for commands, including multiple paths separated by colons.
PROMPT_COMMAND		Specifies the command to be run before displaying each primary prompt (does not apply to ksh).
PS1	prompt	Specifies the primary prompt.
PS2		Specifies the default second-level prompt.
PS3		Specifies the prompt for the select command in scripts.
PS4		Specifies the prompt used when tracing execution of a script.
TMOUT		Specifies time in seconds to wait for input before closing the shell.
VISUAL		Specifies the default visual editor—usually the same as EDITOR, but referenced by different programs.

Code Listing 8.3 In the bash and ksh shells, you can add a new environment variable by specifying the variable and its value, then exporting the variable to the system.

```
[ejr@hobbes ejr]$ NNTPSERVER=news.xmission.com
[ejr@hobbes ejr]$ export NNTPSERVER
[ejr@hobbes ejr]$ echo $NNTPSERVER
news.xmission.com
[ejr@hobbes ejr]$
```

Code Listing 8.4 The process for the csh shell is similar to the process for the bash and ksh shells.

```
xmission> set NNTPSERVER=news.xmission.com
xmission> setenv NNTPSERVER news.xmission.com
xmission> echo $NNTPSERVER
news.xmission.com
```

By following the steps in this section, you can add or change environment variables for the current session. As **Code Listing 8.3** shows, for example, you can specify a news server environment variable (called `NNTPSERVER`), that some Usenet News readers require to access the news (`nntp`) server.

To add or change an environment variable in `bash` or `ksh`:

1. `NNTPSERVER=news.xmission.com`

   At the shell prompt, type the name of the environment variable (in this case, `NNTPSERVER`), followed by = and the value you want for the variable (here, `news.xmission.com`), as shown in **Code Listing 8.3**. In this step, you're setting up the variable and its value.

   If the value contains spaces or special characters, put the value in quotes.

2. `export NNTPSERVER`

   Type `export` followed by the name of the variable. By exporting the variable, you make it available to all programs and scripts that run in the current shell session (again, **Code Listing 8.3**).

3. `echo $NNTPSERVER`

   Optionally, type `echo` followed by a `$` and the name of the variable to have the shell tell you what the variable is set to.

To add or change an environment variable in `csh`:

1. `set NNTPSERVER=news.xmission.com`

   At the shell prompt, type `set`, followed by the name of the environment variable, =, and the value you want for the variable, as shown in **Code Listing 8.4**. In this step, you're setting up the variable and its value.

   If the value contains spaces or special characters, put the value in quotes.

2. `setenv NNTPSERVER news.xmission.com`

   Type `setenv` followed by the name of the variable, a space, and the value of the variable. Here, you make the environment variable available to all programs and scripts that run in the current shell session (**Code Listing 8.4**).

3. `echo $NNTPSERVER`

   Optionally, type `echo` followed by a `$` and the name of the variable to have the shell tell you what the variable is set to.

✔ Tips

- If you want to change or add to your environment variables so that the new settings exist from session to session, use the instructions for changing the environment variables in your configuration files, as described throughout the rest of this chapter.
- In many `csh` implementations, only step 2 is necessary to set an environment variable, while step 1 would still be used to set variables within a shell script.
- Find out more about news readers in Chapter 12.

Looking at your bash configuration files

Your first step in modifying or adding bash environment variables in your configuration files is to look at the configuration files, which show you the variables that have been defined. As **Code Listing 8.5** shows, you do this using more or the editor of your choice.

Remember that configuration files run in a specific order:

1. System-wide configuration files (such as /etc/profile) run first upon login.
2. Configuration files specific to your UNIX account (such as ~/.bash_profile or ~/.profile) run next if they're available..

Code Listing 8.5 Your configuration files set up your environment variables and other features of your UNIX experience.

```
[ejr@hobbes ejr]$ more ~/.bash_profile ~/.profile /etc/bash* /etc/profile
::::::::::::::
/home/ejr/.bash_profile
::::::::::::::
# .bash_profile

# Get the aliases and functions
if [ -f ~/.bashrc ]; then
        . ~/.bashrc
fi

# User-specific environment and startup programs

PATH=$PATH:$HOME/bin
ENV=$HOME/.bashrc
USERNAME=""

export USERNAME ENV PATH

/home/ejr/.profile: No such file or directory
::::::::::::::
/etc/bashrc
::::::::::::::
# /etc/bashrc

# System-wide functions and aliases
# Environment stuff goes in /etc/profile
```

(continued on next page)

Code Listing 8.5 (continued)

```
# Putting PS1 here ensures that it gets loaded every time.
PS1="[\u@\h \W]\\$ "

alias which="type -path"
::::::::::::::
/etc/profile
::::::::::::::
# /etc/profile

# System-wide environment and startup programs
# Functions and aliases go in /etc/bashrc

PATH="$PATH:/usr/X11R6/bin"
PS1="[\u@\h \W]\\$ "

ulimit -c 1000000
if [ 'id -gn' = 'id -un' -a 'id -u' -gt 14 ]; then
        umask 002
else
        umask 022
fi

USER='id -un'
LOGNAME=$USER
MAIL="/var/spool/mail/$USER"

HOSTNAME='/bin/hostname'
HISTSIZE=1000
HISTFILESIZE=1000
export PATH PS1 HOSTNAME HISTSIZE HISTFILESIZE USER LOGNAME MAIL

for i in /etc/profile.d/*.sh ; do
        if [ -x $i ]; then
                . $i
        fi
done

unset i
[ejr@hobbes ejr]$
```

To look at your bash configuration files:

1. `more ~/.bash_profile ~/.profile → /etc/bash* /etc/profile`

   At the shell prompt, type `more` followed by each of the possible system configuration file names to view your configuration files. If you don't have all of the files mentioned here, don't worry. Just make note of the ones you do have. **Code Listing 8.5** shows an example of what you might see. Notice that some of the lines will reference other files, like the `ENV=$HOME/.bashrc` line that references the `.bashrc` file, containing other configuration settings.

2. Write down, for your reference, the system configuration files and the order in which they're run. (Remember, settings in the last file run override all previous ones.) Our system configuration files include:
   - `~/.bash_profile` (automatically called by the system)
   - `~/.bashrc` (called by `.bash_profile`)
   - `/etc/bashrc` (called by `~/.bashrc`)
   - `/etc/profile` (automatically called by the system if it exists)

   Keep in mind that the files that you have might differ from the files that we have.

✔ Tips

- Take special note of any lines in any of the files that start with `ENV` and end with a path and file name, or that reference other files directly, with something like `/etc/profile` on a line by itself. Each of those lines references another file that plays a role in getting you set up.
- All lines that start with # are comments, which contain notes to help you better understand the files. Comments don't actually do anything, but they help you see what each file does.

Fill in your bash system configuration files

____

____

____

____

____

____

____

____

Adding to your bash path

One of the most useful changes you can make to your environment is adding to the default path, which is determined by the path statement. The path statement tells the shell where to look for commands, scripts, and programs. That is, if you issue a command, the path statement tells the system to look in each of the named directories in a specific order.

Be sure not to remove anything from your path unless you really know what you're doing, but feel free to add as many additional directories as you want to it.

As the following steps show, you change your `bash` path by first identifying where your path statement is located, then editing the file that contains it (**Code Listing 8.6**).

To change your bash path:

1. `more ~/.bash_profile ~/.bashrc`
   To begin, view your configuration files (just the ones you can edit) in the order they're executed.
   Look through your system configuration files for a path statement. As **Code Listing 8.6** shows, it'll look something like `PATH=/bin:/usr/bin:/usr/local/bin`. If you have more than one path statement, find the last one executed.
   Remember that different systems will have different configurations, so you might need to do a little digging to find your personal path statement(s).
2. `cp .bash_profile`
   `→ .bash_profile_backup`
   Make a backup of the file containing the path statement so that you can recover if you make mistakes. See Chapter 1 if you need more information on copying files.
3. `vi .bash_profile`
   Use your favorite editor to open up the file you'll be changing the path in.

Code Listing 8.6 Your first step is finding out the location of your path statement(s).

```
[ejr@hobbes ejr]$ more ~/.bash_profile
  ~/.bashrc
::::::::::::::
/home/ejr/.bash_profile
::::::::::::::
# .bash_profile

# Get the aliases and functions
if [ -f ~/.bashrc ]; then
        . ~/.bashrc
fi

# User-specific environment and startup
  programs

PATH=$PATH:/usr/local/games
ENV=$HOME/.bashrc
USERNAME=""

export USERNAME ENV PATH

--More--(Next file: /home/ejr/.bashrc)
```

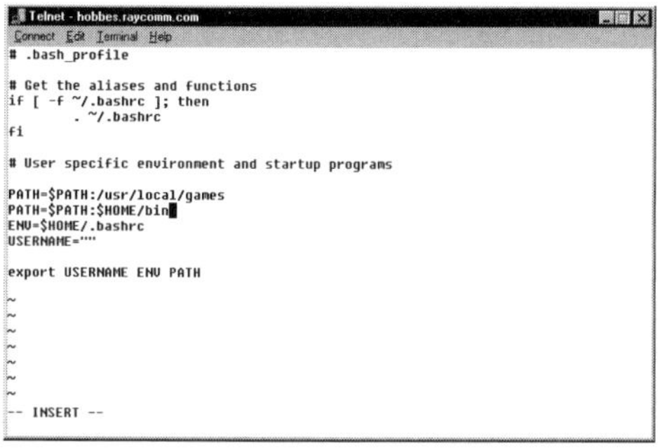

Figure 8.1 You add or modify a path statement in your editor.

Code Listing 8.7 Using echo, you can verify that your new path statement exists.

```
[ejr@hobbes ejr]$ echo $PATH
/bin:/usr/bin:/usr/local/bin:/usr/bin/X11:/
  → usr/X11R6/bin:/usr/local/games:/home/
  → ejr/bin
[ejr@hobbes ejr]$
```

4. `PATH=$PATH:$HOME/bin`

   Add a new path statement immediately below the last path statement. In this example, `$PATH` inserts the current value of the environment variable into the environment variable definition and inserts it into the directory `bin` in your home directory (**Figure 8.1**).

5. Save the file and exit from your editor.

   Refer to Chapter 4 for help if you need it.

6. `su - yourid`

   As you learned back in Chapter 3, this command starts a new login shell so you can test your changes before logging out.

7. `echo $PATH`

   Display the current path environment variable. This should include the addition you just made. It's there, right? (See **Code Listing 8.7.**)

✔ Tips

- If you look through the path statements in your various configuration files, you might find a path statement that includes just a `.` (dot). For example, you might see something like `PATH=/usr/bin:/usr/local/bin:.:` The `.` adds your current directory, whatever it might be, to your path. Keep in mind, though, that it's often safer *not* to have the current directory in the path so you don't unintentionally run a program you're working on.
- You can use `grep` to make it easier to find the configuration files that set your path. `grep PATH .b*` is a good way to start, and `grep PATH /etc/*` is another goodie.
- Your system configuration files will be much less confusing later on if you keep all related changes together. Therefore, you should keep the path statements together, rather than just plugging an entirely random `PATH` statement into your configuration files.

Changing your bash prompt

Depending on your UNIX system, by default you might see as your prompt just a dollar sign (`$`) or perhaps a dollar sign and date, or other information as outlined in the *Setting your* **bash** *prompt promptly* sidebar. You can set your prompt to include information that's handy for you.

You actually have multiple prompts in `bash`:

- The main prompt that you usually think of as the shell prompt. This prompt is called PS1.
- A secondary prompt that you see when the system requires additional information to complete a command. Logically, this prompt is called PS2.

You can change either of these prompts using the following steps. You start by finding your prompt statement (**Code Listing 8.8**), then modify it in your editor (**Figure 8.2**).

To change your bash prompt:

1. `grep PS1 /etc/bashrc ~/.bash_profile → ~/.bashrc`

   To begin, search through the configuration files located in your home directory and in the `/etc` directory to find your prompt statement. It'll look something like `PS1="$ "` or `PS1="[\u@\h \W]\\$ "`, as shown in **Code Listing 8.8**.

   The *Setting your* **bash** *prompt promptly* sidebar will help translate these symbols.

2. `vi ~/.bashrc`

   Because the files with the prompt setting are in the system-wide `/etc` directory, we cannot change them directly, so we have to make the changes to `.bashrc` or a different configuration file in our home directory.

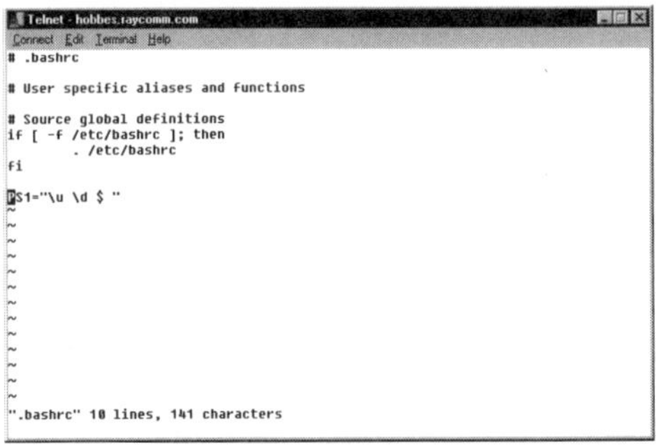

Figure 8.2 Edit your prompt statement in the editor of your choice.

Code Listing 8.8 Use grep to search your configuration files for a prompt statement.

```
[ejr@hobbes ejr]$ grep PS1 ~/.bash_profile
  → ~/.bashrc /etc/bashrc
/home/ejr/.bashrc:PS1="\u \d $ "
/etc/bashrc:PS1="[\u@\h \W]\\$ "
[ejr@hobbes ejr]$
```

3. `PS1="\u \d $ "`

   For example, we often set our prompt to include the userid (because we have enough different accounts on different systems that we need a reminder) and the date (because we're scattered). We're adding this at the end of the file so it will take precedence over the PS1 setting in the `/etc/bashrc` file that is referenced from the `~/.bashrc` file (**Figure 8.2**).

4. Save the file and exit from the editor.

5. `su - ejr`

   Log in again with your changed prompt to try it out.

✔ Tips

- Note the trailing space in the prompt code: `PS1="\u \d $ "`. This space can help make it easier to use the prompt.

- Consider changing your PS1 environment variable at the shell prompt, as discussed in Chapter 3, before you make changes in your configuration files. This way, you can try out a modified shell prompt before you change it in your configuration files.

Setting your bash prompt promptly

You can set your prompt to contain all sorts of information. The following list shows you what code to use to add certain kinds of information to your prompt (as well as helping you translate the code in your existing prompt):

- `\u` shows the userid of the current user—that's you.
- `\w` shows the current working directory with a path, using a ~ notation within your home directory.
- `\W` shows the current directory without the path.
- `\t` shows the time.
- `\d` shows the date.
- `\n` forces a new line, making the prompt appear split on two lines.
- `\h` shows the hostname of the computer.

Looking at your ksh configuration files

As **Code Listing 8.9** shows, you look at your ksh configuration files using more or the editor of your choice. Keep in mind that configuration files are run in a specific order:

1. System-wide configuration files (such as /etc/profile) run first upon login.
2. Configuration files specific to your UNIX account (such as ~/.profile and ~/.kshrc) run next if they're available.

To look at your ksh configuration files:

1. `more /etc/profile ~/.profile → ~/.kshrc /etc/ksh.kshrc`

   Type more followed by the names of traditional Korn shell configuration files. You'll see something similar to **Code Listing 8.9**. As before, look for any other file names or ENV statements in the listings, which would indicate other files that play a role in getting your ksh environment configured.

2. For your own information, list the system configuration files that your system uses and the order in which they're called. For our system, we have:
   - /etc/profile (automatically called by the system)
   - ~/.profile (automatically called by the system)
   - ~/.kshrc (called by .profile)

✔ Tips

- The .profile file is executed when you start a new login shell (by logging in or with su - yourid). The .kshrc file is read each time you start any ksh subshell.
- The techie term (that you'll likely see in these files) for executing a configuration file or a script is to *source* it. That is, when you log in, your .profile sources .kshrc.

Fill in your ksh system configuration files

____

____

____

____

____

____

____

____

Code Listing 8.9 Look for file and path names or ENV statements in the configuration file listings (for the files you have) to identify all of the files that help set up your environment.

```
$ more /etc/profile ~/.profile ~/.kshrc /etc/ksh.kshrc
::::::::::::::
/etc/profile
::::::::::::::
#ident  "@(#)profile   1.17   95/03/28 SMI"   /* SVr4.0 1.3   */

# The profile that all logins get before using their own .profile.

trap ""  2 3
export LOGNAME PATH

if [ "$TERM" = "" ]
then
        if /bin/i386
        then
                TERM=AT386
        else
                TERM=sun
        fi
        export TERM
fi

#       Login and -su shells get /etc/profile services.
#       -rsh is given its environment in its .profile.

case "$0" in
-sh | -ksh | -jsh)

        if [ ! -f .hushlogin ]
        then
                /usr/sbin/quota
                #       Allow the user to break the Message-Of-The-Day only.
                trap "trap '' 2"  2
                /bin/cat -s /etc/motd
                trap "" 2

                /bin/mail -E
                case $? in
                0)
                        echo "You have new mail."
                        ;;
                2)
                        echo "You have mail."
                        ;;
                esac
        fi
esac
```

(continued on next page)

Code Listing 8.9 (continued)

```
umask 022
trap  2 3
::::::::::::::
/home/users/e/ejray/.profile
::::::::::::::
#
PATH=$PATH:$HOME/bin:.                    # set command search path
export PATH
if [ -z "$LOGNAME" ]; then
     LOGNAME='logname'               # name of user who logged in
     export LOGNAME
fi
MAIL=/usr/spool/mail/$LOGNAME             # mailbox location
export MAIL
if [ -z "$PWD" ]; then
     PWD=$HOME                       # assumes initial cwd is HOME
     export PWD
fi
if [ -f $HOME/.kshrc -a -r $HOME/.kshrc ]; then
     ENV=$HOME/.kshrc                # set ENV if there is an rc file
     export ENV
fi
# If job control is enabled, set the suspend character to ^Z (control-z):
case $- in
*m*) stty susp '^z'
     ;;
esac
set -o ignoreeof                     # don't let control-d logout
PS1="$ "
export PS1
export ENV=$HOME/.kshrc
::::::::::::::
/home/users/e/ejray/.kshrc
::::::::::::::
#
# If there is no VISUAL or EDITOR to deduce the desired edit
#  mode from, assume vi(C)-style command line editing.
if [ -z "$VISUAL" -a -z "$EDITOR" ]; then
     set -o vi
fi
/etc/ksh.kshrc: No such file or directory
$
```

Code Listing 8.10 First, find out the location of your path statement(s).

```
$ grep PATH ~/.profile ~/.kshrc
/home/users/e/ejray/.profile:PATH=/usr/bin:/
  → usr/local/bin:/usr/sbin:
/home/users/e/ejray/.profile:export PATH
$
```

Changing your ksh path

The path statement tells the shell where to look for commands, scripts, and programs. For example, if you issue a command, the path statement tells the system to look in the named directories in a specific order.

As the following steps show, you change your `ksh` path by first identifying where your path statement is located, then editing the file that contains it (**Code Listing 8.10**).

To change your ksh path:

1. `grep PATH ~/.profile ~/.kshrc`
   To begin, check for path statements in the configuration files located in your home directory. If you wanted, you could also review the `/etc/profile` file, but you cannot edit that one.
2. Look through your system configuration files for a path statement. As **Code Listing 8.10** shows, it'll look something like `PATH=/bin:/usr/bin:/usr/local/bin`. Remember, if you have more than one path statement, find the last one executed. If you don't have a path statement in your personal configuration files at all, then add one.
3. `cp ~/.profile ~/.profile.backup`
   Make a copy of the file containing the path statement so that you can recover if you make mistakes. See Chapter 1 if you need more information on copying files.
4. `vi ~/.profile`
   Use the editor of your choice to edit the configuration file with the path statement.
5. `PATH=$PATH:$HOME/bin`
   Add a new path statement immediately below the last path statement. In this example, `$PATH` inserts the current value of the environment variable into the envi-

ronment variable definition and inserts it into the directory `bin` in your home directory (**Figure 8.3**).

6. Save the file and exit from your editor.

   Refer to Chapter 4 for help if you need it.

7. `su - yourid`

   As you learned back in Chapter 3, this command starts a new login shell so you can test your changes before logging out.

8. `echo $PATH`

   Display the current path environment variable. This should include the addition you just made. (See **Code Listing 8.11.**)

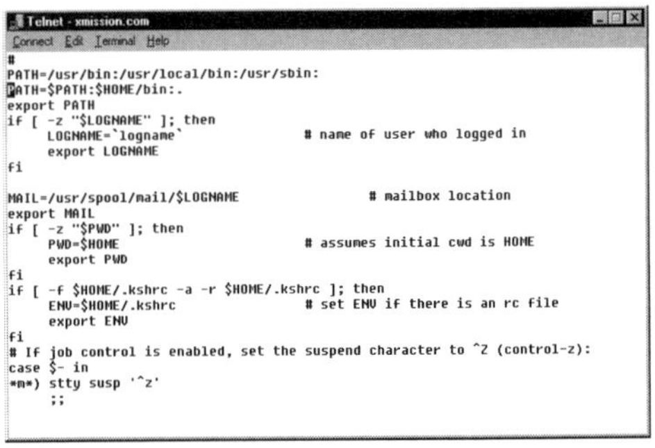

Figure 8.3 Add or modify a path statement in your editor.

Code Listing 8.11 Verify that your new path statement exists.

```
$ echo $PATH
/usr/bin:/usr/local/bin:/usr/sbin:/home/
  → users/e/ejray/bin:.
$
```

Code Listing 8.12 List your configuration files and look for a prompt statement.

```
$ grep PS1 /etc/profile ~/.profile ~/.kshrc
/home/users/e/ejray/.profile:PS1="$ "
/home/users/e/ejray/.profile:export PS1
$
```

Setting your ksh prompt promptly

You can set your ksh prompt to contain all sorts of information. The following list shows you what code to use to add certain kinds of information to your prompt (as well as helping you translate the code in your existing prompt):

- `$LOGNAME` shows the userid of the current user—that's you.
- `${PWD##*/}` shows the current working directory without the path.
- `$PWD` shows the current working directory with the path.
- `$HOST` shows the hostname of the computer.

Changing your ksh prompt

Like `bash`, `ksh` also has two prompts you can edit:

- The main prompt that you usually think of as the shell prompt. This prompt is called PS1.
- A secondary prompt that you see when the system requires additional information to complete a command. Logically, this prompt is called PS2.

You can change either of these prompts using the following steps (we'll modify PS1 in the example). You start by finding your prompt statement (**Code Listing 8.12**), then modify it in your editor.

To change your ksh prompt:

1. `grep PS1 /etc/profile ~/.profile` → `~/.kshrc`

   To begin, search through the configuration files located in your home directory and in the `/etc` directory for your prompt statement. It'll look something like `PS1="$ "` or `PS1="$PWD  $ "`, as shown in **Code Listing 8.12**. Keep in mind that you can only edit the files in your home directory, not those in the `/etc` directory. The *Setting your* `ksh` *prompt promptly* sidebar will help translate these symbols.

2. `vi .profile`

   Use your favorite editor to edit the configuration file with the PS1 setting in it or to add a PS1 setting to a configuration file in your home directory.

3. `PS1="$LOGNAME in $PWD $ "`

   Change the prompt to display the information you want—in this case, the user name and the current working directory.

✔ Tip

- Note the trailing space in the prompt code: `PS1="$ "`. This makes the prompt much easier to use than it would be without the space.

Looking at your csh configuration files

As **Code Listing 8.13** shows, you can use `more` or the editor of your choice to peek at your `csh` configuration files. As with other shells, the `csh` configuration files run in a specific order:

1. System-wide configuration files (such as `/etc/csh.cshrc`) run first upon login.
2. The main configuration files specific to your UNIX account (`~/.cshrc`) run next if they're available.
3. The `~/.login` configuration file runs last.

To look at your csh configuration files:

- `more .cshrc .login`

  Type `more` followed by `.cshrc` and `.login`, which are the only possible names for `csh` configuration files. You'll see something similar to **Code Listing 8.13**. For our system, we have:
  - `~/.cshrc` (automatically called by the system)
  - `~/.login` (automatically called by the system)

✔ Tip

- The `.cshrc` file is executed when you start a new `csh` shell of any kind. The `.login` file is executed when you start a new login shell (by logging in or with `su - yourid`).

Fill in your csh system configuration files

____

____

____

____

____

____

____

____

Code Listing 8.13 Look for references to other paths or files in the listings, which might indicate other files used to set up your environment.

```
xmission> more .cshrc .login
::::::::::::::
.cshrc
::::::::::::::
# <@>(#)Cshrc 1.6 91/09/05 SMI

set path = (/usr/local/bin /usr/local/bin/X11 /usr/openwin/bin /usr/bin
        /usr/ucb /usr/etc /usr/local/games .)

alias pwd           'echo $cwd'
umask 066

if ($?USER == 0 || $?prompt == 0) exit

set filec
set history=40
set prompt="'hostname'> "

# Edit the following lines as you wish
setenv EDITOR "pico -t"
setenv OPENWINHOME /usr/openwin
setenv MANPATH /usr/man:/usr/local/man:/usr/openwin/man
setenv LD_LIBRARY_PATH /usr/local/lib:/usr/openwin/lib
setenv PAGER more

limit coredumpsize 0

#          commands for interactive shells
alias ls        'ls -F'
alias cd        'cd \!*;echo $cwd'
alias home      'cd ~'

# MS-DOS aliases
alias dir       'ls -alg'
alias del       'rm -i'
alias delete    'rm -i'
alias copy      'cp -i'
alias md        'mkdir'
alias move      'mv -i'
alias cls       'clear'
alias clr       'clear'
alias type      'more'

# Terminal settings

setenv TERM vt100
/usr/bin/stty rows 24
/usr/bin/stty cols 80
```

(continued on next page)

Code Listing 8.13 (continued)

```
/usr/bin/stty erase '^?'
::::::::::::::
.login
::::::::::::::
# <@>(#)Login 1.14 90/11/01 SMI

#        general terminal characteristics

#/usr/bin/stty -crterase
#/usr/bin/stty -tabs
#/usr/bin/stty crt
#/usr/bin/stty erase '^h'
#/usr/bin/stty werase '^?'
#/usr/bin/stty kill '^['
#/usr/bin/stty new

#        environment variables

#setenv EXINIT 'set sh=/bin/csh sw=4 ai report=2'
#setenv MORE '-c'
#setenv PRINTER lw

#        commands to perform at login

#w        # see who is logged in

notice     # system information that must be read

#
# If possible, start the windows system.  Give user a chance to bail out
#
if ( 'tty' != "/dev/console" || $TERM != "sun" ) then
        exit    # leave user at regular C shell prompt
endif
xmission>
```

Code Listing 8.14 Use grep to find the path statement in your configuration files.

```
xmission> grep path ~/.cshrc ~/.login
.cshrc:set path = (/usr/local/bin
  → /usr/local/bin/X11 /usr/openwin/bin
  → /usr/bin)
xmission>
```

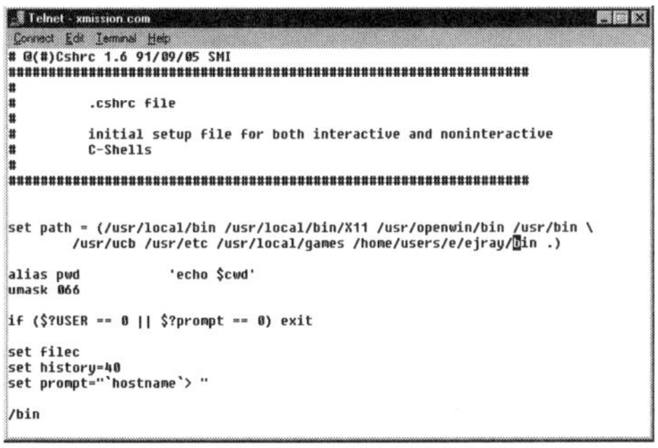

Figure 8.5 Edit your path statement to add your home directory.

Changing your csh path

The path statement tells the shell where to look for commands, scripts, and programs. So if you issue a command, the path statement tells the system to look in the named directories in a specific order. As the following steps show, you change your `csh` path by first identifying where your path statement is located, then editing the file that contains it (**Code Listing 8.14**).

To change your csh path:

1. `grep path ~/.cshrc ~/.login`

   To begin, list the configuration files located in your home directory and in the `/etc` directory. Look through your system configuration files for a path statement. As **Code Listing 8.14** shows, it'll look something like `set path = (/usr/local/bin /usr/local/bin/X11 /usr/openwin/bin /usr/bin)`. If you have more than one path statement, find the last one executed.

2. `cp ~/.cshrc ~/.cshrc.backup`

   Make a copy of the file containing the path statement so that you can recover if you make mistakes. See Chapter 1 if you need more information on copying files.

3. `vi .cshrc`

   Use the editor of your choice to edit the file with the path statement in it.

4. `set path = (/usr/local/bin /usr/bin → /usr/ucb /usr/etc → /home/users/e/ejray/bin)`

   Edit the path statement to add the full path to the `bin` subdirectory in your home directory, as shown in **Figure 8.5**.

5. Save the file and exit from your editor.

   Refer to Chapter 4 for help if you need it.

6. `su - yourid`

   As you learned back in Chapter 3, this command starts a new login shell so you can test your changes before logging out.

7. `echo $path`

   Display the current path environment variable. This should include the addition you just made. Lo and behold! There it is! (See **Code Listing 8.15.**)

Code Listing 8.15 Here's your new path statement!

```
xmission> echo $PATH
/usr/local/bin:/usr/local/bin/X11:
  → /usr/openwin/bin:/usr/bin:/usr/ucb:
  → /usr/etc:/usr/local/games:/home/users/e/
  → ejray/bin:.
xmission>
```

Changing your csh prompt

Your system's default prompt might be just a dollar sign ($) or perhaps a dollar sign and date, or other information as outlined in the *Set your csh prompt promptly* sidebar. You can change this prompt using the following steps. You start by finding your prompt statement (**Code Listing 8.16**), then modify it in your editor (**Figure 8.6**).

To change your csh prompt:

1. `grep path ~/.cshrc ~/.login`

   To begin, list the configuration files located in your home directory and in the `/etc` directory. Look through your system configuration files for your prompt statement. It'll look something like `set prompt="> "` or `set prompt="'hostname'> "`. It's likely in your `.cshrc` file, as shown in **Code Listing 8.16**.

   The *Setting your csh prompt promptly* sidebar will help you translate this code.

Code Listing 8.16 The prompt statement will likely be in your .cshrc file.

```
xmission> grep prompt ~/.cshrc ~/.login
/home/users/e/ejray/.cshrc:if ($?USER ==
  → 0 || $?prompt == 0) exit
/home/users/e/ejray/.cshrc:set
  → prompt="'hostname'> "
/home/users/e/ejray/.login:     exit    #
  → leave user at regular C shell prompt
xmission>
```

Code Listing 8.17 Test out your new prompt to see if you like it.

```
xmission> su - ejray
Password:
Sun Microsystems Inc.   SunOS 5.5.1     Generic May 1996
You have mail.
NOTE! As of 7/15/98, "tin" has been backed out its prior version.  NNTP
      support was compiled in directly as well.  We hope that this will
      stabilize its problems.


--------------------------------------------------------------------------------
  General questions email to "help" or "help@xmission.com".
  Problems with the system mail to "support" or "support@xmission.com".

  Type "acctstat" for a summary of your current account information.
  Type "quota -v" to view your existing disk quota.
  Type "help" for a list of online programs or "menu" for the assisted menu.
ejray>
```

2. `vi .cshrc`

   Use the editor of your choice to edit the configuration file with the prompt setting in it.

3. `set prompt="$LOGNAME > "`

   Set your prompt to something more suitable, as shown in **Figure 8.6**.

4. Save the file and exit from the editor.

5. `su - yourid`

   Log in again to try it out (**Code Listing 8.17**).

✔ Tips

- Note the trailing space in the prompt code: `set prompt="$LOGNAME > "`. This extra space makes the prompt easier to use.

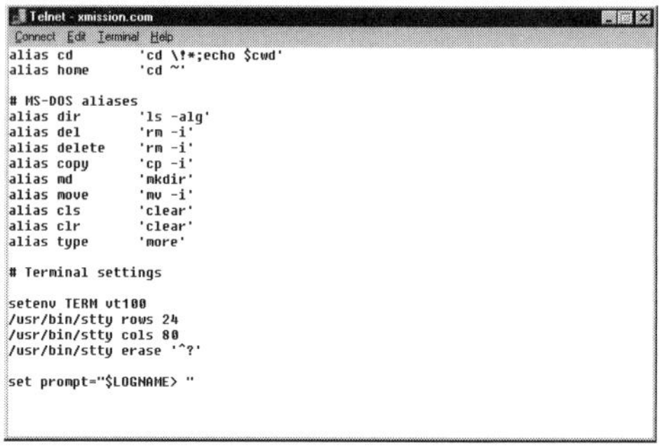

Figure 8.6 Edit your prompt to include the details you want.

Setting your csh prompt promptly

You can set your `csh` prompt to contain some types of information, but not as many as the `bash` or `ksh` prompts. The following list shows you what code to use to add certain kinds of information to your prompt (as well as helping you translate the code in your existing prompt):

- `$LOGNAME` shows the userid of the current user—that's you.
- `${cwd}` shows the current working directory with a path.
- `'uname -n'%` shows the hostname of the computer.

Or, use any other environment variables of your choice.

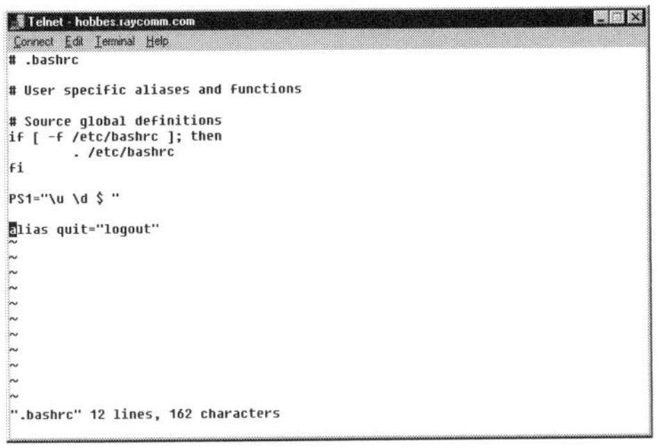

Figure 8.7 Setting aliases can keep you from typing long names and code.

Code Listing 8.18 Type alias at the shell prompt to see a list of aliases you've set.

```
xmission> alias
cd       cd !*;echo $cwd
clr      clear
cls      clear
copy     cp -i
del      rm -i
delete   rm -i
dir      ls -alg
home     cd ~
ls       ls -F
md       mkdir
move     mv -i
pwd      echo $cwd
type     more
xmission>
```

Setting aliases with alias

Aliases are nicknames of sorts that you use to enter commands more easily. For example, if you frequently use the command `mail -s "Lunch today? deb < .signature`, you could set an alias for this command and call it `lunch`. Then, in the future, all you have to do is type in `lunch`, and the result is the same as if you typed in the longer command (**Figure 8.7**).

To set an alias with alias:

1. Choose the appropriate file to edit, depending on which shell you're using.
   - `bash` users should use `~/.bashrc.`
   - `ksh` users should use `~/.kshrc.`
   - `csh` users should use `~/.cshrc.`

   If you don't have the appropriate file, use a different configuration file.
2. `vi .bashrc`

   Edit the configuration file you've selected.
3. `alias quit="logout"`

   Type `alias` followed by the term you want to use as the alias, =, and the command you're making an alias for (in quotes). Here, we're setting the word `quit` as an alias for the system command `logout`, so we can type `quit` instead of `logout` (**Figure 8.7**).
4. Add as many other aliases as you want. See the sidebar called *Good aliases to set* in this section for more ideas.
5. Save the file and exit from the editor.

   See Chapter 4 for details about saving and exiting in `vi` and `pico`.
6. `su - yourid`

   Start a new login shell to test out the alias.
7. `alias`

   Type `alias` at the shell prompt for a listing of all the aliases you have defined (**Code Listing 8.18**).

✔ Tips

- You can put aliases in other files, but it's customary to put them in the `.bashrc` (or other appropriate `rc` file, such as `.kshrc` or `.cshrc`), so they'll be set automatically when you log in, rather than having to be manually set.
- You can also issue `alias` commands from the shell prompt to set aliases for the current session.
- Be sure to make a backup copy of any configuration files you plan to change before you change them. That way, if you mess up, you still have the original file to work with.

Good aliases to set

Here are a few aliases that you might find it worthwhile to set on your system:

- `alias rm="rm -i"` causes the system to prompt you about all deletions.
- `alias quit="logout"` lets you use `quit` as a synonym for `logout`.
- `alias homepage="lynx` → `http://www.raycomm.com/"` lets you use `homepage` to start the lynx browser and connect to the Raycomm home page (substitute your home page as necessary).

Or, if you're coming from a DOS background, you might find the following aliases handy:

- `alias dir="ls"` lets you use `dir` to list files.
- `alias copy="cp"` lets you use `copy` to `copy files.`
- `alias rename="mv"` lets you use `rename` to `move or rename` files.
- `alias md="mkdir"` lets you use `md` to `make a directory.`
- `alias rd="rmdir"` lets you use `rd` to remove a directory.

Running Scripts and Programs

9

Throughout this book, you've been running scripts and programs by typing in commands and pressing Enter. The commands zoom along to the UNIX system, which responds by obediently doing whatever the command or script dictates. In doing this, you run the commands and scripts—called *jobs* in this context—right then and there.

You can also, though, complete jobs at specified times, run them on a schedule you set up, or start, stop, or delete them as you choose. Plus, you can find out when they are scheduled to run, time how long they take, or monitor them as they run. Sound cool? Great! Let's take a look....

Chapter contents

Scheduling one-time jobs with at

Occasionally, you may need to schedule jobs to run one time, at a time you designate. For example, you could schedule an e-mail message to yourself, reminding you to attend a staff meeting. Or, you could schedule a meeting reminder for your coworkers that includes a meeting agenda. You can schedule these and other one-time jobs using `at`, which lets you designate a time at which a job (or jobs) should run. **Figure 9.1** demonstrates scheduling an e-mail about that all-important staff meeting.

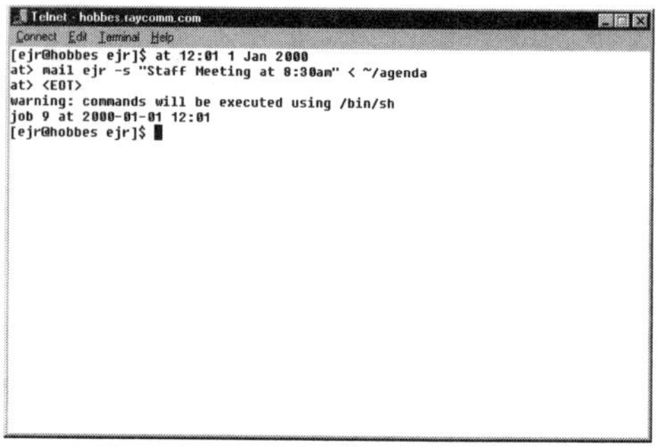

Figure 9.1 To schedule a one-time job, all you have to do is specify the time and the job to run.

To schedule a one-time job with at:

1. `at 12:01 1 Jan 2000`

   To begin, specify when you want the job to run, using `at` plus a time statement (**Figure 9.1**). In this example, we specify a time, month, date, and year, although you can create a variety of other time statements, like these:

   - at noon tomorrow
   - at 01/01/99
   - at 3:42am
   - at now + 3 weeks
   - at teatime

   Yes, teatime is a valid option. It's at 4 P.M., by the way.

2. `mail -s "Staff Meeting at 8:30am"`
   `→ ejr < ~/agenda`

   Specify the job. In this case, it sends e-mail to the user (`ejr`), specifies the subject "Staff Meeting at 8:30am" and sends the contents of the file called `agenda`. See Chapter 11 for the full scoop on using `mail`.

3. Ctrl D

   Indicate that you've finished issuing commands.

Code Listing 9.1 To schedule sequential one-time jobs, just specify the time and the jobs in the order you want them to run.

```
[ejr@hobbes ejr]$ at midnight
at> tar -icf ~/bigdog.tar ~/HereKittyKitty
at> gzip ~/bigdog.tar
at> uuencode ~/bigdog.tar.gz bigdog.tar.gz |
  → mail  -s "Read this by lunch time" deb
at>
at> <EOT>
warning: commands will be executed using
  → /bin/sh
job 12 at 1998-08-28 00:00
[ejr@hobbes ejr]$
```

To schedule sequential one-time jobs with at:

1. `at midnight`

   Specify when you want the sequential jobs to run, using `at` plus a time statement. You can use a variety of time statements, as shown in the previous example.

2. `tar -icf ~/bigdog.tar`
   `→ ~/HereKittyKitty`

   Enter the first job you want to run. This job collects all of the files from the directory called `~/HereKittyKitty` into a single file called `~/bigdog.tar`. Chapter 13 will tell you more about archiving with `tar`.

3. `gzip ~/bigdog.tar`

   Enter the next job to run. This compresses the `~/bigdog.tar` file, making it easier to store and e-mail.

4. `uuencode ~/bigdog.tar.gz`
   `→ bigdog.tar.gz | mail -s`
   `→ "Read this by lunch time!" deb`

   Specify the next job in the sequence. Here, we've uuencoded the compressed file and specified a name for it (`uuencode ~/bigdog.tar.gz bigdog.tar.gz`), and we've piped the uuencoded file to the `mail` command (`mail -s "Read this by lunch time!" deb`). See Chapter 12 for more on mailing, and 13 for more on uuencoding.

5. Ctrl D

   TaDaaaa! Use this key combination to finish the sequence (**Code Listing 9.1**).

To delete a scheduled job:

1. `atq`

   For starters, show the list of jobs waiting in the `at` queue with `atq` (**Code**

SCHEDULING ONE-TIME JOBS WITH at

Listing 9.2). The second column, which shows the scheduled time, should jog your memory about which job is which. The first column, which specifies the job number for each job, lets you identify which job to delete in the next step.

2. `atrm 3`

   Remove the queued job by typing in `atrm` and the job number—in this case, job number 3.

✔ Tips

- `atq` is also handy for reviewing jobs that you've scheduled.
- If you have a long list of commands that you want to run periodically, consider making them into a brief shell script, then using `at` to run the shell script. It's less work in the long run, and you don't have to concentrate on getting the commands just right as you do when telling `at` what to do. See Chapter 10 for the full scoop on shell scripts.

Code Listing 9.2 Delete scheduled jobs by specifying the job number.

```
[ejr@hobbes ejr]$ atq
4       1998-08-28 12:01 a
9       2000-01-01 12:01 a
13      1998-08-27 16:00 a
12      1998-08-28 00:00 a
[ejr@hobbes ejr]$ atrm 12
[ejr@hobbes ejr]$ atq
4       1998-08-28 12:01 a
9       2000-01-01 12:01 a
13      1998-08-27 16:00 a
[ejr@hobbes ejr]$
```

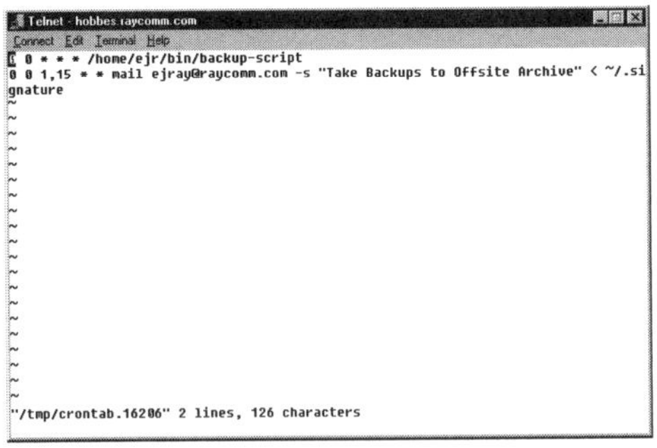

Figure 9.2 The cron file, which is where you specify the cron job, opens in your default editor. If you've previously specified crontab jobs, they'll show up in the editor.

What are those funky numbers?

When entering a `crontab` job, you specify:

- Minutes (0–59)
- Hours (0–23)
- Day of the of month (1–31)
- Month (1–12)
- Days of the week (0–6, with Sunday as 0)

If you replace the number with a `*`, `crontab` will match all possible values, so, if a job is scheduled for

- `1 * * * *`, it will happen at one minute after every hour
- `15 3 * * *`, it will happen at 3:15 A.M. every day
- `59 23 31 * *`, it will happen at 11:59 P.M., 7 times a year (once in each of the months with a 31st)
- `0 12 * * 0`, it will happen at noon on Sundays

Additionally, you can use a comma to separate multiple values. For example, if you want something to happen on the hour and half-hour throughout December, you might use `0,30 * * 12 *`.

Scheduling regularly occurring jobs with crontab

Suppose you want to send yourself a reminder message just before you go home at the end of each day—say, a reminder to turn off the coffeepot. Or, suppose you want to make a backup copy of specific files each week. You can do this by using `crontab` to schedule commands or scripts to run regularly at times you specify. In doing so, you can schedule tasks to occur on specific days at specific times, and know that the jobs will happen unattended (**Figure 9.2**).

To schedule a regularly occurring job with crontab:

1. `crontab -e`

   At the shell prompt, type `crontab`, followed by the `-e` flag, which lets you edit your *cron file*. As shown in **Figure 9.2**, your `cron` file will magically appear in your default editor. It's likely to be empty (if you haven't set up `cron` jobs before), but you might have some content in there.

2. `55 16 * * * mail -s "Go home now!"` → `ejray@raycomm.com`

   On the first line of the cron file, enter values for minutes, hours, day of the month, month, and day of the week, then the command you want to run. See the sidebar called *What are those funky numbers?* for more details about specifying times and days. In this example, we're sending an e-mail to `ejray` every day at 4:55 P.M. reminding him to go home.

3. Save and close the file.

   Chapter 4 will give you a quickie reminder about saving and closing with `pico` and `vi`.

If you set the times and dates correctly (that is, if you didn't accidentally set them to happen in the 59th hour of the day or whatever) you'll see a message like the one near the end of **Code Listing 9.3**, confirming that you're all set. (You'll get an appropriate error message if you scheduled something to happen at 55 hours, 12 minutes, on the 9th day of the week.)

✔ Tip

- When scheduling `crontab` jobs, you need to specify full and absolute paths to the files—that is, specify `/home/ejray/file` rather than `file`. Also, if you write a shell script and reference it in a cron job, you'll need to specify paths in the shell script as well. `crontab` doesn't check out your personal environment variable settings when it runs, so the full path name is essential.

Code Listing 9.3 This job reminds ejray to go home every day. The message toward the end indicates that the cron job has been successfully entered.

```
59 16 * * * mail -s "Go Home Now!"
  → ejray@raycomm.com  < /dev/null
~
~
~
~
~
~
~
~
~
~
~
~
~
~
~
~
~
~
~
"/tmp/crontab.16206" 3 lines, 192 characters
  → written
crontab: installing new crontab
[ejr@hobbes ejr]$
```

Suspending jobs

Suppose you've just started a job that requires no input from you—say, downloading multiple files with `ftp`—and you suddenly realize that you've got to finish something else *right now*. Instead of waiting for the stinkin' files to download or stopping the job completely, you can, instead, just suspend the job and resume it later (**Code Listing 9.4**). In doing so, you can make the UNIX system work your way—that is, you don't lose the progress you've made toward getting the job done, and you can do the other stuff you need to do as well.

To suspend a job:

- Ctrl Z
  While the job is running, press these keys to suspend the process (**Code Listing 9.4**). Ctrl Z doesn't actually terminate the process; it pauses the job in much the same way that pressing the Pause button on your CD player pauses the CD.

✔ Tips

- After you've suspended a job, you can restart it in the background using `bg`, restart it in the foreground using `fg`, check on its status using `jobs`, or delete it

Code Listing 9.4 Suspending jobs is just like pushing the Pause button on your CD player.

```
[ejr@hobbes ejr]$ ftp calvin.raycomm.com
Connected to calvin.raycomm.com.
220 calvin Microsoft FTP Service (Version 2.0).
Name (calvin.raycomm.com:ejr): anonymous
331 Anonymous access allowed, send identity (e-mail name) as password.
Password:
230 Anonymous user logged in.
Remote system type is Windows_NT.
ftp>
[1]+  Stopped                 ftp calvin.raycomm.com
[ejr@hobbes ejr]$
```

completely using `kill`. Refer to the appropriate sections in this chapter for details on using these commands.

- You can suspend as many jobs at a time as you want. Just use Ctrl Z to do so, then use `jobs` to check the status of each suspended job if you need to.
- Because it's pretty easy to forget that you've suspended a job, most shells will remind you that "there are stopped jobs" when you try to log out of the system. You'll need to either resume the job or kill it before you can log out. Yes, the UNIX system uses the terms "stopped jobs" and "suspended jobs" more or less interchangeably.

Checking job status with jobs

Occasionally, you may have multiple jobs running or suspended and need a quick update about the jobs' status. Using `jobs`, you can find out whether a job is running, stopped, or waiting for input (with `tty`, for example), as shown in **Code Listing 9.5**.

To check job status with jobs:

- `jobs`

  At the shell prompt, type `jobs`. You'll see a list of the current jobs (that is, processes that you've suspended or otherwise controlled) either running or stopped, as shown in **Code Listing 9.5**. Using the job numbers on the left, you can choose to run the jobs in the background or foreground, to resume them, or to kill the jobs, as described in the next few sections in this chapter.

✔ Tip

- Depending on your shell, you can often kill jobs with `kill` followed by a `%` and the job number or command name—for example, you could kill the ftp job in **Code Listing 9.5** with `kill %ftp` or `kill %1`. See *Deleting processes with `kill`* later in this chapter for more on killing jobs.

Code Listing 9.5 Viewing jobs lets you know which jobs you have suspended and what their status is.

```
[ejr@hobbes ejr]$ jobs
[1]-  Running              ftp calvin.raycomm.com &
[2]+  Stopped (tty input)   telnet
[3]   Stopped (signal)     lynx http://www.raycomm.com/
 [ejr@hobbes ejr]$
```

Running jobs in the background with bg

If you're running a job that doesn't require input from you, consider running it in the background using bg (**Code Listing 9.6**). In doing so, you can keep the program running while working on other UNIX activities at the same time.

To run jobs in the background with bg:

1. `jobs`

   At the shell prompt, type `jobs` to see the list of all jobs, running or stopped. Note the job numbers on the left.

2. `bg 2`

   Type bg, followed by the number of the job you want to run in the background (**Code Listing 9.6**).

✔ Tips

- If you want to put the most recently suspended job into the background, just type bg (without the number) at the prompt.
- You can also put jobs directly into the background without first suspending them. Just type the name of the job to run, a space, and & (as in `bigdog &`). The & moves the job directly into the background.

Code Listing 9.6 Restarting suspended jobs in the background lets you do two things at once—or more. To move a job to the background, just type bg followed by the job number.

```
[ejr@hobbes ejr]$ jobs
[1]-  Stopped (tty input)
  → ftp calvin.raycomm.com
[2]   Stopped (tty input)     telnet
[3]   Stopped (signal)
  → lynx http://www.raycomm.com/
[4]+  Stopped                 man telnet
[ejr@hobbes ejr]$ bg 1
[1]- ftp calvin.raycomm.com &
[ejr@hobbes ejr]$
```

Code Listing 9.7 Typing fg plus the job number brings that job into the foreground. When you bring suspended jobs into the foreground, you'll sometimes see the job activities onscreen. At other times, you'll only see a prompt and will need to summon help to see anything of the program.

```
[ejr@hobbes ejr]$ jobs
[1]+  Stopped                 ftp ftp.cdrom.com
[ejr@hobbes ejr]$ fg
ftp ftp.cdrom.com
```

Running jobs in the foreground with fg

When you're ready to resume a suspended job, you can do so using `fg`. Remember, when you suspend a job, what you're doing is moving the job into limbo. `fg` just moves the job into the foreground again (**Code Listing 9.7**), for example, so you can see what it's doing or provide input.

To run jobs in the foreground with fg:

1. `jobs`

   At the shell prompt, type `jobs` to list all stopped or running jobs. Note the job numbers at the left.

2. `fg 1`

   Enter `fg` followed by the number of the job that you want to bring back to the foreground (**Code Listing 9.7**).

   Depending on the job you're bringing back into the foreground, you may or may not get to see the job running onscreen. Sometimes you'll be plunked back into the job and be able to enter information as prompted. Other times, you'll just see the prompt for the program you returned to the foreground. If this is the case, try typing ? (for help), which often forces the program to display something onscreen and refresh the display.

✔ Tip

- You can bring the last suspended job into the foreground by typing `fg` (with no job number) at the shell prompt.

Controlling job priority with nice

Suppose you need an enormous file from the Internet that would take practically all afternoon to download. By downloading it, you would hog system resources and make the system response time much slower for other users. OK, bad example. Suppose your coworker needs to download an enormous file and would hog system resources all afternoon. You'd hope that she'd have the courtesy to not tie up system resources that you need to use.

Fortunately, she can, using `nice`, which lets her control job priority. As **Code Listing 9.8** shows, you rank your job's priority using numbers from 1 to 19, with 1 being somewhat nice and 19 being fabulously nice. The UNIX system uses the number you provide to determine how much attention to devote to the job.

To control job order with nice:

- `nice -n 19 slowscript`

  At the shell prompt, type `nice`, followed by the `-n` ("niceness") flag, the appropriate number (19, here), and the name of the job (**Code Listing 9.8**).

✔ Tips

- To find out how nice you need to be, you might check out how many processes (and which kinds) are currently running on the UNIX system. You can do this using `ps`, as described in the next section.
- You could use `nice` and run a job in the background—for example, use `nice 12` → `funscript &` to run `funscript` in the background with a niceness level of 12.
- You can just type `nice` plus the job name (as in `nice sortaslow`). Doing so will automatically specify 10 as the niceness level (the default setting).
- If you are the system administrator and logged in as root, you can use negative numbers with `nice` to increase the priority (`nice -16 priorityjob`).

Code Listing 9.8 By using nice plus a number, you can let UNIX determine how hard to work on your job.

```
[ejr@hobbes ejr]$ nice -19 slowscript
```

CONTROLLING JOB PRIORITY WITH nice

Code Listing 9.9 Enter time plus the full job command to find out the job time.

```
[ejr@hobbes running]$ time slowscript
0.05user 0.06system 0:50.12elapsed 0%CPU
[ejr@hobbes running]$ time ls
bigdog.tar.gz  slowscript     testing.gif
0.03user 0.00system 0:00.03elapsed 78%CPU
[ejr@hobbes running]$ time nice -19 ls
bigdog.tar.gz  slowscript     testing.gif
0.03user 0.03system 0:00.06elapsed 93%CPU
[ejr@hobbes running]$
```

Code Listing 9.10 time output varies from system to system. Here, we get a bunch of garbage to decipher in addition to the time information.

```
$ time slowscript
0.07user 0.05system 0:50.13elapsed 0%CPU
  → (0avgtext+0avgdata 0maxresident)k
0inputs+0outputs (219major+59minor)pagefaults
  → 0swaps
$
```

Timing jobs with time

Sometimes, you might want to know how long a job takes to complete. You can do so using the `time` command, which times jobs according to the built-in UNIX timer. As **Code Listing 9.9** shows, all you have to do is enter `time` followed by the job you want to time.

To time a job using time:

◆ `time script`

At the shell prompt, type `time`, followed by the complete job command. After the command finishes, the system will tell you how long it took, as shown in **Code Listing 9.9**.

To compare job times with time:

1. `time ls`

   At the shell prompt, type `time` followed by a job (here, `ls`).

2. `time nice -n 19 ls`

   Then, type `time` followed by another job. In this example, we're comparing a regular `ls` command to a `nice ls` command. As **Code Listing 9.9** shows, the elapsed time for the `nice ls` command was considerably longer than the regular `ls` command.

✔ Tips

- Keep in mind that the time a job takes to run may vary according to the system's current load or capacity. For example, a job might take less time to run at 2 A.M., when few people are using the UNIX system, compared to 2 P.M., when many more people are using the system.
- Different systems produce slightly different `time` outputs. On some systems, you'll get real (clock) time, user time, and system time. Real time is how many seconds on the clock elapsed while the program was running, while user and system time both refer to different measures of how long it took the system to run the job. On other systems, you might get a ton of garbage, as shown in **Code Listing 9.10**, but the gist of the information is the same.

Finding out what processes are running with ps

The jobs that we've been talking about so far are actually types of processes. *Processes* are programs, scripts, or commands—including anything you do in the UNIX system. All jobs are processes, but not all processes are jobs.

Occasionally, you may want to find out what processes are running on the UNIX system. You can do this using ps, as shown in **Code Listing 9.11**.

To find out what processes are running with ps:

- ps
  At the shell prompt, type ps to see the list of the current processes that you're running, including processes for your current shell as well as any other jobs (**Code Listing 9.11**).

Code Listing 9.11 Using ps, you can find out what processes are currently running.

```
$ ps
  PID TTY STAT TIME COMMAND
15043  p0 S    0:00 /bin/login -h calvin raycomm.com -p
15044  p0 S    0:01 -bash
15911  p1 S    0:00 /bin/login -h calvin raycomm.com -p
15914  p1 S    0:01 -bash
16216  p1 T    0:00 telnet
16217  p1 T    0:00 lynx http://www.raycomm.com/
16267  p1 T    0:00 man telnet
16268  p1 T    0:00 sh -c (cd /usr/man ; (echo -e ".pl 1100i"; cat /usr/man/man1
16269  p1 T    0:00 sh -c (cd /usr/man ; (echo -e ".pl 1100i"; cat /usr/man/man1
16270  p1 T    0:00 sh -c (cd /usr/man ; (echo -e ".pl 1100i"; cat /usr/man/man1
16271  p1 T    0:00 /usr/bin/gtbl
16272  p1 T    0:00 cat /usr/man/man1/telnet.1
16273  p1 T    0:00 sh -c (cd /usr/man ; (echo -e ".pl 1100i"; cat /usr/man/man1
16344  p0 T N  0:00 sh ./slowscript
16345  p0 T N  0:00 sleep 50
16441  p0 R    0:00 ps
$
```

The exact information you see will vary from system to system. In general, though, you'll find the PID (process identification) number at the far left and the process name at the right.

✔ Tips

- You can find out what processes other people are running by typing `ps a` at the shell prompt, and what processes the system is running (also called daemons) with `ps x`.
- You can sometimes, depending on the system, get a broader look at currently running processes by typing `ps f`. The `f` flag indicates "forest" view, which lets you see not only the processes, but how they relate to each other, as shown in **Code Listing 9.12**.
- The results `ps` offers vary depending on the UNIX flavor you're using. Type `man ps`

Code Listing 9.12 The forest view gives you a broader look at running processes.

```
$ ps f
  PID TTY STAT TIME COMMAND
15043  p0 S    0:00 /bin/login -h calvin raycomm.com -p
15044  p0 S    0:01  \_ -bash
16344  p0 T N  0:00      \_ sh ./slowscript
16345  p0 T N  0:00      |   \_ sleep 50
16449  p0 R    0:00      \_ ps f
15911  p1 S    0:00 /bin/login -h calvin raycomm.com -p
15914  p1 S    0:01  \_ -bash
16216  p1 T    0:00      \_ telnet
16217  p1 T    0:00      \_ lynx http://www.raycomm.com/
16267  p1 T    0:00      \_ man telnet
16268  p1 T    0:00          \_ sh -c (cd /usr/man ; (echo -e ".pl 1100i"; cat /
16269  p1 T    0:00              \_ sh -c (cd /usr/man ; (echo -e ".pl 1100i"; c
16270  p1 T    0:00                  \_ sh -c (cd /usr/man ; (echo -e ".pl 1100i
16272  p1 T    0:00                  |   \_ cat /usr/man/man1/telnet.1
16271  p1 T    0:00                  \_ /usr/bin/gtbl
16273  p1 T    0:00                  \_ sh -c (cd /usr/man ; (echo -e ".pl 1100i
$
```

at the shell prompt to find out more about your specific ps capabilities.

- You might be wondering why we don't use dashes before the flags with ps. You can use them, but with ps, that's the old fashioned way and you get a warning about sticking with the program. Just in case you want some UNIX trivia though, if you're set on using ps with the hyphen-format flags, you can set the I_WANT_A_BROKEN_PS environment variable and it'll quit warning you of the error of your ways.

Deleting processes with kill

In addition to suspending jobs and running them in the foreground and background, you can also choose to just delete them completely. For example, you might realize midway through a job that you goofed and need to redo it. Or perhaps you've accessed and suspended a `man` page and no longer need to reference it.

Using `kill`, you can delete essentially any process running or suspended on the UNIX system. As **Code Listing 9.13** shows, you delete a process by first listing the processes, then using the `kill` command.

To kill a job with kill:

1. `jobs`

   At the shell prompt, type `jobs`, then note the number or name of the job you want to kill.

2. `kill %ftp`

   In most shells, you can kill jobs with `kill` followed by `%` and the job number or command name—for example, you could kill

Code Listing 9.13 Using kill plus the PID number, you can delete practically any process running or suspended on the system.

```
$ ps f
  PID TTY STAT TIME COMMAND
15911  p1 S    0:00 /bin/login -h calvin raycomm.com -p
15914  p1 S    0:01  \_ -bash
16216  p1 T    0:00      \_ telnet
16217  p1 T    0:00      \_ lynx http://www.raycomm.com/
$ kill -9 16217
$ ps f
  PID TTY STAT TIME COMMAND
15911  p1 S    0:00 /bin/login -h calvin raycomm.com -p
15914  p1 S    0:01  \_ -bash
16216  p1 T    0:00      \_ telnet
$
```

an `ftp` job with a job number of 1 using `kill %ftp` or `kill %1`. If your shell doesn't cooperate, read on.

To delete a process with kill:

1. `ps`

   At the shell prompt, type `ps` to see the list of all your current jobs (**Code Listing 9.13**). Note the PID (process identification) number of the process you want to delete.

2. `kill 16217`

   Type `kill` followed by the PID number of the job you're deleting.

✔ Tips

- Occasionally, you'll use `kill` and find that the process just keeps going. Try `kill -9` followed by the PID number to delete the process.
- Be careful not to kill your current shell process, or you'll abruptly find your connection broken. Doing so would be like sawing off the branch you're sitting on.

10

Writing Basic Scripts

So far in this book, you've been typing in commands (or perhaps combining commands), pressing Enter, then waiting for UNIX to execute the command(s) you specified...and typing in commands, pressing Enter, and waiting for UNIX...and typing in commands.... You get the idea, and you probably have tired fingers by now.

Using *shell scripts*, you can create a series of commands, save them as a single file, then execute them anytime you want—without having to re-create the commands or do all that tedious typing over and over again. For example, suppose you want to do a complex search and replace on all the `.htm` files in your home directory. With a shell script, you can take the time to structure the commands just one time, save the commands as a single file, then apply it to any directory at any time. Essentially, you do the hard work one time, then can reuse the script any time you need to.

In this book we'll discuss creating scripts using the `sh` (Bourne) shell.

In this chapter, we'll show you how to get started creating and using shell scripts. We won't go into the gory details about scripting (thank goodness, right?!), but we will give you enough information to create your own scripts and apply them to your particular uses.

Chapter contents

Creating a shell script

A shell script is nothing more than a list of commands for UNIX to execute. To write a shell script, you'll

1. Open your favorite editor and start a script file.
2. Start the shell script with `#! /bin/sh`.
3. Add the shell script code one line at a time. This code will look strangely familiar—it's similar to code you've already used in this book.
4. Save and close the file.

In the following steps, we'll show you how to try out this process by writing a script that prints three lines onscreen (**Figure 10.1**). Yeah, we know—whoopie!—but you have to start somewhere, and you can apply the same principles to other shell scripts you create.

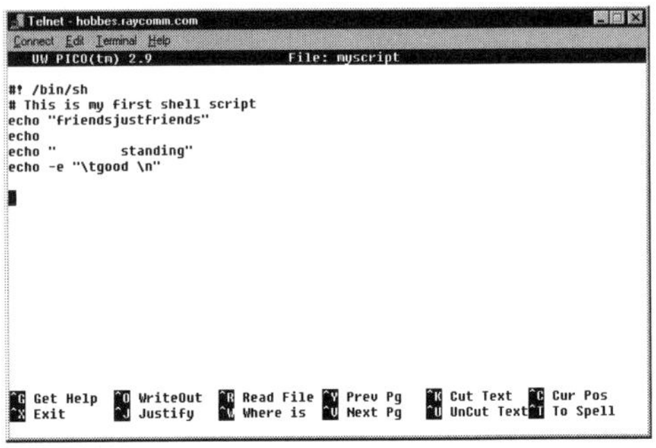

Figure 10.1 You create shell scripts in an editor one line at a time.

To create a shell script:

1. `pico myscript`

   For starters, access the editor of your choice and start a new file. In this case, we call it `myscript`.

2. `#! /bin/sh`

   On the first line of the script, enter `#! /bin/sh`, which specifies the complete path to the shell that should run the script.

3. `# this is my first shell script`

   On the next line, type a # (to indicate a comment), then add any other notes you want to make. It's always a good idea to use extensive comments in your scripts to help you see what's going on. Remember, comments are for your reference only and won't show up onscreen or do anything.

4. `echo friendsjustfriends`

   On the next line of the script, type `echo`, followed by the text you want to see

Code Listing 10.1 Using echo options, you can get good under standing. Or, perhaps, a good understanding just between friends.

```
[ejr@hobbes scripting]$ sh myscript
friendsjustfriends

        standing
        good
```

Getting fancy with echo

In addition to the basic print-to-screen function that `echo` offers, you can also use these formatting flags with `echo`:

- `\b` moves whatever is printed onscreen back one space.
- `\c` forces the following command to appear on the same line as the current command.
- `\f` forces the following command to appear on the next line at a specified horizontal location.
- `\n` forces the following command to appear on a new line.
- `\t` indents the following command output by one tab.

For example, `echo -e "\tGreetings! \c"` would move "Greetings!" one tab space to the right (as specified by the `\t`) and not insert a new line for any command following it (as specified by the `\c`).

onscreen. Here, `echo` tells UNIX to display `friendsjustfriends` onscreen—a message just between friends.

5. `echo`

   Add another line with `echo` and nothing else, to display a blank line.

6. `echo "        standing"`

   Add another `echo` command. Note that if you use leading spaces or tabs, as we've done here, you must use quotes, as **Figure 10.1** shows.

7. `echo -e "\tgood"`

   Using the `-e` flag plus `\t`, you can insert a tab character. See the sidebar called *Getting fancy with* **`echo`** in this section for more `echo` options.

8. Save and close your script.

   Check Chapter 4 if you need help saving a file and closing your editor.

9. `sh myscript`

   Use `sh myscript` to run your new script. In doing so, you get good under standing, as shown in Code Listing 10.1.

   TaDaaaaa! You just wrote your first shell script! (See the following section for more information and details on running scripts.)

✔ Tip

- Unless you have some compelling need to use a different shell (for example, if you're taking advantage of commands that exist only in `bash`), just stick with `sh` for your scripts.

Running a shell script

After you've created a script in your editor and saved the script file, your next step is to *run* it, which means to execute every command in the script in the order provided. (Yes, you did this in the last section, but we'll expand on it here.) As **Figure 10.2** shows, you do this using the `sh` command (or the name of the shell you're using), followed by the name of the shell script you want to run.

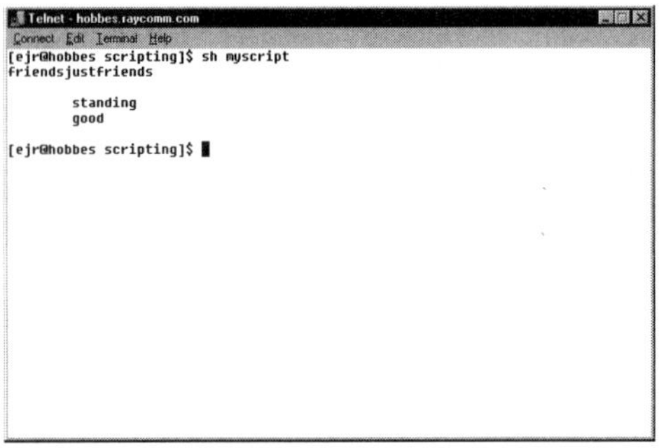

Figure 10.2 Running a script is as easy as typing `sh` plus the file name of the script.

To run a script:

◆ `sh myscript`

At the shell prompt, type `sh` (or the name of the shell, like `ksh` or `csh`, you want to run the script), followed by the name of the script. In this case, you're really just telling `sh` to run and to use the list of commands in the `myscript` file. You'll see the results of the script—in this case, words appear onscreen as shown in **Figure 10.2**.

✔ Tip

■ Note that in this example, you're explicitly telling UNIX the name of the script to run (`myscript`). When you do so, the `#! /bin/sh` line at the top of the script in the previous section is technically superfluous. It's only essential when the script is executable, as in the following section.

Code Listing 10.2 After a little one-time preparation, you can run executable scripts by typing the script name at the shell prompt.

```
[ejr@hobbes scripting]$ head -2 myscript
#! /bin/sh
# This is my first shell script
[ejr@hobbes scripting]$ chmod u+x myscript
[ejr@hobbes scripting]$ pwd ; echo $PATH
/home/ejr/scripting
/usr/local/bin:/bin:/usr/bin:/usr/X11R6/bin:
  → /usr/local/games:/home/ejr/bin:/home/ejr/
  → scripting
[ejr@hobbes scripting]$ myscript
friendsjustfriends


        standing
        good


[ejr@hobbes scripting]$
```

Making a script executable

In the last section, we showed you that you can run a shell script by typing `sh` followed by the name of the shell script file. You can also make a script *executable*, which means that you can run it simply by typing the script name at the shell prompt (omitting the name of the shell). Doing so is handy because it allows you to use the script as conveniently as you'd use any other command. As **Code Listing 10.2** shows, you must set up a little before you can just execute the script.

1. `head -2 myscript`

   At the shell prompt, check to verify that your script does have the `#! /bin/sh` line at the top to specify the shell that runs it. Remember from Chapter 6 that `head -2` will list the top two lines of the file specified.

2. `chmod u+x myscript`

   Here, use the `chmod` command to give the user (that's you) execute permission. See the section in Chapter 5 called *Changing permissions with* `chmod`, for details on setting permissions.

3. `pwd ; echo $PATH`

   Display the name of your current directory and the full path and verify that the current directory is in the path. The current directory (the one in which you just granted yourself execute permission) must contain the path; otherwise, the script will not be executable from the shell prompt.

4. `myscript`

   At the shell prompt, type the name of the script. Assuming that your current directory is in the path, the script will run.

✔ Tips

- Every time you open up a new script, check to verify that the first line is `#! /bin/sh` so the file will run correctly. Also, check the permissions and your path to make sure you can run the script from the shell prompt. (You'll almost always find it more convenient to use executable scripts than to specify the shell each time you want to run a script.)
- If the current directory isn't in the path (either explicitly or through a `.` notation, as in `PATH=/usr/bin:.:`), you'll have to take an additional step to execute the script. You could:
  - Add the current directory to the path with something like `PATH=$PATH:/home/yourid/tempdir`. Read more about this option in Chapter 8.
  - Execute the script with `./myscript` instead of just `myscript`.
  - Move the script to a directory in the path.

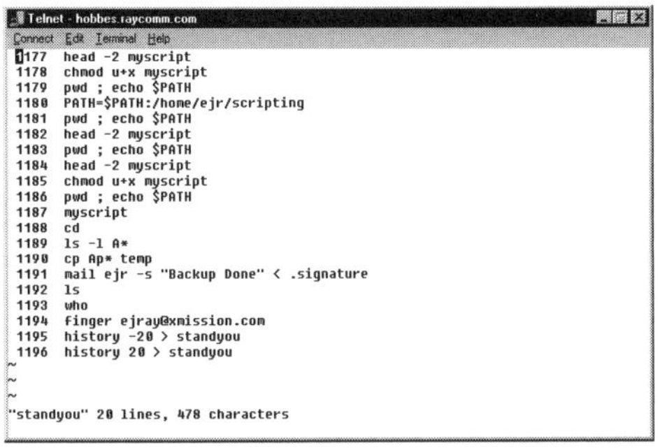

Figure 10.3 You can enter a series of commands, then use the code provided with history to help create a shell script.

Jump-starting scripts with history

If you find yourself performing a particular process over and over again, consider making that process into a script. An easy way to create a script is to work from the session history as shown in **Figure 10.3**. Basically, all you have to do is complete the procedure one time, then use the session history to help build the script for you.

To jump-start your script with history:

1. Go through the process that you want to include in the script.

   We'll wait.

2. Keep a rough count of the commands you issue.

   Don't worry about the exact number of commands you use, but have an idea as to whether it's 3, 30, or 300 commands.

3. `history 20 > standyou`

   When you've finished the process, type `history`, followed by the approximate number of commands for your script. When estimating the number of commands, err on the high side, as it's easier to delete extra commands than to add in missing ones. Then, redirect the output to the desired file name, and see your in-the-making script stand before you.

4. `vi standyou`

   Use the editor of your choice to edit your script file, deleting the initial line numbers and spaces and generally whipping that script into shape. See the section *Creating a shell script* earlier in this chapter for more details.

✔ Tip

- If you use `vi`, do a global search and replace to get rid of the line numbering (that `history` introduced) at the left—just use `Esc:%s/^ .*  //g` (one space after the ^, and two before //), and you're in business. See Chapter 4 for more about clever `vi` tricks.

Embedding commands

Suppose you create a script that will automatically run when you log in each day. The script might, for example, print "Greetings!" onscreen and possibly deliver a cleaver message: "Say, you're looking sharp today!". You could easily do this with the information you've learned so far in this chapter.

What would be handy here would be to add a line to the script that tells UNIX to do all those things plus name the most recently used file—for those of you who need a reminder about what you were last working on. You could just use an `ls` command, but that would only list the file names and not integrate the information with the rest of your morning greeting. Instead, a better (and more attractive) idea would be to bundle a couple of commands and use them with `echo` (**Figure 10.4**) to embed the information right into the greeting.

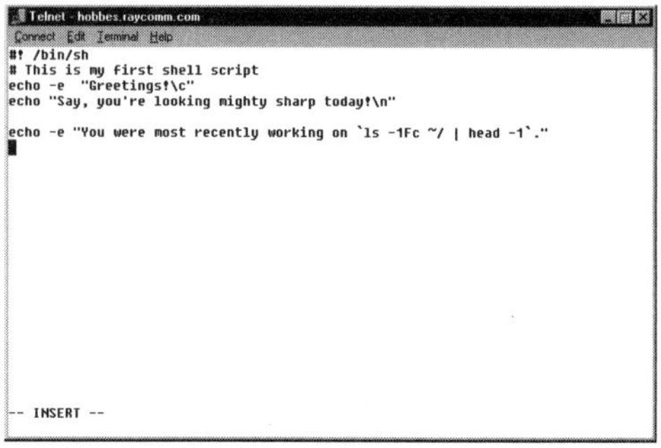

Figure 10.4 Embedding commands just requires an additional couple of lines in the script.

To embed a command:

1. `vi myscript`

   To begin, open `myscript` or another script in your favorite editor. Your script might look like **Figure 10.4**, with the greeting onscreen.

2. `echo "You were most recently working → on `ls -1Fc ~/ | head -1`."`

   Type `echo`, followed by the descriptive text you want to see. Then embed the `ls` command (`` `ls -1Fc ~/ | head -1` ``) within the descriptive text. Note that the embedded code begins and ends with `.

   The embedded command here lists just the most recently changed file or directory in the home directory. 1 provides for one entry per line, F formats the directory names with a / so we can tell whether we're working in a subdirectory or on a file, and c sorts by the modification date.

Code Listing 10.3 The results of embedded commands can be impressive.

```
[ejr@hobbes scripting]$ myscript
Greetings!  Say, you're looking mighty sharp
  → today!

You were most recently working on figlet.
[ejr@hobbes scripting]$
```

Using clever dates

You can use the `date` command to deliver any date with any format. In general, use `date +"Today is %A"`, but you can use any or all of the following bits:

- `%d` includes the date.
- `%y` includes the two-digit year.
- `%Y` includes the four-digit year.
- `%m` includes the numeric month.
- `%b` includes an abbreviated month.
- `%B` includes the full month name.
- `%a` includes the abbreviated day of the week.
- `%A` includes the full day of the week.
- `%R` includes the time in hours and minutes.
- `%D` includes the date in month/date/year format.

Check the `man` pages for the remaining several dozen options.

We then pipe the output to `head -1`, which displays the top line of the file.

3. Save your script and exit the editor, then try it out, as in **Code Listing 10.3**.

✔ Tips

- You can embed dates into scripts, too! Try `echo -e "Today is `date +%A`"` if you work so much that you forget what the day of the week is. See the sidebar *Using clever dates* for more date details.
- When you embed commands that are directory-dependent—such as `ls` or `find`—be sure to specify the complete path. If you don't, you'll get paths relative to where the script is rather than relative to where you're running the script from.
- Embedded commands are useful in many ways. You can use them any time that you want to have one program act based on the output of another program, just as `echo` displays something based on the output of a program.

Looping your scripts

Suppose you've created a script that you'd like to apply to several files. For example, say that at the end of each day you need to make backup copies of all `.html` files in your `www` directory. You could make a backup of each individual `.html` file, but that's a lot of work. An easier way would be to create a short script to copy an `.html` file, then *loop* the script to apply to all `.html` files in your `www` directory (**Figure 10.5**). You create one short script; UNIX does the tedious work for you.

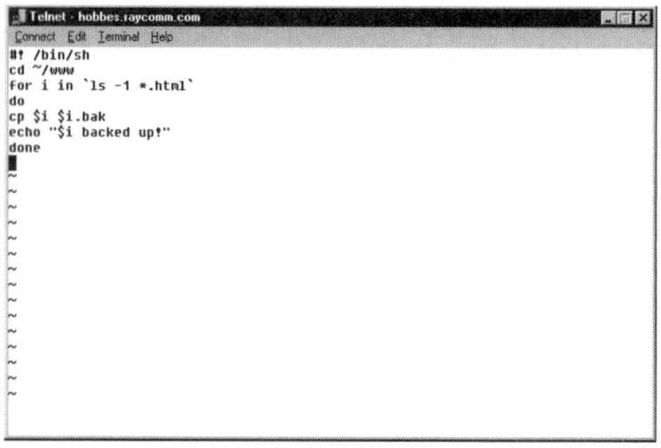
Telnet - hobbes.raycomm.com
Connect Edit Terminal Help
#! /bin/sh
cd ~/www
for i in `ls -1 *.html`
do
cp $i $i.bak
echo "$i backed up!"
done

Figure 10.5 Using a loop with an embedded command, you can automatically apply a script to several files.

To make a loop:

1. `vi head_ache`

   At the shell prompt, start your editor and open the script you want to loop. In this case, we're using `vi` and the `head ache` file. (Of course, you could name the script `html-backup` or something mundane like that.)

2. `#! /bin/sh`

   Tell your UNIX system which shell to use to run the shell script. In this example, we're telling it (with `#!`) to run the shell script with `/bin/sh`.

3. `cd ~/www`

   Make sure that you're in the directory in which the loop will take place. In this example, our shell script resides in our home directory, but the files the loop will apply to reside in the `www` directory.

4. ``for i in `ls -1 *.html` ``

   OK, don't panic. Read this as: "Look `for` `items` `in` the `list` of `.html` files." In this code, we're providing the output of the embedded command (`` `ls -1 *.html` ``) to the `for` loop (the `.html` files), as shown in **Figure 10.5.** The `-1` flag on the `ls` command, by the way, forces a single list of output, which is ideal for script use, rather than several columns, which is easy to read on screen but doesn't work well for scripts.

Code Listing 10.4 This loop reports progress as it backs up each file.

```
[ejr@hobbes scripting]$ more head_ache
#! /bin/sh
cd ~/www
for i in `ls -1 *.html`
do
cp $i $i.bak
echo "$i backed up!"
done

[ejr@hobbes scripting]$ ./head_ache
above.html backed up!
file1.html backed up!
html.html backed up!
reference.html backed up!
temp.html backed up!
[ejr@hobbes scripting]$
```

5. `do`

   On the line immediately after the for statement, type `do`. This tells the UNIX system that the following information will be the loop to apply.

6. `cp $i $i.bak`

   Here, we copy (`cp`) the specified items (`$i`) to a backup file (`$i.bak`)—that is, one backup file per file copied. So, if you have 72 `.html` files to begin with, you'll end up with those original 72, plus 72 new backup files.

7. `echo "$i backed up!"`

   Add `echo "$i backed up!"` so that the system displays onscreen what it's done.

8. `done`

   On the next line, announce that you're done with the loop.

9. Save it and try it out.

   This example script will make backup copies of all `.html` files in the `www` directory.

✔ Tips

- Loop instructions can be much more complex. For example, you could make a loop to spell-check each of the chapter files in the directory and report how many misspelled words there are in each file. To do that, use this line in the loop: `echo -e "$i has \t `cat $i | spell → | wc -l` misspelled words"`. Again, here, just build the loop one step at a time.
- Loops are particularly handy for searching and replacing throughout multiple documents. For example, if you're the new Webmaster and want to replace the old Webmaster's name at the bottom of all `.html` files with your name, you can do so using a loop with `sed`. Check out Chapter 6 for more information about `sed`, which will help with complex searches, and Chapter 16, which introduces `sed` to loops.

Creating if-then statements

The basic principle of if-then statements is that if a certain condition is met, then one thing happens; if the condition is not met, then another thing happens. That is, if you walk into your office in the morning and you see your daily ToDo list, then you sit down and work. If you walk into your office in the morning and you don't see your ToDo list, then you get to lounge all day. Or something like that.

As **Figure 10.6** shows, you can create if-then statements using `if`, `then`, and `else` commands. When you set up these conditional statements, the computer then has to *test* the condition to determine whether it's true or false, and act accordingly. In the next example, we set up a fairly simple if-then conditional statement, requiring the computer to test whether or not a file exists and tell us what it finds. Use the following steps to get started with if-then statements, and see the sidebar called *"More on if-then* in this section to learn how to expand your if-then statements.

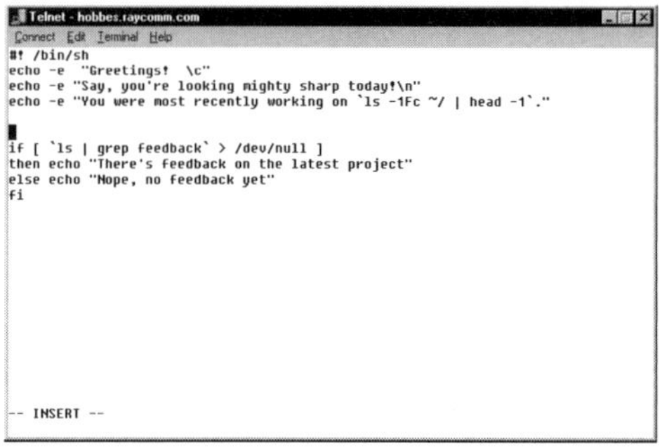

Figure 10.6 Using if-then conditional statements, you can let the computer determine if something is true or not, then act accordingly.

To write an if-then conditional statement:

1. `vi deef`

   To begin, access your editor and the script file. Here we're adapting an existing script (for feedback) in `vi`.

2. `if [ `ls | grep feedback` >`
   `→ /dev/null ]`

   Start the loop with `if`, then follow it with the conditional statement, in this case `if ls | grep feedback`. Read this as: "List the files in my home directory and search for a file named `feedback`. If that file exists (is greater than `/dev/null`, or more than nothing), then the expression is true." (See the whole script in **Figure 10.6**.)

Code Listing 10.5 The last line produced by the feedback script differs, depending on the files found.

```
[ejr@hobbes scripting]$ ./deef
Greetings!  Say, you're looking mighty sharp
  → today!

You were most recently working on scripting/.
Nope, no feedback yet
[ejr@hobbes scripting]$ touch feedback
[ejr@hobbes scripting]$ ./deef
Greetings!  Say, you're looking mighty sharp
  → today!

You were most recently working on scripting/.
There's feedback on the latest project
[ejr@hobbes scripting]$
```

3. `then echo "There's feedback on the → latest project"`

   On the line immediately after the `if` statement, enter the command to be carried out or message to be displayed if the `if` statement is true. In this example, a true `if` statement would result in "There's feedback on the latest project" being printed onscreen.

4. `else echo "Nope, no feedback yet"`

   On the next line, use `else` followed by an statement specifying what should happen if the `if` statement is false. Here, we specify that "Nope, no feedback yet" would be printed onscreen if the `deef` file were not found or had nothing in it.

5. `fi`

   Immediately after the `else` statement, announce that you're finished with `fi`.

6. Save the script and try it out.

   In this example, the script will check to see if `feedback` exists, and print a different message depending on what it finds (**Code Listing 10.5**).

More on if-then

Using the steps provided in this section, try some of these other if-then possibilities:

- `[ -a filename ]` checks to see whether a file exists.
- `[ ! -a filename ]` checks to see whether a file does not exist. The `!` symbol (not) makes this test report "true" when the previous example would be "false".
- `[ -d name ]` checks to see whether a name exists and is a directory.
- `[ first -nt second ]` checks to see whether the modification date of the first file is newer than the second.
- `[ first -ot second ]` checks to see whether the modification date of the first file is older than second.
- `[ -n string ]` checks to see whether the string has a length greater than 0.
- `[ -z string ]` checks to see whether the string is null length.
- `[ string1 = string2]` checks to see whether the first string is equal to the second.
- `[ string1 != string2]` checks to see whether the first string is not equal to the second.
- `[ string1 < string2]` checks to see whether the first string comes alphabetically before the second.
- `[ string1 > string2]` checks to see whether the first string comes alphabetically after the second.
- `[ \( condition1 \) -a \( condition2 \) ]` checks to see whether both conditions are true (conditions can include other conditions).
- `[ \( condition1 \) -o \( condition2 \) ]` checks to see if either condition1 or condition2 is true.

Type `man test` for more information about creating conditional statements.

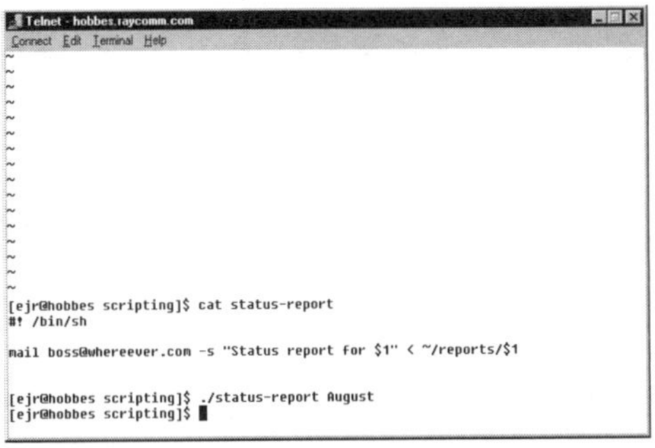

Figure 10.7 Using command line input, you can add flexibility to a script and still have the script do the grunt work for you.

Code Listing 10.6 By providing command line input, you can control what the script does.

```
[ejr@hobbes scripting]$ more status-report
#! /bin/sh

mail boss@whereever.com -s "Status report for
  → $1" < ~/reports/$1

 [ejr@hobbes scripting]$ ./status-report
  → August
[ejr@hobbes scripting]$
```

✔ Tips

- To see the information provided at the command line, echo it back out with `echo $*`. The `$*` variable provides all of the command line input, with `$1`, `$2`, and `$3` containing the individual items.
- You can also accept input at specified points while a script is running. See the next section for more details.

Accepting command line input in your scripts

Suppose that at the end of every month you need to send a progress report to your bosses. You might set up a script to address an e-mail message to your boss, provide an appropriate Subject line, and send the file containing the progress report. You'd likely have this script automatically address a message to your boss and put in the Subject line, but you'd want to use *command line input* to tell the script which file you want to send. By using command line input, you can give your scripts a bit more flexibility and still have much of a process automated for you. You run the script and specify the input at the shell prompt, as shown in **Figure 10.7**.

To accept command line input in a script:

1. `vi status-report`

   Use your favorite editor to edit your script.

2. `mail -s "Status report for $1"`
   `→ boss@whereever.com < ~/reports/$1`

   Enter a command, with `$1` appearing in each place you want to use the first item of input from the command line. In this example, the script starts a message to the boss, fills in the Subject line (adding the month automatically) and sends the appropriate monthly report (the one specified on the command line) from the reports directory under your home directory.

3. Save and exit, then run the script (**Code Listing 10.7**), though you might have to find a boss to take your status report and have to provide the content for the status report first.

Accepting input while a script is running

In the last section, we showed you that you can require that information be provided along with the script in order for the script to run, but it's easy to forget to input the information and thus not get the results you expected. You can also require input while a script is running. The script runs, you input some information, then the script continues (probably) using the information that you input (**Figure 10.8**). In this case, the script counts misspelled words, but you can apply it to anything you want.

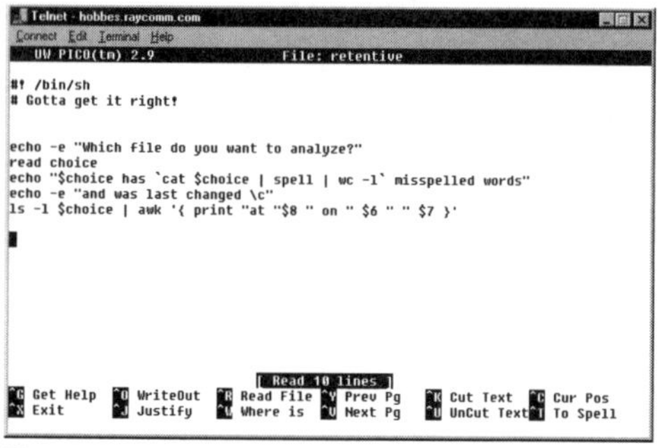

Figure 10.8 You can also input information while a script is running.

To accept input while a script is running:

1. `pico retentive`

   Use your favorite editor to edit your script.

2. `echo -e "Which file do you want to ➝ analyze?"`

   Specify the text for the prompt that you'll see onscreen. Here, the onscreen text will read "Which file do you want to analyze?".

3. `read choice`

   At whatever point in the script where you want the script to accept information, type `read`, followed by the name of the variable to accept the input. Here, we name the variable `choice`.

4. ``echo "$choice has `cat $choice | ➝ spell | wc -l` misspelled words"``

   Echo a phrase (and embedded command) to check the spelling, count the misspelled words, and report the number for the file specified. At each place where the file name should appear, substitute `$choice`.

Code Listing 10.8 Accepting input while a script runs helps ensure that you don't forget to type it in, and still gives customized results.

```
[ejr@hobbes scripting]$ ./retentive
Which file do you want to analyze?
testfile
testfile has       11 misspelled words
and was last changed at 05:08 on Sep 12
[ejr@hobbes scripting]$
```

5. `echo -e "and was last changed \c"`

   Echo another line with text and (because of the `\c`) no line break at the end of the line.

6. `ls -l $choice | awk '{ print "at "$8 → " on " $6 " " $7 }'`

   This very long and complex line uses `awk` to pluck the time, month, and day of the month fields out of the `ls -l` listing for the file given as `$i` (**Figure 10.8**). See Chapter 6 for details about `awk`.

7. Save and exit.

   You have the hang of this by now.

8. `./retentive`

   Run the script (after making it executable and specifying the current directory, if necessary) and provide a file name when prompted, as shown in **Code Listing 10.8**.

✔ Tips

- A great example of a use of prompted input is configuration files. See *Using input to customize your environment* in Chapter 16 for details and a specific example.
- See Chapter 8 for more information about setting up configuration files and starting scripts upon login.
- You can use a set of lines like `echo -e "Please enter the name: \c"` and `read $name` to have the input line and the introduction to it both appear on the same line.

Debugging scripts

As you're developing scripts, you'll no doubt encounter a few problems in getting them to run properly. As **Figure 10.9** shows, you can help debug your scripts by printing the script onscreen as it runs. That way, you can follow the script as it runs and see where the problems might be.

To print the script onscreen as it runs:

- `sh -x retentive`

  At the shell prompt, type `sh -x` followed by the script name (and any additional information you need to provide). The `-x` tells the shell to both execute the script (as usual) and print out the individual command lines as shown in **Figure 10.9**.

✔ Tip

- Use the name of any shell, followed by `-x`, followed by the script name for this kind of debugging output. For example, try `bash -x retentive`.

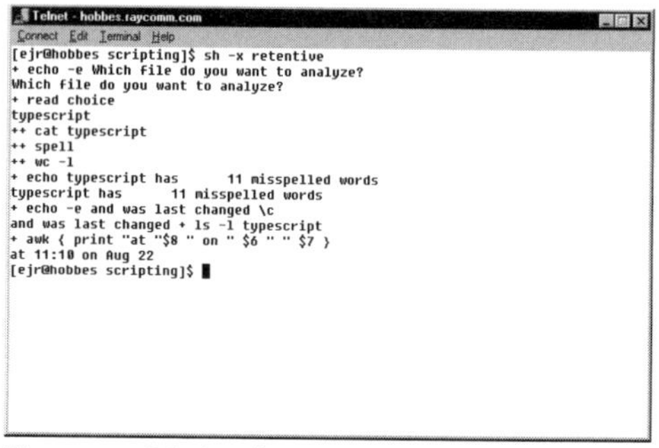

Figure 10.9 Printing the script onscreen as it runs is a great way to debug it.

11 Sending and Reading E-mail

If you're anything like us, your whole day revolves around getting goodies in your e-mail inbox and sending "highly important" messages (of course, they're important, right?). In any case, sending and receiving e-mail will probably be pretty common tasks in your UNIX experience.

In this chapter, we'll introduce you to a few UNIX e-mail programs and show you how to get started with them. (Of course, just use the instructions that apply to the program you're using!) Then, we'll show you some clever things you can do with e-mail in UNIX, such as creating signature files and sending automatic vacation e-mail replies.

Chapter contents

Choosing an e-mail program and getting started

In general, you'll have a choice of two kinds of programs for sending and receiving e-mail on a UNIX system:

- An e-mail program installed on your local computer or network that interacts with the UNIX system for you. You might know these programs as *POP mail* programs and might have used ones like Eudora, Outlook Express, or Netscape's mail program in Communicator, Messenger. These are handy because they usually have a spiffy interface and can handle attachments without a lot of hassle on your part, but they're not really UNIX e-mail programs. These programs also let you store your mail on your personal computer.
- An e-mail program that you access and use directly on the UNIX system. These programs, such as `pine`, `elm`, and `mail`, let you send and receive e-mail easily. Additionally, `pine` lets you send attachments with not a lot of hubbub. Because the mail remains on the UNIX system, you can access your mail from any place you can access the Internet.

In this chapter, we'll focus on the e-mail programs that you access directly from the UNIX system, as these are the true UNIX e-mail programs. Although there are a bazillion different ones available, you'll likely have access to one (or more) of these:

- `pine`: This program is intuitive to use and lets you send and receive e-mail and attachments very easily. `pine` is our recommendation if you have it available. **Figure 11.1** shows its relatively simple interface. Just use the menu commands listed at the bottom of the screen.

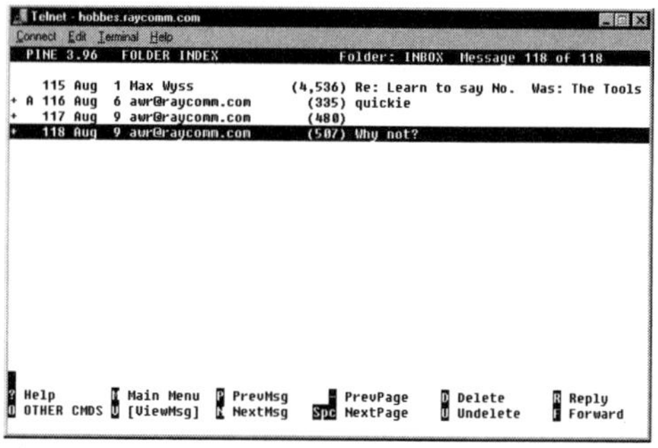

Figure 11.1 pine's interface and features are intuitive and easy to use.

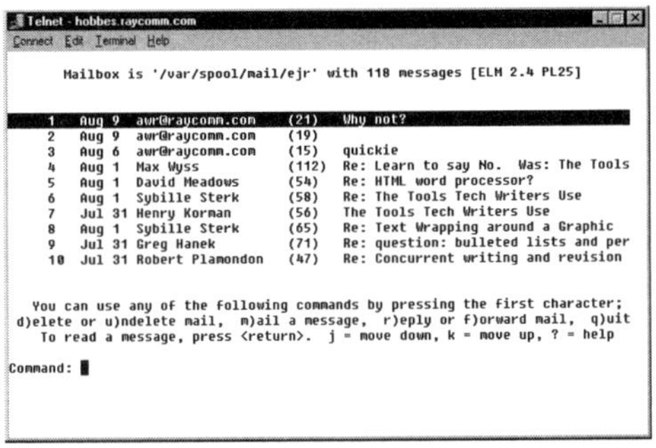

Figure 11.2 elm's interface and features are fairly easy to use, but not as easy as pine's.

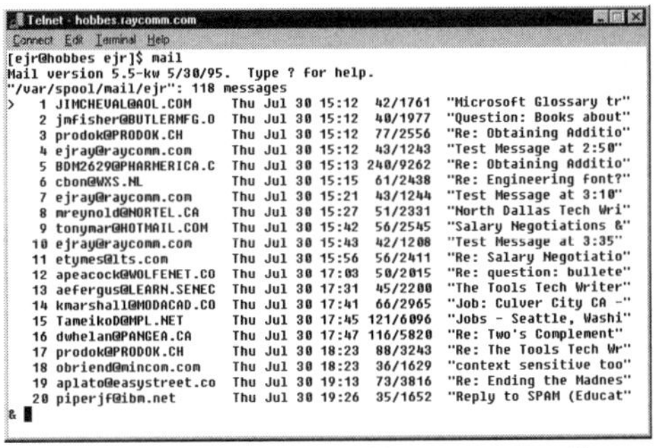

Figure 11.3 mail's interface and features are, well, kind of a pain to use.

Code Listing 11.1 Read with great interest the line that says "You have mail" when you log in.

```
Red Hat Linux release 5.1 (Manhattan)
Kernel 2.0.34 on an i486
login: ejr
Password:
Last login: Sun Aug  2 07:41:00 on tty4
You have mail.
[ejr@hobbes ejr]$
```

- `elm`: This program is a bit less user-friendly, but lets you send and receive e-mail and can deal with attachments, after a fashion. `elm` is our distant second choice, if `pine` is not available. **Figure 11.2** shows its interface, which provides ample features for most purposes.
- `mail`: This program is available on practically every UNIX system; however, it's fairly difficult to use and does not provide intuitive options or commands, as **Figure 11.3** shows. We recommend choosing another e-mail program if at all possible.

✔ Tips

- How do you know whether someone has sent you something? The UNIX system will often announce (but not audibly) "You have mail" or "You have new mail" when you log in, as shown in **Code Listing 11.1**. That is, if you do in fact have e-mail waiting for you.
- You're not limited to using just a regular UNIX e-mail program or a POP mail program; you can use either or both, depending on your specific preferences and needs. You're also not limited to using just one UNIX e-mail program if you have more than one available, although reading mail from two different UNIX programs can make it a little hard to keep track of what's where. Try them out and see which program or combination of programs meets your needs.
- If you end up contacting your system administrator for help with any UNIX e-mail program, be sure you know what tree-name e-mail program you're using. If you claim to be using `maple`, they'll think you're using a high-end mathematical program. If you claim to be using `oak`, they'll think you're missing a few acorns.

Reading e-mail with pine

It's likely that your first step in using `pine` will be to read e-mail. As **Figures 11.4** through **11.7** show, you start by entering the `pine` command, then work screen by screen, depending on what you want to do.

To read e-mail with pine:

1. `pine`

   At the shell prompt, type `pine` to start the program. The first time you use `pine`, it will ask you if you want to view a help file (see **Figure 11.4**) before you get started. Thereafter, you'll see the normal main screen, as shown in **Figure 11.5**.

   If you get an error message about the `pine` command not being found, look around on the system and try to find the program. See Chapter 1 for details on where to look.

2. `l`

   Type `l` to view the folder list, which includes an Inbox folder as well as (eventually) other folders that you set up.

3. Use the ↑ and ↓ keys to move up and down in the folder list (if you have other folders).

4. `v`

   Type `v` to view the selected folder. Note that the default selection in the bottom menu is shown with [brackets] (see **Figure 11.6**). Rather than using arrow keys to select the default, you can, instead, press Enter.

5. Use the ↑ and ↓ keys to move up and down in the message list.

   Your unread messages will appear at the bottom of the list by default.

6. Enter

   Press Enter to read the selected message.

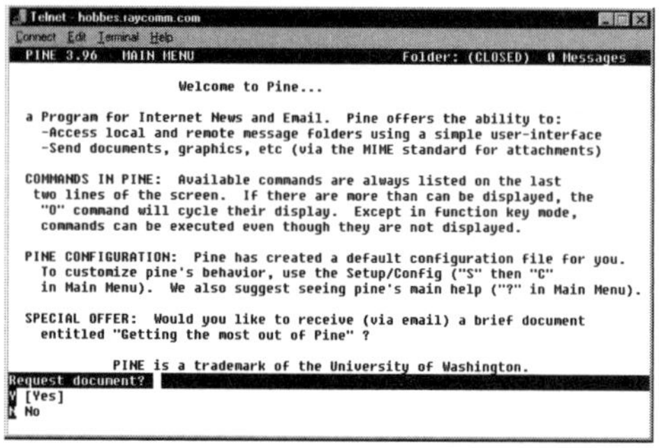

Figure 11.4 When you start pine for the first time, it will ask whether you want help before you begin.

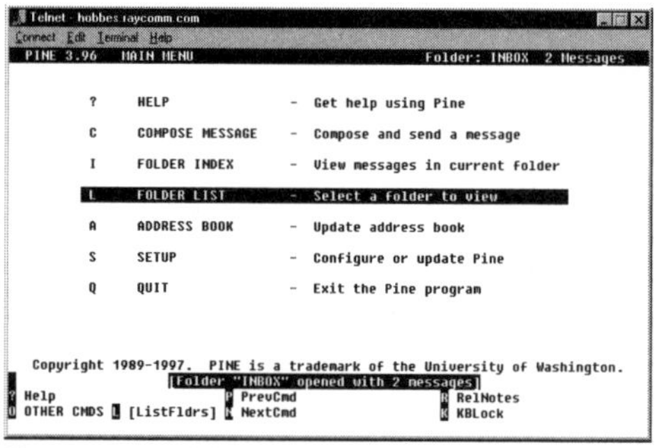

Figure 11.5 You'll become well acquainted with pine's main screen.

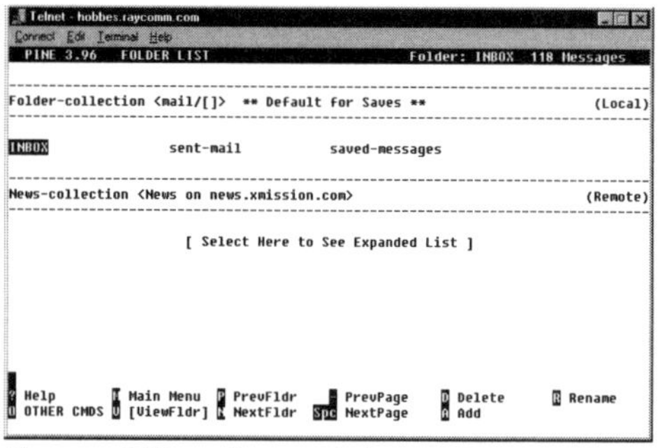

Figure 11.6 All you have to do is press Enter to select the default selection, which is shown at the bottom in [brackets].

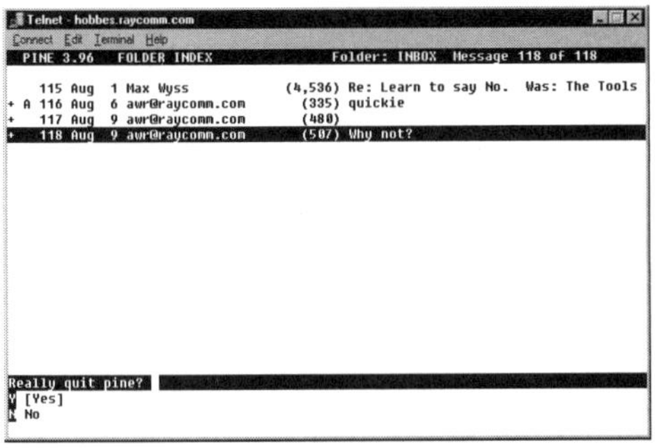

Figure 11.7 Do you really want to quit pine? Just checking.

7. Hmmm. Uh-huh. Wow. Marvy.

Read your messages. Use `i` to get out of the current message and back to the message list for the current folder.

8. `q`

Type `q` when you're ready to quit `pine`. You'll be prompted to verify that you want to quit, as shown in **Figure 11.7**. Just type `y` to quit, or `n` if you really didn't want to quit.

✔ Tips

- Notice the menu commands listed at the bottom of the `pine` screen. You can choose any of these options by pressing the appropriate key, and `pine` is conveniently case insensitive, so either lower or uppercase commands will work.
- Start with `pine -i` to start in your inbox, rather than at the main menu.
- As you're perusing your e-mail, you can use Tab to jump to the next unread message in the folder.
- Delete messages by typing `d`, either when the message is highlighted in the message list or when the message is open onscreen. When you quit the program, `pine` will verify that you want to discard the deleted messages. Just type `y` to confirm the deletion, or `n` if you really didn't want to get rid of the messages.
- Don't miss the sidebar called *Printing with `pine`* in this section.
- You can reply to messages by typing `r` with a message selected or while reading a message.
- When using `pine`, keep your eyes open for an `O` in the menu at the bottom of the screen indicating that there are other options.

Printing with pine

Although many UNIX e-mail programs don't let you print to your local printer, `pine` does. All you have to do is choose `Y` (for "prYnt," according to pine), take the default printout on "attached to ansi," as `pine` suggests, and your printout will most likely appear on your regular printer. Printing to a local printer this way doesn't work with some communications programs (notably Windows Telnet), but it does work with most.

Sending e-mail with pine

Our next favorite thing to do with `pine` is to send new messages. Commonly, you'll send messages after you've already started `pine` (**Figure 11.8**), but you can also start a new message directly from the shell prompt (see the tips).

Figure 11.8 Preparing a message in pine is as easy as filling in the blanks.

To compose and send a message using pine:

1. `pine`

   Type `pine` at the shell prompt to start `pine`, if it isn't already running.

2. `c`

   Type `c` to compose a new message.

3. [Tab]

   Press to move through the message header fields. Fill in carbon copy recipients (`cc:`) and the `Subject:` line. See the sidebar called *Our $.02 on the subject of Subjects* for details about including Subject lines.

   If you're sending an attachment, type in the UNIX file name (and path, if appropriate) on the `Attchmnt:` line. For example, type `~/myfile`, which includes the full path name and the file name.

4. ```
   Hi, John,
   When should we schedule that golf
   game -- er, um -- business meeting?
   ```

   In the message window, type in your message. **Figure 11.8** shows our message, complete with the header information and the message body.

5. [Ctrl][X]

   When you're ready to send, press [Ctrl][X]. `pine` will ask you to confirm that you really want to send the message. Type `y` (or press [Enter]) to send it, or `n` if you don't want to send it.
   ```

✔ Tips

- Rather than typing in someone's lengthy e-mail address (such as `joeblow@acme` → `fancompany.com`), set up an alias, with which you'd be able to just type in `Joe` or whatever. To set up aliases, use the address book (`A` from the main menu) and follow the instructions given.
- If you're at the shell prompt and want to send e-mail without bothering with the main `pine` interface, type `pine` followed by the e-mail address you want to send mail to (for example, `pine bigputz@ray` → `comm.com`). If you want to send e-mail to multiple addresses, just separate them with commas but no spaces, as in `pine unixvqs@raycomm.com,info@raycomm.com`.

Our $.02 on the subject of Subjects

- Always include a descriptive Subject line that succinctly summarizes the message's contents. Rather than saying "Here you go," say "Comments on the Baskins proposal."
- Never leave the Subject line blank. Many people toss Subject-less messages, thinking that they might be spam or otherwise not important enough to read.
- Never use ALL CAPS in the Subject line (or anywhere else, for that matter), as recipients may perceive this as being YELLED AT VERY LOUDLY.
- Be aware of how spam filters work. Many ISPs use them to reduce the amount of spam (bulk messages, like junk mail, that are sent out to hundreds or thousands of people at one time) that goes through. Some filters are set to toss messages with Subject lines typed in ALL CAPS. Others toss ones with lots of !!!!! in the Subject.

Customizing pine

Although pine is pretty intuitive to use, it is also pretty powerful, giving you ample options for customizing it. **Figure 11.9** shows pine's customization screen, as well as a few of the options you can choose.

To customize pine:

1. pine

   At the shell prompt, type pine to start the program.

2. m

   Type m to visit the main menu.

3. s

   Type s to summon the setup menu.

4. c

   Type c to access the configuration setup menu, which is shown in **Figure 11.9**.

5. Scroll through the configuration list using the [Page Up] and [Page Down] keys.

   pine offers you gobs of options to configure. **Table 11.1** describes the ones you might find most useful.

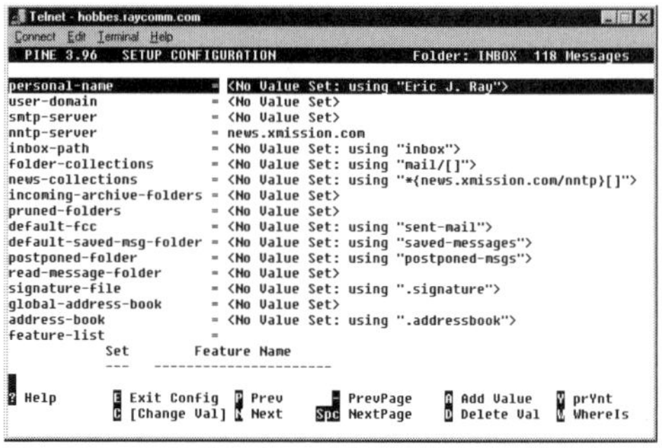

Figure 11.9 By using the configuration setup menu, you can tailor pine to your needs.

Table 11.1

Commonly Used Configuration Options

Option	Description
initial-keystroke-list	Specifies key commands for pine to use when starting, just as if you'd typed them in directly.
nntp-server	Sets the news server name so you can read Usenet news in pine, as mentioned in Chapter 12.
quit-without-confirm	Allows you to exit pine without the "are you sure" message.
signature-at-bottom	Puts your automatic signature at the end of the message you're replying to, rather than above it.
saved-msg-name-rule	Sets pine to automatically file your saved messages in a specific folder, based on the characteristics (sender, etc.) of the message.
fcc-name-rule	Sets your file copy of outgoing messages to be saved in a particular folder. We like the by-recipient option, which files messages according to who we sent them to.
use-only-domain-name	Sets pine to send all outgoing messages with just the domain name and not the machine name on the From line. For example, our messages come from @raycomm.com, not from @hobbes.raycomm.com.

6. [Enter]

   Press [Enter] to select the option you want to change.

7. Make your selection or fill in the necessary information.

8. e

   Type `e` to exit the configuration menu and return to the setup menu. You'll be prompted to save your changes. If you want to do so, type `y`; if not, type `n`. You'll then whiz back to the main menu.

✔ Tip

- You can customize `pine` so that it automatically opens up your inbox whenever you start it. In the initial keystroke list, just type `l,v`, then press [Enter], to specify the initial characters.

Reading e-mail with elm

If you're using `elm`, you'll probably find that reading e-mail messages is pretty straightforward. As **Figure 11.10** shows, you just scroll through your list of messages and press Enter to open the message you want to read.

To read e-mail with elm:

1. `elm`

   Type `elm` at the shell prompt to start the program. The system might ask you if you want it to create folders for you, as shown in **Code Listing 11.2**. We say: Let it do the work for you and press `y`. Press `n` if you don't want folders created. **Figure 11.10** shows the main `elm` screen.

2. Use the ↑ and ↓ keys to move up and down in your list of e-mail messages.

   Your unread messages will be at the top of the list.

3. Enter

   Press Enter to open a message to read.

4. `i`

   Type `i` to return to the list of messages (index) or press the Spacebar to scroll down through the current message. **Figure 11.10** shows the menu of commands, which should help you remember how to navigate in `elm`.

5. `q`

   Type `q` (for quit), then wave goodbye to `elm`. You might be prompted with questions to answer (for example, about discarding deleted messages or moving read messages to your read-mail folder). Answer `y` only if you'll be using `elm` as your mailer in the future.

Code Listing 11.2 elm will create e-mail boxes for you.

```
[awr@hobbes awr]$ elm
Notice:
This version of ELM requires the use of a
→ .elm directory in your home directory to
→ store your elmrc and alias files. Shall I
→ create the directory .elm for you and set
→ it up (y/n/q)? n
```

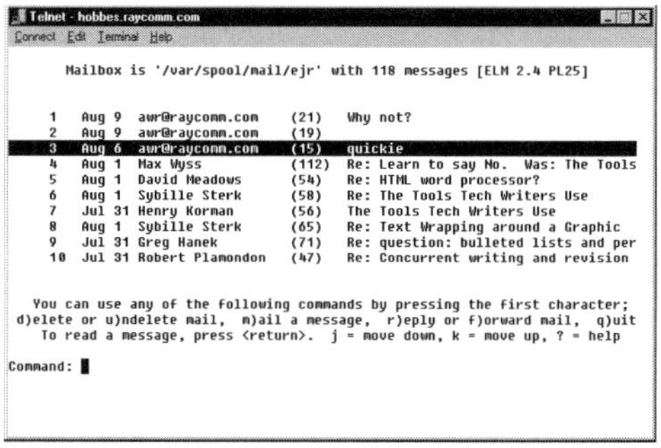

Figure 11.10 elm's main index screen shows many of your options.

✔ Tips

- You can customize some aspects of `elm` by typing `o` from the index screen. Although `elm` doesn't offer many customization options, it does let you change the sort order of read and unread messages, toggle the menu off and on, and change the "user level," which give you a few additional power options in the menus.
- You can delete a message by typing `d` when you're viewing it or when it's selected in the message index screen. When you quit `elm`, you'll be asked whether `elm` should "Keep unread messages in incoming mailbox." At that time, type `n` to delete them or `y` to keep them.
- You can reply to messages by typing `r` with the message selected in the message list or while reading the message.
- You can access `elm` help from most any screen by pressing Shift ?.
- You can move to a specific message in the message index by typing the message number.

Sending e-mail with elm

Sending messages with `elm` is similar to sending messages with `pine`. Most commonly, you'll compose a message once you're already futzing around in `elm` (**Figure 11.11**).

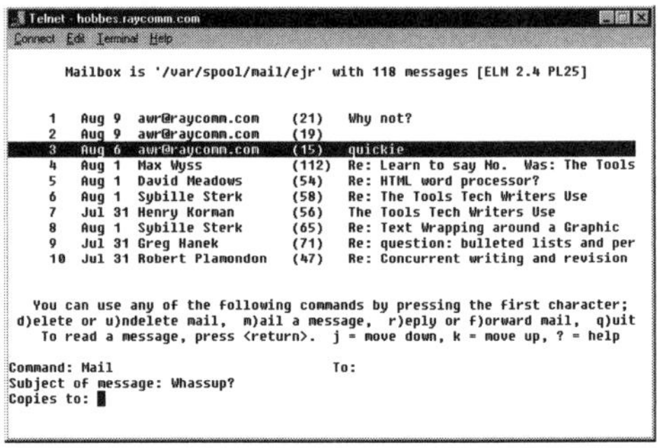

Figure 11.11 You fill in the message header by answering questions, then move on using the Enter key.

To compose and send a message using elm:

1. `elm`

   To begin, type `elm` at the shell prompt to start `elm`.

2. `m`

   Type `m` to start a new message.

3. Enter

   Press Enter after entering each bit of information that `elm` asks for (see **Figure 11.11**). Fill in the Send the message to:, Subject:, and Copies to: lines. See the sidebar called *Our $.02 on the subject of Subjects* earlier in this chapter for highly interesting details about Subject lines.

4. Say hello to `vi`.

   Huh? After you tab through the message header contents (filling in what you want), you'll be plunked right into `vi`, facing the top of a very blank message. See Chapter 4 for a quickie reminder about using `vi`.

5. ```
   John,
   I was having this dream that I had
   my alarm clock installed in my stom-
   ach. I remembered this because, when
   my alarm went off, I found myself
   pushing my belly button trying to
   turn off the noise. Good grief...I
   need a vacation!
   ```

   Type your message, whatever it may be.

6. Esc

   When you're finished, press Esc (to get into command mode).
   ```

7. `:wq`

Then type `:wq` to save your work and exit the editor.

8. `s`

Type `s` to send the message. If you decide you don't want to share details about your belly button after all, you can type `e` to edit your message or press `f` to forget the whole thing.

✔ Tips

- You might be able to change the default editor from `vi` to something else available on your UNIX system. All you have to do is set the `EDITOR` environment variable to the full path to another editor on your system, as in `/usr/local/bin/pico`. See Chapter 8 for more information about changing environment variables.
- You cannot send attachments using `elm`, although wouldn't it be cool if you could? The best alternative is to manually uuencode files and send them from the command prompt, using `mail`. Check out Chapter 13 for uuencoding details.
- To send a quick message from the shell prompt, type `elm` followed by the recipient's e-mail address, as in `elm winches` → `ter@raycomm.com`. If you want to send e-mail to multiple addresses, just separate them with commas but no spaces, as in `elm unixvqs@raycomm.com,info@ray` → `comm.com`.

Reading e-mail with mail

In general, using `mail` is a bit less intuitive than using either `pine` or `elm`; however, reading e-mail with `mail` is particularly—umm—challenging. Although we'd recommend using another program to read e-mail if at all possible, here are the steps for reading e-mail with `mail` if you're daring enough or if you have no other options. **Figure 11.12** illustrates this fairly quick task.

To read e-mail with mail:

1. `mail`

   Type `mail` at the shell prompt. You'll get a list of messages and a prompt (**Figure 11.12**).

2. `3`

   Type the number of the message you want to read.

3. `Marvelous...he's such a jerk...oh, that's neat....`

   Read your messages. Use `n` to move to the next message, or `more` to page through the message a screen at a time.

4. `q`

   Type `q` to quit `mail` when you're ready.

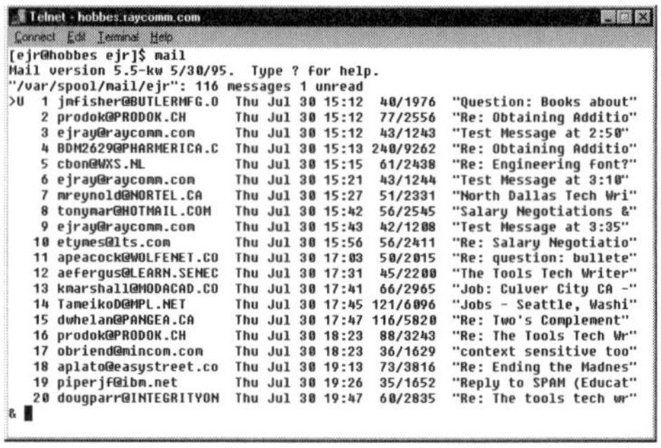

Figure 11.12 The mail screen is anything but intuitive, but you can see the messages you have.

✔ Tips

- If somebody really long-winded sends you a long message, your UNIX system might just whirrr the message on by, leaving you reading only the bottom few lines. To read the message in its entirety, either type `more` to page through the message, or type `s` followed by the message number to save it to a file, then use the editor of your choice read it.
- Type `h` followed by a message number to see different message headers. For example, type `h 117` to see the messages leading up to number 117.
- Find a different mail program if at all possible—it's useful to be able to cope with `mail` for times of need, but it's not a good long-term solution.

Code Listing 11.3 Using mail, you can dash off a quick note by including the recipient's address and the message text.

```
[ejr@hobbes ejr]$ mail debray
Subject: You're in big trouble now!
So, anyway, Winchester had perched
himself on my stereo turntable (those were
sooooo low-tech, weren't they?!). He was
waiting for me to turn on the stereo so he
could go back to sleep while spinning in
circles. I used to let him sleep that way
at night. Well, that was until one night
when the lid closed on him...
EOT
[ejr@hobbes ejr]$
```

Sending e-mail with mail

Despite `mail`'s unintuitive interface and features, it is a great program to use if you just want to dash off a quick message without fussing with niceties. As **Code Listing 11.3** shows, you can send messages while in `mail` or from the shell prompt. You can also use `mail` to send files fairly easily.

To compose and send a message using mail:

1. `mail unixvqs@raycomm.com`

   At the shell prompt, type `mail` followed by the recipient's address. If you want to send e-mail to multiple addresses, just separate them with commas but no spaces, as in `mail putz@raycomm.com,` → `putz2@raycomm.com`.

   If you're already in `mail`, just use `m` followed by the address or addresses, like `m putz@raycomm.com, deb@raycomm.com`.

2. `So anyway, Winchester had perched himself on my stereo turntable (those were soooo low-tech, weren't they?!). He was waiting for me to turn on the stereo so he could go back to sleep while spinning in circles. I used to let him sleep that way at night. Well, that was until one night the lid closed on him...`

   Type in your message text (see **Code Listing 11.3**).

3. Ctrl D

   Announce that you're done with either a `.` by itself on the last line or with Ctrl D, and the message will zip off to the recipient(s).

To send files with mail:

- `mail unixvqs@raycomm.com <` → `sendit.txt`

  At the shell prompt, type `mail` followed by the recipient's address. Then use `<`

and the file name to redirect the file (< `sendit.txt`), which tells UNIX to send the file to the address provided (**Code Listing 11.4**).

✔ Tips

- See *Scheduling regularly occurring jobs with* `crontab`, in Chapter 8, for a spiffier way of using `mail` to send messages directly.
- See the section in Chapter 1 called *Redirecting input and output* for a refresher on redirection.
- You'll notice that the `mail` interface does not provide for a Subject line. You can add one by including `-s` plus the Subject text, like this: `mail -s "An old ➝ Winchester story...dumb cat!" ➝ unixvqs@raycomm.com`.

Code Listing 11.4 To send a text file through the mail, you just redirect the file to mail.

```
[ejr@hobbes ejr]$ mail unixvqs@raycomm.com <
  ➝ sendit.txt
[ejr@hobbes ejr]$
```

Figure 11.13 Your signature file can contain any information you want. Be creative, but keep it concise!

Creating a signature file

If you've been reading e-mail for any length of time, you've undoubtedly noticed *signature files*, which appear at the bottom of messages and include contact information, company names, and perhaps a short funny quote or saying. You can add a signature to your outgoing messages by creating a `.signature` file (**Figure 11.13**).

To create a signature file:

1. `pico ~/.signature`

   At the shell prompt, type an editor's name (here we use `pico`, but you can use the editor of your choice), specify the home directory (with `~/`), then specify the `.signature` file name. Note the leading dot in the file name, which makes the file hidden.

2. ```
   Eric J. Ray    ejray@raycomm.com
   My thoughts are my own...is that
   okay, honey?
   ```

   Go ahead, type your signature information. We recommend that your `.signa` → `ture` file include, at minimum, your name and e-mail address. You can also add funny sayings ("You know you're a geek when you refer to going to the bathroom as 'downloading'") or disclaimers ("My opinions are mine and not my company's"). Whatever you want, really. Keep your signature to no more than four or five lines; signatures any longer than this are hard to wade through (**Figure 11.13**).

3. Save and exit the file.

   If you're using `pico` or `vi`, you can get a quickie reminder about this in Chapter 4.
   ```

✔ Tip

- If you want to get really fancy with your signature, use a *figlet*, which is a text representation of letters, as shown in **Code Listing 11.5**. Check out `www.yahoo.com` and search for "figlet" or "figlet generator" for more information about creating your own.

Code Listing 11.5 Figlets are fun and fancy.

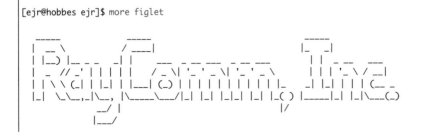

```
[ejr@hobbes ejr]$ more figlet

  _____             _____                                  _____
 |  __ \           / ____|                                |_   _|
 | |__) |__ _ _   _| |     ___  _ __ ___  _ __ ___         | |  _ __   ___
 |  _  // _' | | | | |    / _ \| '_ ' _ \| '_ ' _ \        | | | '_ \ / __|
 | | \ \ (_| | |_| | |___| (_) | | | | | | | | | | | |_   _| |_| | | | (__ _
 |_|  \_\__,_|\__, |\_____\___/|_| |_| |_|_| |_| |_|_( ) |_____|_| |_|\___(_)
               __/ |                                 |/
              |___/
```


Creating a Signature File

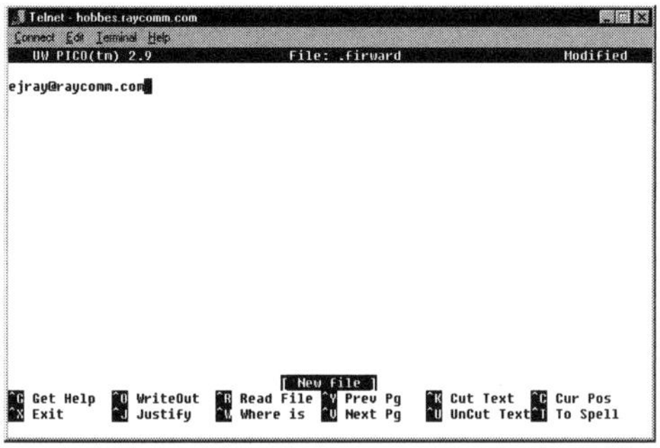

Figure 11.14 All you have to do is tell UNIX where you want your messages forwarded to.

■ Forwarding messages is also handy when you change ISPs. You can forward all messages sent to your old address to your new one, which helps tremendously in ensuring that you receive all your important messages while your friends and coworkers update their files.

Forwarding incoming messages

Suppose you're the boss of a big project, and everyone sends you all the important related e-mail messages. You can tell UNIX to automagically forward these incoming messages to the people who will actually do something about them. Hey, you're the boss, right? As **Figure 11.14** shows, all you have to do is create a `.forward` file.

To forward incoming e-mail messages:

1. `vi ~/.forward`

   To begin, type `vi` at the shell prompt (or the appropriate command for whichever editor you are using), indicate your home directory (with ~/), then put `.forward` as the file name.

2. `mynewid@raycomm.com`

   Add, as the first line of the file, the address to which you want your e-mail forwarded (**Figure 11.14**). In addition to forwarding to a single address, you can also use a `.forward` file with multiple addresses on multiple lines to send incoming e-mail to several addresses at once.

3. Save and close the file.

   Check out Chapter 4 for details about saving and closing files using `pico` or `vi`.

✔ Tips

■ If you want, you can keep a copy of all incoming messages (in your incoming e-mail box, just where it'd usually be) *and* forward them to unsuspecting recipients. Just type `\yourid, other@address.com` (filling in your id on the current system for yourid, and the address to which to forward the mail for the other one).

Announcing an absence with vacation

Cal-i-forn-ya here you come! If you're planning a vacation and will be away from your e-mail for a while, let UNIX announce your absence for you (**Figure 11.15**). Using the `vacation` program, you can have UNIX send a reply saying that you're out of the office to everyone who sends you e-mail.

Keep in mind that `vacation` is quite variable among different UNIX systems and ISPs. What you have might be quite different from the "standard" form used here. Be sure to check with your system administrator for specific instructions if you have any problems.

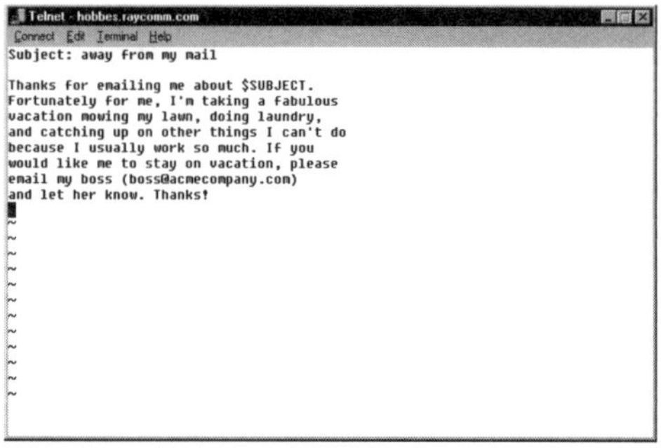

Figure 11.15 Using a template, you can customize the vacation message—even extensively, as we've done.

To send "I'm on vacation" messages using vacation:

1. `vacation`

   At the shell prompt, type `vacation`. You'll see a short template for the response that people should receive when they e-mail you, as shown in **Figure 11.15**.

2. ```
   Subject: Not here now, sorry!
   Thanks for e-mailing me about
   $SUBJECT. Fortunately for me,
   I'm taking a fabulous vacation
   mowing my lawn, doing laundry, and
   catching up on other things I
   can't do because I usually work
   so much. If you would like me to
   stay on vacation, please e-mail
   my boss (boss@acmecompany.com)
   and let her know. Thanks!
   ```

   Edit the text to say what you want.

   The `$SUBJECT` term in the text will be replaced with the actual subject of the e-mail sent to you.

3. Save your text and exit the editor.

   Chapter 4 has the gory details about saving and exiting in `pico` and `vi`.
   ```

Code Listing 11.6 Your .forward file should reference the vacation file.

```
[ejr@hobbes ejr]$ cat .forward
\ejr, "|vacation ejr"
[ejr@hobbes ejr]$
```

4. `vacation -I`

   Type `vacation -I` at the shell prompt to start `vacation` and tell it to respond to all incoming messages. You'll still get the incoming messages in your inbox. In fact, they'll pile up in your mailbox and wait for you to return.

5. `cat ~/.forward`

   Look at the `.forward` file in your home directory to verify that it contains a reference to the `vacation` program. Your `.forward` file specifies what should happen to your mail upon receipt, and in this example, it should be processed by `vacation`. The reference to `vacation` is usually automatically inserted by the `vacation` program, but if it's not there, you'll need to edit the `.forward` file and add text like `\yourid, "|vacation → yourid".` Of course, substitute your real userid for the placeholder above, and possibly include the full path to `vacation` (`/usr/bin/vacation` on our system). (See **Code Listing 11.6.**)

Stopping vacation e-mails:

- `mv .forward vacation-forward`

  At the shell prompt, move the `.forward` file that references the vacation program to a different name (in this case, `vacation-forward`). You could just delete it or remove the reference to `vacation`, but it's easier to save it so you can reuse it for your next vacation.

✔ Tips

- Remember to unsubscribe to all mailing lists before you start `vacation`. If you don't, you'll send a vacation announcement to a whole list of people who likely don't care (not to mention that you'll really irritate the list administrator!). Or, worse, you might cause a *mail loop* (in which your messages to the list are acknowledged by the server, and the acknowledgements are in turn sent vacation announcements), causing hundreds or thousands of messages to accumulate in your account.

- Your `EDITOR` environment variable determines which editor will be used to edit the vacation message in step 1. If you'd rather manually choose the editor, just save and close the message, then specify the editor you want to use to edit the text in the `.vacation.msg` file, as in `pico .vacation.msg`. Learn more about environment variables in Chapter 8.
- Start `vacation` with `vacation -j` to automatically respond to all messages. Without the `-j` flag, `vacation` responds only to one message each week from any specific sender.

12 Accessing the Internet

So far in this book, you've been working with files and scripts located on the UNIX system. In this chapter, we'll show you how to venture beyond your UNIX system and take advantage of the information on the Internet.

Chapter contents

- Getting familiar with UNIX-Internet lingo
- Logging in to remote systems
- Communicating with other users (two methods)
- Getting files from the Internet
- Sharing files on the Internet
- Surfing the Web
- Checking connections
- Tracing connections
- Matching domain names
- Choosing a News reader
- Reading News (two methods)

Getting familiar with UNIX-Internet lingo

Before you venture out onto the Internet using the information in this chapter, you should become familiar with some concepts and terminology.

A *server* is a computer that stores files and "serves" them whenever requested. For example, you might think of a Web server as a big storehouse for `.html` files. Its job is to store `.html` files, wait for another computer to request files, then find the requested files and "serve" them to the requesting computer. And, yes, your UNIX system might be a Web server, but it doesn't have to be.

A *client* is a program that runs on your UNIX system and is used to access files on a server. For example, your `lynx` Web browser is a client—that is, it runs on your UNIX system and is used to access files on a Web server.

An *IP number* (Internet protocol number) is the address of a specific computer. This address identifies a computer, much the way your street address identifies your home. You use IP numbers, for example, every time you access a Web page. You may type in `www.raycomm.com` (which is called the *domain name*), but behind the scenes, that's translated into a specific IP number, such as `204.228.141.12`. You probably will use domain names (such as `www.ibm.com` or `www.compaq.com`) more often, because they're easier to remember than a string of numbers. Whether you type in a character address or a number address, all you're doing is accessing a specific address for a specific computer.

Protocols are the languages that computers use to communicate with one another. For example, ftp (file transfer protocol) is used to transfer files from one computer to another.

Table 12.1

Internet Ports and Protocols

Port	Protocol
21	ftp
23	telnet
70	gopher
80	http
119	nntp
8080	http (usually for test servers)

http (hypertext transfer protocol) is used to transfer data on the World Wide Web.

Ports are like a computer's ears—they're "places" that computers listen for connections. Most Web servers run at port 80, and if you connect to `http://www.raycomm.com:80/`, you're explicitly saying that you want to talk to the `www.raycomm.com` computer, at port `80`, using the http protocol. You could specify a different protocol (ftp, for example) or a different port (`8080`, for example) to communicate with the same computer in a different way, as **Table 12.1** shows.

Logging in to remote systems with telnet

You might already be using telnet to connect to your UNIX system. You can, though, use it to connect to and use practically any other computer system on the Internet (assuming you have rights to log in to it), as **Figure 12.1** shows.

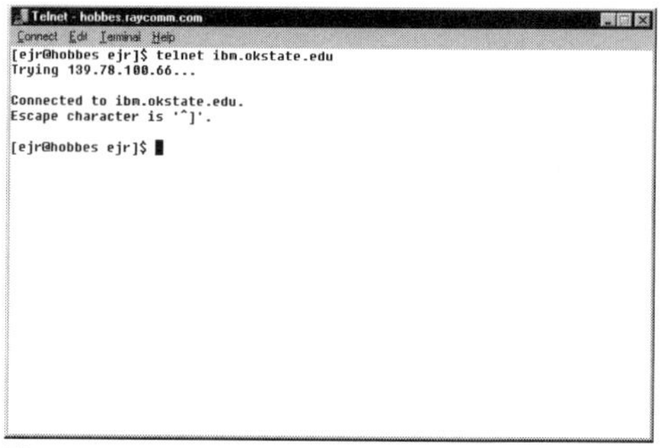

Figure 12.1 Note the Escape character as it flashes by.

To connect to another computer using telnet:

1. `telnet ibm.okstate.edu`

   At the shell prompt, type `telnet` followed by the name of the system you want to connect to. In this example, we're connecting to the Oklahoma State University online library catalog.

2. Make note of the Escape character announced when you log in—look quickly, as it'll whirr by onscreen. The Escape character is what you'll press should your telnet connection stall or the system lock up. In our example, the Escape character is Ctrl [, which will return us to the telnet prompt so we can `quit` the connection (**Figure 12.1**).

3. Log in using the instructions you have for accessing the system.

   Presumably, if you're accessing a system over the Internet, you have some reason to do so and permission to do so. In some cases, you'll type the name of the application. In our example, we type `pete`, which is the name of the card catalog. In most other systems, you'll log in with a userid and password, just as you log in to your UNIX system (**Figure 12.2**).

4. After you've finished using the remote system, log out according to the instructions and policies of the remote system.

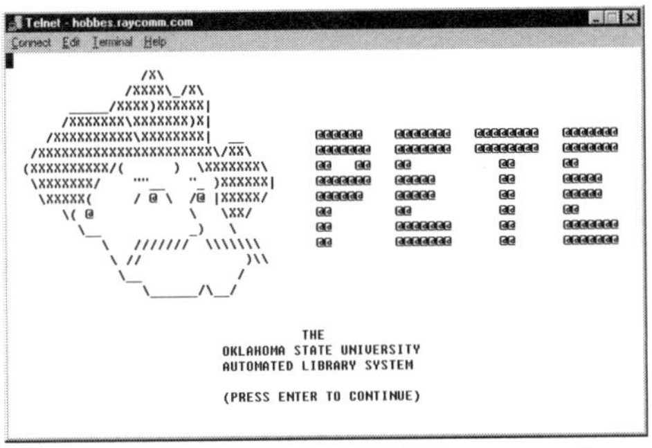

Figure 12.2 After you're connected, you can use the remote system just like your own.

✔ Tips

- For help with `telnet`, type `telnet` at the shell prompt, then enter a ? at the `telnet>` prompt. `open`, `close`, and `exit` will be the most useful tools for you.
- You'll find that telnet connections to libraries and other mainframe computers are often difficult to use because of oddities in keyboard emulations. Your best bet is to contact the site owner and ask for a FAQ list (with answers!). You'll assuredly not be the first to have questions.
- A program closely related to telnet, `tn3270`, is designed specifically for communicating with IBM mainframes, such as ones commonly used for college library catalogs as well as other professional and academic systems. If you know that you're communicating with an IBM mainframe, `tn3270` will probably be better to use.

Communicating with other users using write

Most of the time when you connect to a UNIX system, you'll be communicating with the computer. You can, though, communicate with other people logged in to the same system. `write` is ideal for getting a quick message to another user, kind of like putting a yellow sticky note on their computer, as **Figure 12.3** shows.

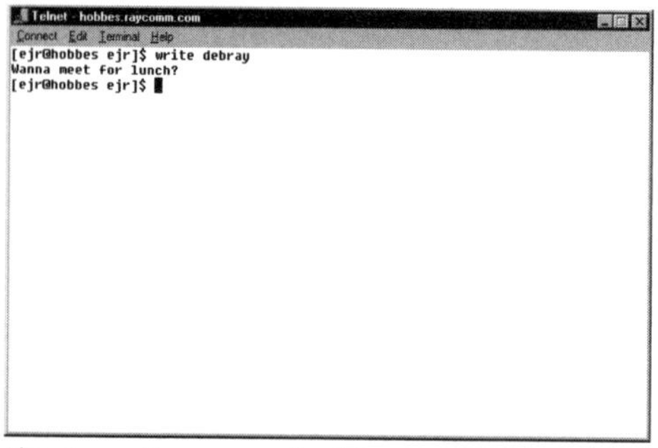

Figure 12.3 You can send quick messages to another user on your system with write.

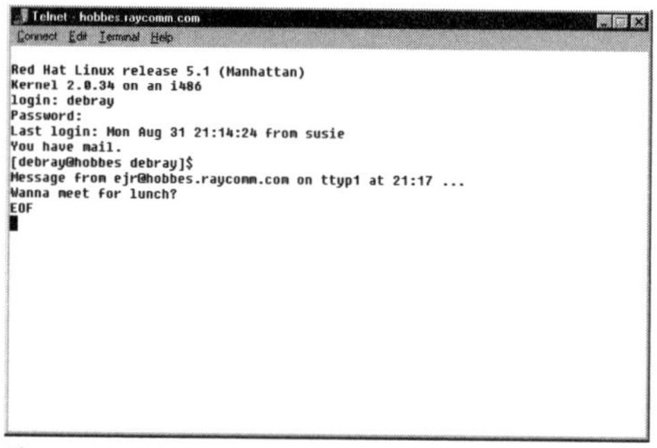

Figure 12.4 The message suddenly appears on the user's screen.

To communicate with other users using write:

1. `write userid`

   At the shell prompt, type `write` followed by the userid of the person you want to send a message to. You'll get a blank line with a blinking cursor on it, just waiting for you to type something.

2. `Wanna meet for lunch?`

   Go ahead and type your message (**Figure 12.3**).

3. Ctrl D

   When you're finished typing, press Ctrl D to send the message. What you typed will appear on the other user's screen (**Figure 12.4**).

✔ Tips

- Keep in mind that `write` message will suddenly appear on the recipient's screen and can be an intrusive surprise!
- If you don't want to receive `write` messages, type `mesg n` at the shell prompt. This command will keep other people from sending you `write` messages for the current session. Type `mesg y` to enable `write` again.
- You can use the `wall` command to send `write`-type messages to everyone logged in to the system. `wall` is commonly used by system administrators if they need to warn of the system being brought down or something like that.

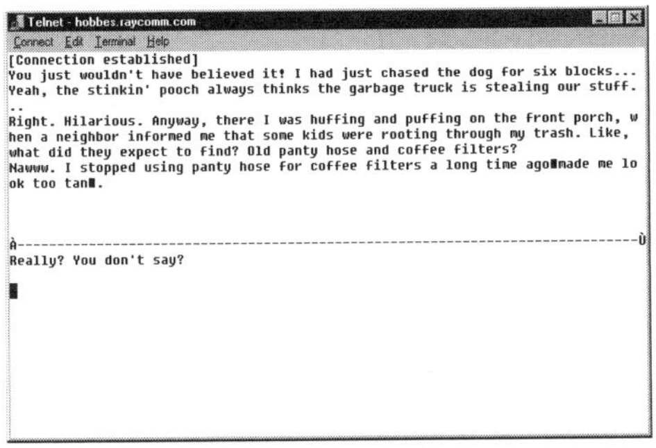

Figure 12.5 talk lets you have a real-time, two-way online conversation.

Communicating with other users using talk

You can also have a real-time, two-way conversation with another user logged in to the system by using `talk`. As **Figure 12.5** shows, you type your messages, the other person types theirs, and you can both see the exchanges onscreen.

To communicate with other users using talk:

1. `talk deb`

   At the shell prompt, type `talk` and the userid of the person you want to talk to. The other user will be prompted to enter `talk` and your userid. Then, you'll see the `talk` screen, as shown in **Figure 12.5**.

2. ```
   You just wouldn't have believed it!
   → I had just chased the dog for six
   → blocks...
   Yeah, the stinkin' pooch always
   → thinks the garbage truck is
   → stealing our stuff...
   Right. Hilarious. Anyway, there I
   → was huffing and puffing on the
   → front porch, when a neighbor
   → informed me that some kids were
   → rooting through my trash. Like,
   → what did they expect to find? Old
   → panty hose and coffee filters?
   Nawww. I stopped using panty hose
   → for coffee filters a long time
   → ago. It made me look too tan.
   ```

   Type anything you want. Each keystroke will show up on the other person's screen, so they'll see exactly how quickly (and how well) you type.

3. Ctrl C

   When you're finished, break the connection.

✔ Tips

- You can also talk to people logged in to other UNIX systems. Just use `talk userid@whereever.com`. Of course, fill in the other person's actual userid and address, which will often be the same as their e-mail address.
- If someone requests a `talk` with you, just type `talk` and their userid (or their `userid@whereever.com`, if their hostname isn't the same as yours).
- As with `write`, you can type `mesg n` and `mesg y` at the shell prompt to turn `talk` off and on for the current session.
   ```

Getting files from the Internet with ftp

Some of the Internet's great information resources are ftp sites, which contain hundreds of thousands of files from all over the Internet. ftp sites are similar to Web sites, but are directory-oriented and speak a different protocol. They're less fun than the Web usually is, but often more practical.

One of the easiest ways to access information on ftp sites is to use anonymous `ftp`, which lets you access the sites and download files to your computer (**Code Listing 12.1**).

Getting a single file through anonymous ftp:

1. `ftp calvin.raycomm.com`

   At the shell prompt, type `ftp` followed by the name of the ftp site you're connecting to. Of course, if the computer has an IP number but no name, type the IP number instead. You'll be prompted to log in, as shown in **Code Listing 12.1**.

2. `anonymous`

   For the user name, type `anonymous`. (Type `ftp` if you get tired of typing `anonymous`—it nearly always works.)

3. `you@whereever.com`

   Use your e-mail address for the password. It's polite to identify yourself to the people who provide the ftp service.

4. `cd /pub/files`

   Use standard UNIX `cd` commands to move through the directory tree to the file you want.

5. `binary`

   Specify the file type—in this case, `binary`, because we're downloading a gzipped

Code Listing 12.1 Use anonymous ftp to get files from archives across the Internet.

```
[ejr@hobbes ejr]$ ftp calvin.raycomm.com
Connected to calvin.raycomm.com.
220 calvin Microsoft FTP Service (Version 2.0).
Name (calvin.raycomm.com:ejr): anonymous
331 Anonymous access allowed, send identity (e-mail name) as password.
Password:
230 Anonymous user logged in.
Remote system type is Windows_NT.
ftp> cd /pub/files
250 CWD command successful.
ftp> binary
200 Type set to I.
ftp> hash
Hash mark printing on (1024 bytes/hash mark).
ftp> get jokearchive.gz
local: jokearchive.gz remote: jokearchive.gz
200 PORT command successful.
150 Opening BINARY mode data connection for jokearchive.gz(1481035 bytes).
################################################################################
################################################################################
################################################################################
################################################################################
################################################################################
################################################################################
################################################################################
################################################################################
################################################################################
################################################################################
################################################################################
################################################################################
################################################################################
################################################################################
################################################################################
################################################################################
################################################################################
################################################################################
######
226 Transfer complete.
1481035 bytes received in 4.07 secs (3.6e+02 Kbytes/sec)
ftp> quit
221
```

archive file. Specify `ascii` for README files, text, and HTML files.

6. `hash`

   Next, you have the option of typing **`hash`** to tell the ftp client to display a hash mark (#) for every 1024 bytes transferred. If you're transferring a small file or using a fast connection, this might not be necessary; however, for large files and slow connections, the hash marks will let you know that you're making progress.

   If you'll be downloading multiple files, check out the sidebar *Getting multiple files* in this section before proceeding. The instructions for getting single and multiple files differ at this point in the process.

7. `get jokearchive.gz`

   At the `ftp>` prompt, type **`get`** and the file name to get the file from the remote system and plunk it into your own account.

8. `quit`

   When it's finished, just type **`quit`**.

✔ Tips

- If the ftp connection seems to get stuck as soon as you log in, try **`-yourid@whereever.com`** as the password. The - character disables system announcements and helps keep your `ftp` client happy.
- Another handy use for - is to view text files onscreen. For example, type **`get filename -`** to have the text just scroll by on the screen.
- Instead of using **`get`**, you could use **`newer`** (as in **`newer goodjokes.gz`**) to get a more recent file with the same name as one you already have.
- If you start downloading a file and the ftp connection breaks, type **`reget`** and the

file name to continue the transfer from wherever it left off. (You'll have to re-establish the connection first, of course.)

- After you've downloaded files, you might check your disk quota (type `quota -v` at the shell prompt) to make sure you haven't exceeded your allotted space.
- You can tell the ftp client to make sure that all the transferred files have unique names by using `runique` instead of `get`. This way, you can ensure that files don't overwrite existing files on your local system.
- Use regular UNIX commands like `ls`, `pwd`, and `cd` to move around in the remote system, and preface them with an l to apply to your system. For example, `cd ..` would change to the next higher directory on the other system, and `lcd ..` (from within the FTP client) would change to the next higher directory on the local system. The current local directory is where your files will be saved.

Getting multiple files

If you'll be getting multiple files with `ftp`, follow steps 1 through 6 in this section, then:

- `prompt`

  Optionally, type `prompt` to tell the ftp client *not* to prompt you for each individual file that you want to get. You'll be informed that prompt is set to no. If you want to turn it back on, issue `prompt` again.

- `mget start*`

  At the `ftp>` prompt, type `mget` (for "multiple get") followed by the string or filenames to match. In this example, we use `start*` to get all files with names that begin with "start". You could also use `mget *.gz`, for example, to get files with the `.gz` file extension. See Chapter 1 for more about using wildcards.

- `quit`

  When you're finished getting files finished, just type `quit`.

Sharing files on the Internet with ftp

Sharing files on the Internet with ftp is similar to getting files; instead of retrieving files, however, you give files to other people (**Code Listing 12.2**).

To share files on the Internet with ftp:

1. `ftp ftp.raycomm.com`

   Open the ftp connection as shown in the previous section.

2. `youruserid`

   Log in with your userid.

3. `password`

   Enter your password.

4. `cd incoming`

   Use standard UNIX directory commands (`ls`, `cd`, and so on) to move into the directory you want to put the files into (**Code Listing 12.2**). `incoming` is often the right directory name to use, particularly on public ftp servers.

5. `binary`

   Set the file type. You'll want to use the `binary` file type for any files other than text or HTML files; use `ascii` for text or HTML.

6. `put myjokes.gz`

   Type `put`, followed by the name of the file you're making available.

7. `quit`

   Type `quit` when you're done.

Code Listing 12.2 Using put, you can share your files with other people on the Internet.

```
[ejr@hobbes ejr]$ ftp ftp.raycomm.com
Connected to www.raycomm.com.
220 ftp.raycomm.com FTP server (NcFTPd 2.1.2,
  → registered copy) ready.
Name (ftp.raycomm.com:ejr): ejray
331 User ejray okay, need password.
Password:
230-You are user #8 of 100 simultaneous users
  allowed.
230-
230 Logged in.
Remote system type is UNIX.
Using binary mode to transfer files.
ftp> cd incoming
250 "/home/ftp/pub/users/e/ejray/incoming" is
  → new cwd.
ftp> binary
200 Type okay.
ftp> put myjokes.gz
local: myjokes.gz remote: myjokes.gz
200 PORT command successful.
150 Opening BINARY mode data connection.
226 Transfer completed.
128889 bytes sent in 15.5 secs (8.1
  → Kbytes/sec)
ftp> quit
221 C-ya!
[ejr@hobbes ejr]$
```

✔ Tips

- On public ftp servers that accept incoming files, you might not be able to list the files in the `incoming` directory or see anything in there. In this case, you essentially just cast your file into a big open room and close the door. This allows ftp administrators to screen the incoming files before making them available for downloading.
- You can use the `mput` command to make multiple files available.
- If you're transferring a lot of files at once—say, for example, you're moving all of your files from your old ISP to your new one—consider using `tar` and `gz` to collect and zip up all of your files, then transferring just a single file. See Chapter 13 for more information about these commands.
- Navigate in your local system (for example, to change to a directory containing files to put) with regular UNIX commands like `ls`, `pwd`, and `cd`, prefaced with an `l`. For example, `pwd` would display the path and name of the current directory on the other system, and `lpwd` would display the path and name of the current directory on the local system.

Surfing the Web with lynx

Using lynx, a text-based Web browser, you can surf the Web just as you might with Netscape Navigator or Internet Explorer. lynx won't provide a fancy interface or let you see all the colorful bells and whistles that graphical interfaces provide, but you can access the wealth of information available on the Web (**Figure 12.6**). The advantage of lynx is that you won't have to deal with slow download times for graphics, annoying sound files, plug-ins, or other showy Web page features.

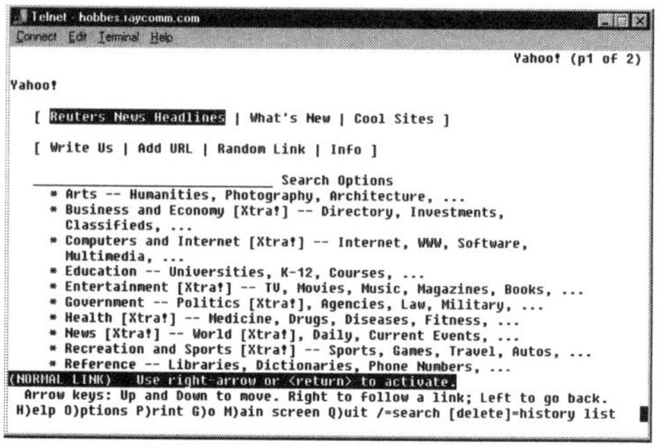

Figure 12.6 You can use lynx to navigate to any site on the Web.

To surf the Web with lynx:

1. `lynx http://www.yahoo.com/`

   At the shell prompt, type `lynx` followed by the name of an `.html` file or a Web site address. Here, we're accessing the Yahoo! Web site (**Figure 12.6**).

   If you only type in `lynx`, you'll get the default page for your system, which is likely the `lynx` home page or the main page for your ISP.

2. Surf, surf, surf!

   See the sidebars called *Navigating with lynx* and *Useful keystrokes* in this section for details.

3. `q`

   Type `q` to quit and return to the shell prompt. That's it!

Navigating with lynx

- [→] (or [Enter]) follows the currently highlighted link to a new page.
- [←] returns to the previous page.
- [↓] moves the highlight down to the next link in the document.
- [↑] moves the highlight up to the previous link in the document.
- [M] returns you to the first screen you accessed in the session—the one you saw in step 1.
- [Spacebar] scrolls down to the next page.
- [B] scrolls up to the previous page.

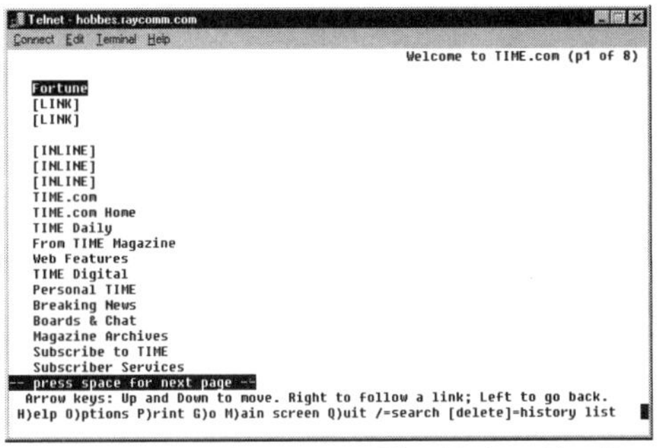

Figure 12.7 Some sites are considerably less friendly than others if you're not using graphics.

✔ Tips

- If you access a `lynx`-unfriendly page, like the one shown in **Figure 12.7**, press the Spacebar to scroll down a few times. Usually you'll be able to find the content.
- `lynx` is a great way to get a spiffy plain text file out of an HTML document. Try `lynx -dump http://url.com/good` → `page.html > newname.txt` to start lynx and direct it to send the display to standard output, then redirect the output to the file called `newname.txt`. This will give you the text from the page, without HTML codes, in a file in your UNIX account.

Useful lynx keystrokes

- `/findme` finds text within the file. (Replace `findme` with the text you're looking for.)
- ? lets you access help.
- d downloads the current link.
- g goes to an address or file. You enter the address at the prompt.
- G lets you edit the current address.
- A adds the current link to your bookmark list.
- V lets you view the bookmark list.
- Backspace lets you see a list of pages you've visited (your history).
- \ lets you toggle back and forth between viewing the formatted page and viewing the HTML source.
- Ctrl R reloads the current page and refreshes the screen.

Checking connections with ping

Think of using `ping` as saying "Are you there?" to a remote computer. For example, suppose you're trying to connect to a Web page but are getting no response from the computer. Rather than waiting and wondering what's going on, type `ping` to find out if the computer is up and functional (**Code Listing 12.3**).

To check a computer with ping:

- `ping www.raycomm.com`

  At the shell prompt, type `ping` and the hostname to test the connection to a specific host, as shown in **Code Listing 12.3**.

  Depending on your UNIX system, it may check the connection one time and report the results. Or, it may continue to pester the other computer every second or so until you tell it to stop. If that's the case, just press Ctrl C to stop it.

✔ Tip

- If you're having problems connecting to a particular computer, you might consider using `traceroute`, which pings all the computers on the path between point A and point B. While `ping` tells you if a host responds or not, `traceroute` will give you an idea where the problem might lie. See the next section for more details about `traceroute`.

Code Listing 12.3 Using ping, you can find out whether you can connect to a specific computer or not.

```
[ejr@hobbes ejr]$ ping www.raycomm.com
PING www.raycomm.com (204.228.141.12): 56
  → data bytes
64 bytes from 204.228.141.12: icmp_seq=0
  → ttl=251 time=190.3 ms
64 bytes from 204.228.141.12: icmp_seq=1
  → ttl=251 time=197.7 ms
64 bytes from 204.228.141.12: icmp_seq=2
  → ttl=251 time=166.5 ms
64 bytes from 204.228.141.12: icmp_seq=3
  → ttl=251 time=157.5 ms


--- www.raycomm.com ping statistics ---
4 packets transmitted, 4 packets received, 0%
  → packet loss
round-trip min/avg/max = 157.5/178.0/197.7 ms
[ejr@hobbes ejr]$
```

Tracing connections with traceroute

When you're connecting to a remote computer, you're actually connecting through a series of computers (and routers, and other expensive Internet stuff). That is, your computer connects to another computer, which connects to another, which connects to yet another, and so on until your computer connects to the one you're trying to reach.

The data that you're sending or receiving actually meanders through the path in *packets* (little chunks of data) that are reassembled into the correct sequence at the other end. But not all packets take precisely the same route from the sending computer to the destination computer. Communication on the Internet is much more like sending a lot of letters than making a telephone call. It's a bunch of little messages being passed along, not a continuous connection.

Using `traceroute`, you can satisfy your curiousity or, possibly, identify bottlenecks. How? You find out what route the packets take to arrive at the destination computer, as shown in **Code Listing 12.4**. If, for example, you see that the routes to your three favorite (but

Code Listing 12.4 Using traceroute, you can see how data meanders between your computer and a remote computer.

```
ejray> traceroute www.yahoo.com
traceroute to www10.yahoo.com (204.71.200.75), 30 hops max, 40 byte packets
 1  198.60.22.1 (198.60.22.1)  8 ms  2 ms  3 ms
 2  903.Hssi5-0-0.GW1.SLT1.ALTER.NET (157.130.160.141)  18 ms  13 ms  14 ms
 3  124.ATM4-0-0.CR1.SFO1.Alter.Net (137.39.68.9)  68 ms  65 ms  52 ms
 4  311.atm3-0.gw1.sfo1.alter.net (137.39.13.49)  60 ms  50 ms  39 ms
 5  Hssi1-0.br1.NUQ.globalcenter.net (157.130.193.150)  40 ms  39 ms  28 ms
 6  pos0-1-155M.wr1.NUQ.globalcenter.net (206.132.160.25)  30 ms  48 ms  42 ms
 7  pos1-0-622M.wr1.SNV.globalcenter.net (206.251.0.74)  50 ms  67 ms  61 ms
 8  pos5-0-0-155M.cr1.SNV.globalcenter.net (206.251.0.105)  48 ms  40 ms  41 ms
 9  www10.yahoo.com (204.71.200.75)  43 ms  50 ms  53 ms
ejray>
```

currently inaccessible) Web sites all end at a specific computer, that's where the network outage is and who you're waiting for to get things up and running.

To trace a connection with traceroute:

◆ `traceroute www.yahoo.com`

At the shell prompt, type `traceroute` plus the address of the other computer in the connection. You'll see results similar to those shown in **Code Listing 12.4**. Each line in the `traceroute` output represents a computer (or other device) on the Internet that receives your packets and passes them on to the next computer.

✔ Tips

- If you're experiencing connectivity problems, try using `traceroute` to several different, geographically dispersed hosts to isolate the problem. For example, if you're in the Midwest and can `traceroute` all the way to `www.altavista.digital.com` (physically located in Palo Alto, California) but not to `www.mit.edu` (in Boston, Massachusetts), there's likely trouble on the Internet between you and the East Coast.
- You can speed up the `traceroute` process by using the `-n` flag; for example, `traceroute -n hostname`. This checks the path using only IP numbers and does not translate the IP numbers into the DNS addresses you're familiar with.

Code Listing 12.5 You can manually translate a domain name into an IP address using nslookup.

```
ejray> nslookup www.raycomm.com ns1.sierra.net
Server:  ns1.sierra.net
Address:  207.135.224.247

Name:    www.raycomm.com
Address:  204.228.141.12

ejray>
```

Matching domain names with IP numbers using nslookup

When accessing a computer on the Internet, you generally type in a domain name (such as `www.raycomm.com`), which is pretty easy to remember. To connect to another computer, though, your system must translate the domain name into an IP number (such as `204.228.141.12`), which is the actual address of the computer you're connecting to.

As a rule, the translation from domain name to IP number proceeds without a problem. Heck, most of the time, you won't even notice that it happened. Occasionally, though, you'll come across an error message that says something like, "failed DNS (Domain Name Server) lookups." All this message means is that the DNS server (probably on your UNIX system) cannot match the domain name you provided to an IP number.

So, what do you do?

- Just be patient for a day or two until the problem is resolved. (In the meantime, make sure the problem isn't a typo on your part.)
- Use `nslookup`, which manually converts a domain name to the matching IP number (**Code Listing 12.5**). Then you can connect directly to the IP number, rather than using the domain name.

To match a domain name with an IP number using nslookup:

- `nslookup www.raycomm.com` ➝ `ns1.sierra.net`

  At the shell prompt, type `nslookup`, followed by the domain name you want to look up and the server you want to do the looking for you (**Code Listing 12.5**). Remember, if you get one of those pesky "failed DNS lookup" messages, the problem likely resides with your name server; therefore, you'll need to specify a different name server to match the domain name and IP number for you.

✔ Tip

- You can find alternate Domain Name Servers by using the `whois` query server at `rs.internic.net` and looking up the domain name you want. All domain names have to be listed with two different DNSs that are responsible for the domain names. So, either of those listed servers should be able to provide the IP number for the domain name you enter.
- You can also use `nslookup` to find domain names from IP numbers. For example, if a Web page links to an address identified only with a number, you can find the correct name, if it exists. Just enter an IP number instead of a domain name in the steps above.

Choosing a News reader

Usenet News (often called *Netnews* or just *News*) is a collection of over 20,000 different discussion groups on a variety of topics. Several main categories of Usenet newsgroups exist, as well as dozens of local, regional, and esoteric categories. Our ISP carries around 25,000 newsgroups, which is fairly typical. The sidebar called *Common Usenet categories* lists some of the main Usenet categories. The newsgroups you'll have available through your UNIX system depend on which ones your ISP or company subscribes to.

You can read News using a variety of News readers, including `pine` and `tin`, which we'll cover in this section. Both of these are fairly easy to use and available on many UNIX systems.

Common Usenet categories

The main Usenet categories include:

- `comp.` computer-related topics
- `news.` Usenet administration topics, including answers to questions frequently asked by new users
- `rec.` recreational topics
- `sci.` science-related topics
- `soc.` social/sociology topics
- `talk.` discussion for its own sake
- `misc.` anything that's left over

Other common categories include:

- `alt.` practically any topic imaginable
- `bit.` mirrors of discussions from Listserv lists (that were originally on the BITnet network)
- `k12.` education topics, from K–12

Dozens of other categories exist for universities, states, companies, and other purposes. Ask your system administrator about what's available to you, or just take a look for yourself.

Reading News with pine

pine is an excellent choice for reading news, particularly if you already use pine to read and send e-mail. pine provides an easy-to-use interface and a slew of features. To use pine to read News, you'll need to

- Configure pine to read News (**Figure 12.8**)
- Subscribe to one or more newsgroups (**Figure 12.9**)
- Read your newsgroup messages (**Figure 12.10**)

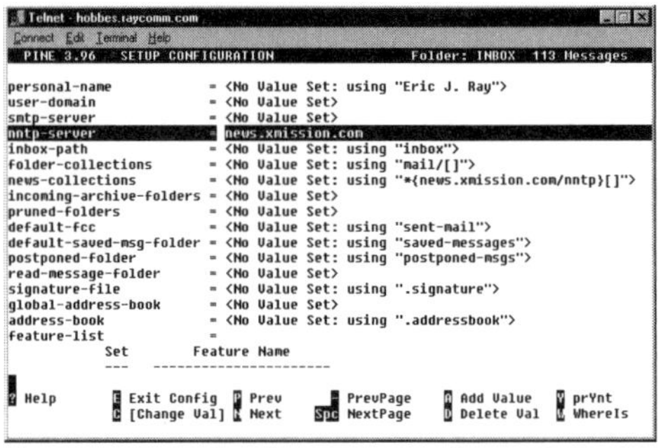

Figure 12.8 You often have to manually set pine so it knows where your news server is.

To configure pine to read News:

1. pine

   At the shell prompt, type pine.

2. m

   Type m to get to pine's main menu.

3. s

   Type s to enter pine's setup menu.

4. c

   As shown in the setup menu, type c to access the configuration screen (**Figure 12.8**).

5. Scroll down to nntp-server and press Enter.

   nntp stands for Network News Transport Protocol, and the server is where you'll find the news.

6. news.yourisp.com

   Type in the news server name—something like news.yourisp.com or news.yourserver.com (with your specific information in there, of course). Check with your system administrator for the specifics.

7. e

   Type e to exit the configuration screen.

Figure 12.9 You have to subscribe to newsgroups before you can read them in pine.

8. y

Confirm that you really want to exit and save your changes by typing y.

9. q

Quit `pine`.

10. y

Confirm that you really want to quit.

To subscribe to newsgroups with pine:

1. `pine`

For starters, type `pine` at the shell prompt.

2. `l`

Choose `l` to see the folder list. You'll notice that you now have a News section at the bottom of the folder list.

3. a

Type a to subscribe to a newsgroup. You have to subscribe for groups to show up in your list.

4. Ctrl T

Press Ctrl T to get a list of all newsgroups, then scroll through the list with the arrow keys until you find one you want to try out, as **Figure 12.9** shows. Note that this can be pretty time-consuming on a slow connection.

5. s

Type s to subscribe to the newsgroup you highlighted in the previous step.

6. Continue subscribing to any groups that look interesting by following the same process.

7. q

Type q (and confirm with y) when you're finished and ready to exit `pine`, or just move to the next section to read your new newsgroups.

To read newsgroup messages with pine:

1. pine

   At the shell prompt, type pine (unless you're still in pine from the previous section).

2. l

   Type l to view the list of folders.

3. Tab Tab Tab. Ah-ha!

   Tab down to the News collection (**Figure 12.10**).

4. v

   Type v to view the folder you choose.

5. Read messages just like you'd read mail.

   Check back with Chapter 11 for a quickie reminder about reading, sending, and replying with pine.

✔ Tips

- When subscribing to newsgroups, you can just enter the name of a newsgroup (or part of the name) after you choose a to add a new subscription, rather than searching through the entire list of newsgroups.
- After you subscribe to a newsgroup, you might have a few initial messages that show up as "No Message Text Available." Just scroll down to other messages.

Figure 12.10 From here, you can choose messages to read.

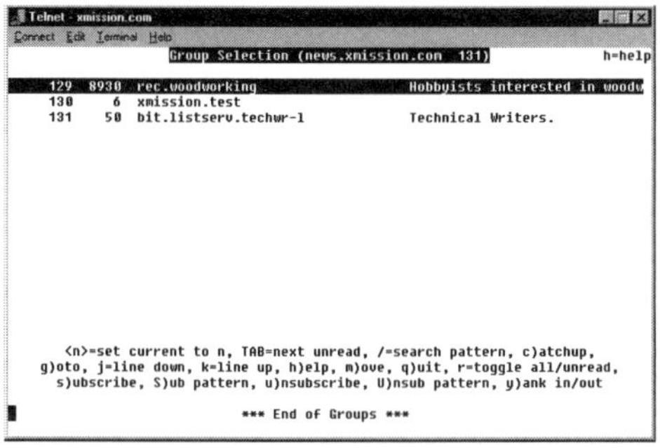

Figure 12.11 The main tin screen is very similar to elm's main screen.

Reading News with tin

Another program you can use to read News is `tin`, which is very similar to the `elm` e-mail program. You'll find that it's fairly intuitive to use (as newsreaders go) and that the menu options and interface are similar to those of `elm`. `tin` is only a News reader (unlike `pine`, which is also an e-mail program), so your only tasks here are subscribing to newsgroups (**Figure 12.11**) and reading newsgroup messages (**Figure 12.12**).

To subscribe to newsgroups with tin:

1. `tin`

   At the shell prompt, type `tin`. You'll see a list (quite possibly empty) of all of the groups you've subscribed to, and a menu at the bottom (**Figure 12.11**).

2. Page Down

   Optionally, type `y` to "yank" the whole list of newsgroups into the reader if you want to see your choices.

3. `s rec.woodworking`

   Type `s` followed by the newsgroup name to subscribe to a newsgroup.

4. Esc

   Keep subscribing to other newsgroups if you want, then press Esc to quit `tin` when you're done.

To read newsgroup messages with tin:

1. `tin`

   At the shell prompt, type `tin`.

2. `2`

   Enter the number of the newsgroup you want to read (the number is in the list of newsgroups that `tin` displays). You can use your ↑ and ↓ keys to navigate and the Spacebar to move to the next screen.

3. 1

Choose the thread you want to read by number as well (**Figure 12.12**). You can use your ↑ and ↓ keys to navigate and the Spacebar to move to the next screen.

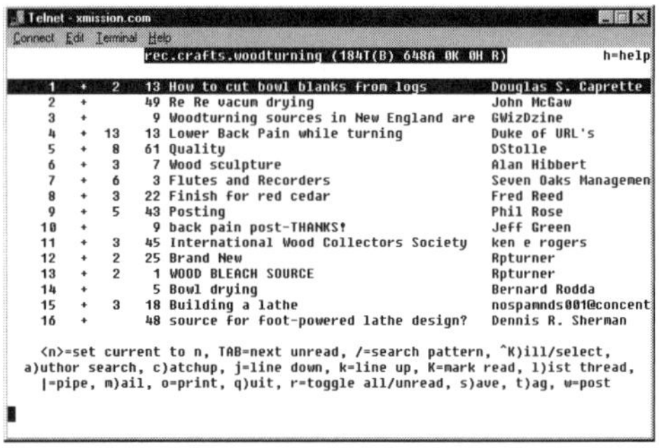

Figure 12.12 Choose a thread from the listing tin provides.

4. Enter

Press Enter an extra time to open a newsgroup message.

5. `n`

Use `n` (for next) and `p` (for previous) to read the messages, and `q` to return to the list of threads.

6. `q`

Type `q` quit `tin`.

✔ Tips

- You can reply to any newsgroup message by typing `r`, which will send your reply only to the person who posted the message. Type your message in the resulting editor screen and use `s` to send the message, `i` to spell-check it, `q` to quit (cancel), or `e` to return to the editor and keep revising.
- If you'd rather reply to the entire newsgroup, type `f` (to follow up) instead of `r`.
- Many "binary" groups post encoded pictures, programs, and sound files. Save the newsgroup posting, then use `uudecode` (from Chapter 13) to restore the file to its original state.
- Type `w` from any `tin` screen to start a new posting to that newsgroup. Fill in the subject and type your message in the resulting editor screen.
- If a newsgroup thread wanders onto a topic you don't want to read about, just type `k` to kill it. All of the articles with that subject will be marked as already read, so you won't see them again.
- You can type `h` from any `tin` page to get help.

Working with Encoded & Compressed Files

13

As you use UNIX, you will likely encounter encoded or compressed files and need to extract, unencode, or otherwise manipulate the files to be able to view or use them. This chapter discusses different ways of encoding and compressing files that meet various needs.

Chapter contents

Encoding files with uuencode

You'll use encoding whenever you're sending a *binary file* (a non-text file) through e-mail or posting one to a newsgroup. Although many e-mail programs and news readers will take care of encoding for you (and, therefore, you won't need to mess with the information here), you may occasionally need to do it yourself.

Files must be encoded so that they can pass through Internet e-mail and news gateways unscathed. If you don't encode a file and your program doesn't do it for you, the file will arrive as a bunch of unusable gibberish (because the gateways assume that all text passing through uses 7-bit words, while binary files use 8-bit words, thus binary files are bargled). To prevent gibberish, just `uuencode` your files before you send them along, as shown in **Code Listing 13.1**.

To encode a file using uuencode:

- `uuencode ournewhouse.jpg house.jpg` `→ > house.uue`

  At the shell prompt, type `uuencode`, followed by
  - The name of the unencoded file (`ournewhouse.jpg`, in this case).
  - The name you want the (eventually) unencoded file to have (`house.jpg`). We deliberately chose a short file name so our Windows 3.1 and DOS friends can easily access the file on their systems.
  - A command to redirected the output to a new file name (`> house.uue`). You add this bit so the file will be saved on disk and not displayed on the screen instead. We've used the `.uue` extension so we'll more easily remember that the file is uuencoded.

Code Listing 13.1 lists the files in a directory (to verify the name) and then uuencodes the file. Also, notice that it shows what the top of a uuencoded file looks like.

To encode with uuencode and e-mail at once:

- `uuencode ournewhouse.jpg house.jpg` ➝ `| mail -s "Here's the new picture"` ➝ `debray@raycomm.com`

  At the shell prompt, use uuencode, followed by
  - The name of the unencoded file (`ournewhouse.jpg`. in this case).
  - The name you want the (eventually) unencoded file to have (`house.jpg`).
  - A command to pipe the output (`|` ➝ `mail -s "Here's the new picture"` ➝ `debray@raycomm.com`). This mails the file to a specific e-mail address with specific text in the Subject line, which the `-s` flag sets. See Chapter 11 for

Code Listing 13.1 Use uuencode to encode files and, optionally, to redirect the output to disk.

```
[ejr@hobbes compression]$ ls
Folder          bigfile.uue     folderzip.zip    home.gz.uue
Zipadeedoodah   file1.htm       fortunes1.txt    newzip.zip
bigfile.gz      file2.html      fortunes1.zip    ournewhouse.jpg
bigfile.new.gz  folder.tar      gzip             temp
[ejr@hobbes compression]$ uuencode ournewhouse.jpg ourhouse.jpg >  house.uue
[ejr@hobbes compression]$ head house.uue
begin 664 ourhouse.jpg
M"<@>H@("'@("'@("'@("'@("'@("'@("'@("'@("'@("'@("'@("'@("'@("
M("'@4F%N9&]M(%5.25@@1F]R='5N97,A"@H*"@I)9B!Y;W4G<F4@;F]T('!A
M<G0@;V8@=&AE('-O;'5T:6]N+"!Y;W4G<F4@<&%R="!O9B!T:&4@<')E8VEP
M:71A=&4N"@H*"@I4:&4@;VYL>2!R96%L;'D@9V]O9"!P;&%C92!T;R!B=7D@
M;'5M8F5R(&ES(&%T(&$@<W10<F4@=VAE<F4@=&AE(&QU;6)E<@IH87,@86QR
M96%D>2!B965N(&-U="!A;F0@871T86-H960@=&]G971H97(@:6X@=&AE(&9O
M<FT@;V8@9G5R;FET=7)E+'IF:6YI<VAE9"P@86YD('!U="!I;G-I9&4@8F]X
M97,N"B'@("'@("'@("'@("'M+2!$879E($)A<G)Y+"''B5&AE(%1A;6EN
M9R!O9B!T:&4@4V-R97<B"@H*"@HB1&ES8V\@:7,@=&\@;75S:6,@=VAA="!%
[ejr@hobbes compression]$
```

more about mailing files and mailing from the shell prompt.

Code Listing 13.2 shows this command and gives a glimpse into a uuencoded file.

✔ Tip

- If you're sending a file to someone with a MIME-compliant e-mail program, you might try `base64` encoding, using `uuencode -m`. See Chapter 11 for more about e-mail and MIME types.
- Also check out Chapter 11 for information about e-mail programs that will automatically encode files for you.
- You must (either manually or automatically) encode all binary files (graphics, programs, compressed files, etc.) before emailing them. Plain text (text files, scripts, or HTML documents) don't need to be encoded.

Code Listing 13.2 You can uuencode and mail all in one step to work more efficiently.

```
[ejr@hobbes compression]$ uuencode
  → ournewhouse.jpg house.jpg | mail -s
  → "Here's the new picture"
  → debray@raycomm.com
```

Decoding files with uudecode

You'll decode files whenever you receive binary files through e-mail—it's the only way you can use encoded files. Although some programs will take care of decoding files for you (and, therefore, you won't need the information here), you may need to do it manually on occasion. (Hint: If you open up a file or an email message and see something like **Code Listing 13.4**, you've got a little decoding to do, as shown in **Code Listing 13.3**) To avoid the gibberish, decode your files, as shown in **Code Listing 13.3**.

Code Listing 13.3 Uudecoding files is straightforward.

```
[ejr@hobbes compression]$ uudecode rowboat.uue
[ejr@hobbes compression]$ ls -l row*
-rw-rw-r--   1 ejr      users      128886
  → Jul 27 09:52 rowboat.jpg
-rw-r--r--   1 ejr      users      177606
  → Jul 27 09:51 rowboat.uue
[ejr@hobbes compression]$
```

To decode files with uudecode:

◆ `uudecode rowboat.jpg`

  At the shell prompt, type **uudecode** followed by the name of the file to decode (**Code Listing 13.3**).

✔ Tips

- If you have a file that you suspect is uuencoded, use **head** plus the file name to view the top ten lines of the file. If it's really uuencoded, you'll see a line saying so at the top, as shown in **Code Listing 13.4**. The 644 in the list is the file's permissions and `rowboat.jpg` is the file name that the extracted file will have. See Chapter 5 for highly interesting details about file permissions.
- When you receive an encoded file, you might have to uncompress or unzip it in addition to decoding it. See the appropriate sections later in this chapter for details.

Code Listing 13.4 Use the head command to view the top of a file. The "begin" line is the tipoff that it's a uuencoded file, with 644 permissions and the name of rowboat.jpg.

```
[ejr@hobbes compression]$ head rowboat.uue
begin 664 rowboat.jpg
M"<@>H@("'@("'@("'@("'@("'@("'@("'@("'@("'@("'@("'@("'@("'@("
M("'@4F%N9&]M(%5.25@@1F]R='5N97,A"@H*"@I)9B!Y;W4G<F4@;F]T('!A
M<G0@;V8@=&AE('-O;'5T:6]N+"!Y;W4G<F4@<&%R="!O9B!T:&4@<')E8VEP
M:71A=&4N"@H*"@I4:&4@;VYL>2!R96%L;'D@9V]O9"!P;&%C92!T;R!B=7D@
M;'5M8F5R(&ES(&%T(&$@<W1O<F4@=VAE<F4@=&AE(&QU;6)E<@IH87,@86QR
M96%D>2!B965N(&-U="!A;F0@871T86-H960@=&]G971H97(@:6X@=&AE(&90
M<FT@;V8@9G5R;FET=7)E+'IF:6YI<VAE9"P@86YD('!U="!I;G-I9&4@8F]X
M97,N"B'@("'@("'@("'@("'M+2!$879E($$)A<G)Y+"''B5&AE(%1A;6EN
M9R!O9B!T:&4@4V-R97<B"@H*"@HB1&ES8V\@:7,@=&\\@;75S:6,@=VAA="!%
[ejr@hobbes compression]$
```

Archiving with tar

Occasionally, you'll want to take a bunch of files and make them into one file, when you're archiving information, for example. You might think of it as tossing a bunch of toys into a toy box—that is, taking a bunch of related things and storing them all in one place.

Using `tar` (which came from *t*ape *ar*chive), you can take a bunch of files and store them as a single, uncompressed file (see **Code Listing 13.5**). You'll use `tar` files not only to store information, but also to create a single source for compressing and gzipping files, which are discussed later in this chapter.

Code Listing 13.5 Tarring files binds them all together into a single file.

```
[ejr@hobbes compression]$ ls -l
total 2290
drwxrwxr-x   2 ejr      users       1024 Jul 23 10:56 Feather
drwxrwxr-x   2 ejr      users       1024 Jul 23 10:49 Zipadeedoodah
-rw-rw-r--   1 ejr      users      53678 Jul 23 06:42 bigfile.gz
-rw-rw-r--   1 ejr      users      53678 Jul 23 10:16 bigfile.new.gz
-rw-rw-r--   1 ejr      users      73989 Jul 23 10:16 bigfile.uue
-rw-rw-r--   1 ejr      users     128886 Jul 23 11:45 file1.htm
-rw-rw-r--   1 ejr      users     128886 Jul 23 11:45 file2.html
-rw-rw-r--   1 ejr      users     686080 Jul 23 10:41 folder.tar
-rw-rw-r--   1 ejr      users     268156 Jul 23 06:53 folderzip.zip
-rw-rw-r--   1 ejr      users     128886 Jul 23 06:37 fortunes1.txt
-rw-rw-r--   1 ejr      users      55124 Jul 23 06:38 fortunes1.zip
-rw-rw-r--   1 ejr      users          0 Jul 23 11:21 gzip
-rw-rw-r--   1 ejr      users      73978 Jul 23 11:15 home.gz.uue
-rw-r--r--   1 ejr      users     177607 Jul 27 09:34 house.uue
-rw-rw-r--   1 ejr      users      53792 Jul 23 06:52 newzip.zip
-rw-rw-r--   1 ejr      users     128886 Jul 23 08:19 ournewhouse.jpg
-rw-rw-r--   1 ejr      users     128886 Jul 27 09:52 rowboat.jpg
-rw-r--r--   1 ejr      users     177606 Jul 27 09:51 rowboat.uue
drwxrwxr-x   3 ejr      users       1024 Jul 23 12:56 temp
[ejr@hobbes compression]$ tar -cf tarredfilename.tar Feather
[ejr@hobbes compression]$
```

To archive a directory with tar:

1. `ls -l`

   For starters, type `ls -l` at the shell prompt to verify the name of the directory you're going to tar.

2. `tar -cf tarredfilename.tar Feather`

   Type `tar`, followed by
   - The `-cf` flags (to create a file)
   - The name you want the tarred (archived) file to have (`tarredfilename.tar` in this example)
   - The name (or names) of the directory or files to tar (`Feather`, here)

✔ Tips

- See the section called *Combining commands* later in this chapter for time-saving ideas for combining and compressing files all in one swell foop.
- You can add the `v` flag to the `tar` command flags (`-vcf`) to get a verbose description of what's being tarred.
- If you want to sound like a real UNIX geek, refer to tarred files as "tarballs."

Unarchiving files with tar

You'll also use `tar` to unarchive files, where you take all of the individual files out of the single tarred file—like dumping the bunch of toys out of the toy box—as shown in **Code Listing 13.6**.

To unarchive files with tar:

- `tar -xf labrea.tar`

  At the shell prompt, type `tar -xf` (here, `x` means extract), followed by the name of the tarred file you want to unarchive. The bunch of once-tarred files will be separated into the original files or directories, as shown in **Code Listing 13.6**.

To unarchive selected files with tar:

- `tar -xf labrea.tar "*mammoth*"`

  You can also extract only specified files from a `tar` file. You might do this to restore just a couple of files from a backup archive, for example. This command extracts all files that have `mammoth` in their names from the `labrea.tar` file and places them back where they belong (**Code Listing 13.7**).

✔ Tip

- Consider moving tarred files into a temporary directory before you unarchive them. When you unarchive, `tar` overwrites any files with the same names as files that are extracted, but using a temporary directory will prevent this.
- Use `tar -tf` filename to list the files (to check your work, perhaps, or find a backup file) without actually unarchiving the files.

Code Listing 13.6 Untarring files reconstructs the original directory structure.

```
[ejr@hobbes compression]$ tar -xf labrea.tar
[ejr@hobbes compression]$ ls -l Labrea/
total 483
-rw-r--r--   1 ejr      users       53678
  → Jul 27 10:05 bigfile.gz
-rw-r--r--   1 ejr      users      128886
  → Jul 27 10:06 mammoth.jpg
-rw-r--r--   1 ejr      users      177607
  → Jul 27 10:05 house.uue
-rw-r--r--   1 ejr      users      128886
  → Jul 27 10:06 rowboat.jpg
[ejr@hobbes compression]$
```

Code Listing 13.7 Unarchive just a single file to replace a missing or corrupt file.

```
[ejr@hobbes compression]$ tar -xf labrea.tar
  → "*mammoth*"
[ejr@hobbes compression]$ ls -l Labrea/m*
-rw-r--r--   1 ejr      users      128886
  → Jul 27 10:06 Labrea/mammoth.jpg
[ejr@hobbes compression]$
```

Compressing files with compress

Compressing a file just means making it smaller so that it takes up less hard-disk space. It's like filling a toy box, closing the lid, then sitting on it to moosh the contents so that they fit into a smaller space. Any time you create a file that you'll be sending via ftp or that people will access through the Web, you'll want to compress the file so that it takes less time to send, download, or whatever. As **Code Listing 13.8** shows, you compress files using the `compress` command.

To compress a file with compress:

◆ `compress labrea.tar`

At the shell prompt, type `compress` followed by the file name. Here, we're compressing a tarred file, which contains multiple files. As you can see in **Code Listing 13.8**, the compressed file has a new extension (`.Z`) that shows that it's compressed, and it replaces the original, uncompressed file.

✔ Tips

- You can only compress one file at a time. If you have multiple files you want to compress, consider archiving them first using `tar`, then compressing the single archived file. See the section called *Archiving files with* `tar`, earlier in this chapter.
- You can add the `-c` flag to `compress` to leave the original file untouched and send the compressed version to standard output (where you'll probably specify a name and save it to a file). For example, you might use `compress -c labrea.tar > labrea.tar.Z`. See Chapter 1 for some mighty interesting information on redirecting output, as is shown here.

Code Listing 13.8 Listing files before and after compressing them lets you see how much smaller the new file is.

```
[ejr@hobbes compression]$ ls -l l*
-rw-r--r--   1 ejr      users      501760 Jul 27 10:06 labrea.tar
[ejr@hobbes compression]$ compress labrea.tar
[ejr@hobbes compression]$ ls -l l*
-rw-r--r--   1 ejr      users      297027 Jul 27 10:06 labrea.tar.Z
[ejr@hobbes compression]$
```

Uncompressing files with uncompress

Compressing a file is handy for reducing the amount of disk space it uses, but you can't do much with a compressed file—directly, at least. You'll need to uncompress it first. As **Code Listing 13.9** shows, you do so using the `uncompress` command.

To uncompress a file with uncompress:

- `uncompress labrea.tar.Z`

  At the shell prompt, type `uncompress` followed by the full file name of the file to uncompress. The compressed file is replaced by the uncompressed file, which is named like the original, but without the `.Z` (see **Code Listing 13.9**).

✔ Tips

- Remember that uncompressed files take up more space—sometimes lots more space—than compressed files. You might want to check your storage quota with your ISP before you uncompress a file to make sure that you don't exceed your limit. As Chapter 7 explains, you can check your quota by typing `quota -v` at the shell prompt.
- You can add the `-c` flag to `uncompress` to leave the original file untouched and send the uncompressed version to standard output. For example, you might use `uncompress -c tarred.tar.Z > tarred.tar`. See Chapter 1 for more information on redirecting output, as is shown here.
- You can also use `gunzip` to uncompress compressed files. Check out *Unzipping zipped files with* `gunzip` later in this chapter.

Code Listing 13.9 You can uncompress files with a single swift command, and possibly double your disk usage at the same time, as shown here.

```
[ejr@hobbes compression]$ ls -l l*
-rw-r--r--   1 ejr      users      297027 Jul 27 10:06 labrea.tar.Z
[ejr@hobbes compression]$ uncompress labrea.tar.Z
[ejr@hobbes compression]$ ls -l l*
-rw-r--r--   1 ejr      users      501760 Jul 27 10:06 labrea.tar
[ejr@hobbes compression]$
```

Zipping a file or directory with gzip

If you only want to compress a single file or directory, you might choose `gzip`, rather than `compress`. `gzip` is more efficient so you wind up with smaller files than you do with `compress`. As **Code Listing 13.10** shows, you use `gzip` much the same way that you use `compress`.

To zip a file or directory with gzip:

1. `ls -l z*`

   At the shell prompt, use `ls -l` to confirm the name of the file or directory you want to zip. In this example, we're looking for `z` (as in zipadeedoodah) files.

2. `gzip zipadeedoodah.tar`

   Type `gzip` followed by the name of the file or directory to `gzip`. The zipped file will replace the unzipped version and will have a new `.gz` extension

✔ Tips

- You can `tar` a group of files then compress the single file using `gzip`.
- If you want to keep a copy of the original, unzipped file, try `gzip -c filetogzip > ➝compressed.gz`.
- If the compressed files will be accessed by someone using Windows, you should consider using `zip`, which is discussed later in this chapter. Although it'd be more convenient, `gzip` is not the same as good old Pkzip or `.zip` files used in DOS and Windows.

Code Listing 13.10 Use gzip to zip up those bulky tar files.

```
[ejr@hobbes compression]$ ls -l z*
-rw-r--r--   1 ejr      users      501760 Jul 27 10:22 zipadeedoodah.tar
[ejr@hobbes compression]$ gzip zipadeedoodah.tar
[ejr@hobbes compression]$ ls -l z*
-rw-r--r--   1 ejr      users      239815 Jul 27 10:22 zipadeedoodah.tar.gz
[ejr@hobbes compression]$
```

Unzipping a gzip file with gunzip

To access gzipped files, you'll need to unzip them. You do so using gunzip, as **Code Listing 13.11** shows.

To unzip a gzip file with gunzip:

1. `ls *.gz`

   At the shell prompt, verify the name of the gzipped file with `ls *.gz` (**Code Listing 13.11**).

2. `gunzip zipadeedoodah.tar`

   Enter `gunzip` and the name of the file to unzip. `gunzip` will uncompress the file(s) and return you to the shell prompt.

✔ Tips

- When you're unzipping files with `gunzip`, you're not required to enter the file extension. `gunzip zipadeedoodah` would work just as well as `gunzip zipadeedoo` → `dah.tar`.
- Some systems don't recognize the `gunzip` command, so you might need to use `gzip -d` to uncompress the files.
- If you have a compressed file that you know is text—`oldfunnysayingsfromthenet.gz`, for example—you can uncompress it (without deleting the original file) and view it with a single command: `zcat` → `oldfunnysayingsfromthenet | more`.
- `gunzip` understands how to uncompress most (compressed) files, including those compressed with `compress` or zip files from DOS/Windows systems.

Code Listing 13.11 Use gunzip to uncompress zipped files.

```
[ejr@hobbes compression]$ ls -l *.gz
-rw-rw-r--   1 ejr      users       53678 Jul 23 06:42 bigfile.gz
-rw-rw-r--   1 ejr      users       53678 Jul 23 10:16 bigfile.new.gz
-rw-r--r--   1 ejr      users      239819 Jul 27 10:22 zipadeedoodah.tar.gz
[ejr@hobbes compression]$ gunzip zipadeedoodah.tar
[ejr@hobbes compression]$ ls -l z*
-rw-r--r--   1 ejr      users      501760 Jul 27 10:22 zipadeedoodah.tar
[ejr@hobbes compression]$ ls -l *.gz
-rw-rw-r--   1 ejr      users       53678 Jul 23 06:42 bigfile.gz
-rw-rw-r--   1 ejr      users       53678 Jul 23 10:16 bigfile.new.gz
[ejr@hobbes compression]$
```

Code Listing 13.12 Use zip to compress files, particularly those you'll share with Windows users.

```
[ejr@hobbes compression]$ ls -l z*
-rw-r--r--   1 ejr      users      501760
  → Jul 27 10:22 zipadeedoodah
[ejr@hobbes compression]$ zip zipped
  → zipadeedoodah
  adding: zipadeedoodah.tar (deflated 52%)
[ejr@hobbes compression]$ ls -l z*
-rw-r--r--   1 ejr      users      501760
  → Jul 27 10:22 zipadeedoodah
-rw-r--r--   1 ejr      users      239943
  → Jul 27 10:41 zipped.zip
[ejr@hobbes compression]$
```

Zipping files and directories with zip

If you're working with files and directories that will be accessed on the Windows platform, you might need to use `zip` (rather than `gzip`). This `zip` is like DOS or Windows `zip`, so it's a safer option than `gzip`, which can work, but it depends on the software available on the Windows system .`zip` files are compressed to save disk space and sometimes contain multiple files (see **Code Listing 13.12**).

To zip files or directories with zip:

1. `ls -l`

   At the shell prompt, use `ls -l` to confirm the names of the files or directories you want to zip.

2. `zip zipped zipadeedoodah`

   Type `zip`, followed by the name of the zip file you're creating (without an extension), followed by the name of the file or directory to zip. Then just twiddle your thumbs while waiting for UNIX to zip your files (**Code Listing 13.12**).

✔ Tips

- Some UNIX systems don't offer the `zip` command. In this case, if you need to share files with Windows users, use either `gzip` or `compress`, send the file, and tell your colleagues that they can use Winzip, among other programs, to extract the files.
- If you zip a directory, you zip all the files within it.
- If you can't get the tune "Zip-A-Dee-Doo-Dah" out of your head after these examples, try humming "The Candy Man" or "I'd Like to Teach the World to Sing," or whistling the "Colonel Bogey March" (theme from *The Bridge over the River Kwai*).

Unzipping zipped files with unzip

You can unzip zipped files using **unzip**, which is logical because you certainly wouldn't unzip zipped files with unVelcro or unsnap (**Code Listing 13.13**).

To unzip a zip file using unzip:

1. `ls *.zip`

   At the shell prompt, verify the name of the zip file with `ls *.zip`.

2. `unzip zipped`

   Enter `unzip` and the name of the file to unzip (without the .zip extension). `unzip` will uncompress the file(s) and return you to the shell prompt.

✔ Tips

- If you attempt to unzip a file and the file or files to be unzipped already exist, `unzip` will prompt for you each one to determine if you want to overwrite (destroy) the existing file, cancel the unzipping process, or rename the file you're unzipping to a safe name.
- `gunzip` also understands how to uncompress `.zip` files, so you can use `gunzip` instead of `unzip`, if you'd like. On the UNIX side of things, use whatever seems easiest to you, or `gunzip` if you really don't care. If you're providing files to Windows users, `zip` is somewhat more reliable because the format it creates is more standard.

Code Listing 13.13 unzip lets you uncompress files without accidentally obliterating them.

```
[ejr@hobbes compression]$ ls -l *.zip
-rw-rw-r--    1 ejr      users      268156
  → Jul 23 06:53 folderzip.zip
-rw-rw-r--    1 ejr      users       55124
  Jul 23 06:38 fortunes1.zip
-rw-rw-r--    1 ejr      users       53792
  → Jul 23 06:52 newzip.zip
-rw-r--r--    1 ejr      users      239943
  → Jul 27 10:41 zipped.zip
[ejr@hobbes compression]$ unzip zipped.zip
Archive:  zipped.zip
replace zipadeedoodah.tar?
  → [y]es, [n]o, [A]ll, [N]one, [r]ename: y
  inflating: zipadeedoodah.tar
[ejr@hobbes compression]$
```

Combining commands

As we've shown you in this chapter, you use separate commands to encode/unencode, tar/untar, compress/uncompress, and zip/unzip files and directories. A lot of times, however, you can pipe commands together and run them in sequence, saving you time and hassle. For example, as **Code Listing 13.14** shows, you can uudecode and gunzip files at the same time by piping the commands together. You can also uncompress and untar at one time, and you can tar and gzip at one time.

To uudecode and gunzip at one time:

1. `ls -l`

   Use `ls -l` to verify the existence of your uuencoded and zipped file.

2. `uudecode -o /dev/stdout home.gz.uue → | gunzip > home`

   Here, we use `-o /dev/stdout` to send the uudecode output to the standard output, then pipe the output of the uudecode command to `gunzip`, then redirect the output of `gunzip` to the home file. Whew! See **Code Listing 13.14** for the details.

Code Listing 13.14 Decoding and unzipping at once is a little cryptic, but saves your typity typity fingers.

```
[ejr@hobbes compression]$ ls -l h*
-rw-rw-r--   1 ejr      users       73978 Jul 23 11:15 home.gz.uue
-rw-r--r--   1 ejr      users      177607 Jul 27 09:34 house.uue
[ejr@hobbes compression]$ uudecode -o /dev/stdout home.gz.uue | gunzip > home
[ejr@hobbes compression]$ ls -l h*
-rw-r--r--   1 ejr      users      128886 Jul 27 10:48 home
-rw-rw-r--   1 ejr      users       73978 Jul 23 11:15 home.gz.uue
-rw-r--r--   1 ejr      users      177607 Jul 27 09:34 house.uue
[ejr@hobbes compression]$
```

To uncompress and untar at one time:

- `uncompress filename.tar.Z | tar xf -`

  At the shell prompt, type `uncompress` followed by the file name (as usual) and pipe that output to `tar`. Follow the `tar` command and flags with a - so that `tar` will be able to save the file to the intended name (**Code Listing 13.15**).

To tar and gzip at one time:

- `tar cf - Labrea | gzip >` → `labrea.tar.gz`

  At the shell prompt, enter your `tar` command as usual but add a – (and a space) before the file name so the output can be piped. Then, pipe the output to `gzip` and redirect the output of that to a file name with the `tar` and `gz` extensions to show that the file has been tarred and gzipped (**Code Listing 13.16**).

Code Listing 13.15 After you find the compressed files, you can uncompress and untar them at once, then use ls -ld (long and directory flags) to check your work.

```
[ejr@hobbes compression]$ ls -l *.Z
-rw-r--r--   1 ejr      users      297027
  → Jul 27 10:06 labrea.tar.Z
[ejr@hobbes compression]$ uncompress
  → labrea.tar.Z | tar -xf -
[ejr@hobbes compression]$ ls -l l*
-rw-r--r--   1 ejr      users      501760
  → Jul 27 10:06 labrea.tar
[ejr@hobbes compression]$ ls -ld L*
drwxr-xr-x   2 ejr      users        1024
  → Jul 27 10:16 Labrea
[ejr@hobbes compression]$
```

Code Listing 13.16 You can efficiently tar and gzip all at once as well.

```
[ejr@hobbes compression]$ ls -ld F*
drwxrwxr-x   2 ejr      users        1024 Jul 23 10:56 Feather
[ejr@hobbes compression]$ tar -cf - Feather | gzip > feather.tar.gz
[ejr@hobbes compression]$ ls -l f*
-rw-r--r--   1 ejr      users      106752 Jul 27 10:54 feather.tar.gz
-rw-rw-r--   1 ejr      users      128886 Jul 23 11:45 file1.htm
-rw-rw-r--   1 ejr      users      128886 Jul 23 11:45 file2.html
-rw-rw-r--   1 ejr      users      686080 Jul 23 10:41 folder.tar
-rw-rw-r--   1 ejr      users      268156 Jul 23 06:53 folderzip.zip
-rw-rw-r--   1 ejr      users      128886 Jul 23 06:37 fortunes1.txt
-rw-rw-r--   1 ejr      users       55124 Jul 23 06:38 fortunes1.zip
[ejr@hobbes compression]$
```

Installing Your Own Software

14

If you use UNIX long enough, you'll eventually want or need to install new software for your use. Installing software could mean just installing a shell script that you get from a friend, or it could mean installing a full-fledged program that you download from the Internet.

In this chapter, we'll explore the process for installing software on UNIX systems. Work through each section in the order provided, and keep in mind that:

- The process for installing UNIX software is a bit more complicated than doing the same on Windows or Macintosh systems.
- The example we use here will probably differ slightly from the exact process you'll need to use for the programs or scripts you choose for your system. In the example we're installing a program called `rpm`, distributed with RedHat Linux systems, which makes it easier to install software that comes in `rpm` format.
- You should probably check with your system administrator for specifics on what you can and cannot install on the system. Most ISPs will let you install what you want, but others may have specific restrictions or even make it impossible to compile software in your account.

Chapter contents

Understanding UNIX software installation

When installing software on your UNIX system, keep in mind two things. First, most software, including scripts, relies on other programs or scripts being available at specific places within the system. For example, a script might require that the `bash` shell be available and located at `/bin/bash`. Or, a program might expect that it will be in `/usr/local/bin` and that all user home directories will be under `/home`. So, you should pay special attention during the installation process to make sure that all other required scripts or programs are available.

Second, programs (but not scripts) are *compiled*, which means that they're taken from one probably-mostly-readable-to-you language (generically called *source code*) and translated into computer-readable files (often called *binaries*). As software is compiled, hardware and operating system-specific characteristics (or dependencies) are built in. So, a program that's compiled to run on a specific platform and operating system cannot run on other ones—that is, a program compiled on Linux on a Pentium cannot run on Linux on an Alpha, Solaris on a Pentium, or Digital UNIX on an Alpha.

In fact, most UNIX programs are distributed as source code, not as binaries, so you can compile them for your particular system when installing.

✔ Tip

- Before you get started with the next section, you might cruise back to Chapters 1 and 2 for information about exploring your UNIX system and to Chapter 7 for a reminder of how to find out what operating system and hardware you're using.

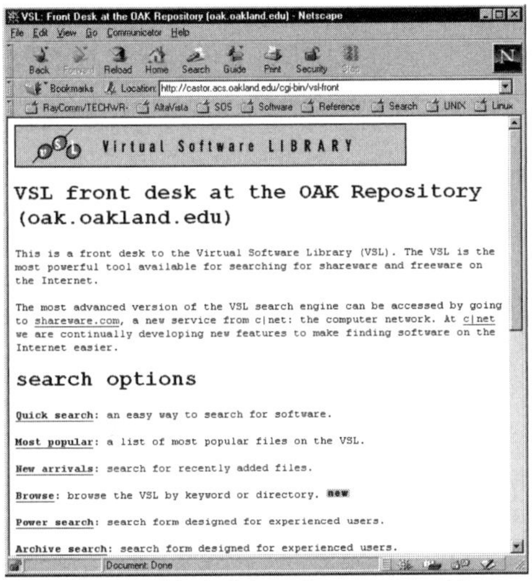

Figure 14.1 You'll find all the software you could ever want on many software archives on the Web.

✔ Tip

- If you'll be downloading and installing a lot of software, and if you have no significant quota limitations, look into downloading and installing `rpm`. It's a neat compression/installation/configuration program that makes installing UNIX software in this special format as easy as installing a program in Windows or on a Macintosh. It's standard on RedHat Linux but has been used on many different UNIX systems. We've chosen to illustrate downloading and installing `rpm` as the example for this chapter.

Finding UNIX software

Before you can install software on your UNIX system, you have to find the software and locate the correct version of the software. We recommend the following places to look:

- Search the Web using Yahoo! (`www.yahoo.com`) or AltaVista (`www.altavista.digital.com`) to find downloadable software.
- Visit specific software sites, such as the Virtual Software Library at `www.shareware.com` or `http://castor.acs.oakland.edu/cgi-bin/vsl-front` (**Figure 14.1**).

In using these resources, you'll come upon the following:

- Code for Perl, shell, or other scripts: You'll generally have to download, uncompress, and unarchive these, then edit some of the files to insert system-specific settings.
- Source code for programs: With these, you'll have to download, uncompress, and unarchive, and set some system-specific settings. Then, you'll have to "make" them, which tells the make program on your system to compile and install the programs.
- Pre-compiled binaries: You'll have to scout through the names available and find the name (and operating system, and platform) that corresponds to the system you want to run the software on. Then, you'll have to download it, decompress it, and put it where you want it. This is the easiest solution, when it works; however, keep in mind that you might download it, uncompress it, and find that it still won't work, leaving you with no choice but to download and compile the source code.

Downloading, placing, and decompressing software

Once you've found software you want to install, your next step is to download it, put it in the proper place, then decompress it (**Code Listing 14.1**). This process includes several tasks that you've already learned in other parts of this book, so we won't go over them in detail here. For this section, we assume that you already know what you want to download and where it can be found. In the example, we're downloading the latest version of `rpm`, from `ftp.cdrom.com`, in the directory `/pub/linux/redhat/code/rpm`, with the name `rpm-2.5.1.tar.gz`.

To download, place, and decompress software:

1. `ftp ftp.cdrom.com`

   Use `ftp` to connect to the software archive (or whatever you're downloading from). (See *Getting files from the Internet with* `ftp`, in Chapter 12 for the specifics.) See **Code Listing 14.1** for the complete `ftp` process.

2. `anonymous`

   Log in as `anonymous`.

3. `yourid@youraddress.com`

   Provide your e-mail address as the password.

4. `cd /pub/linux/redhat/code/rpm`

   Change to the appropriate directory.

5. `binary`

   Set `ftp` to transfer a binary file, because an archive is a compressed file, not a plain text file.

6. `get rpm-2.5.1.tar.gz`

   Issue the `get` command to transfer the software. You may have to wait a little

Code Listing 14.1 The process of downloading software and getting ready to install it is a little long, but not too tricky.

```
[ejr@hobbes ejr]$ ftp ftp.cdrom.com
Connected to wcarchive.cdrom.com.
220 wcarchive.cdrom.com FTP server (Version DG-3.1.21 Fri Jul 31 05:07:36 PDT 19
8) ready.
Name (ftp.cdrom.com:ejr): anonymous
331 Guest login ok, send your email address as password.
Password:
230-Welcome to wcarchive - home FTP site for Walnut Creek CDROM.
230-There are currently 3197 users out of 3200 possible.
230-
230-Most of the files in this area are also available on CDROM.  You can send
230-email to info@cdrom.com for more information or to order, or visit our Web
230-site at http://www.cdrom.com.  For tech support about our products, please
230-email support@cdrom.com.  You may also call our toll-free number:
230-1-800-786-9907 or +1-510-674-0783.  Please keep in mind that we only offer
230-technical support for our CDROM products and not for the files on our
230-FTP server.
230-
230-Please send mail to ftp-bugs@ftp.cdrom.com if you experience any problems.
230-Please also let us know if there is something we don't have that you think
230-we should!
230-
230 Guest login ok, access restrictions apply.
Remote system type is UNIX.
Using binary mode to transfer files.
ftp> cd pub/linux/redhat/code/rpm
250 CWD command successful.
ftp> binary
200 Type set to I.
ftp> get rpm-2.5.1.tar.gz
local: rpm-2.5.1.tar.gz remote: rpm-2.5.1.tar.gz
200 PORT command successful.
150 Opening BINARY mode data connection for 'rpm-2.5.1.tar.gz' (589054 bytes).
226 Transfer complete.
589054 bytes received in 350 secs (1.6 Kbytes/sec)
ftp> quit
221 Goodbye!
[ejr@hobbes ejr]$ mv rpm-2.5.1.tar.gz ~/src/rpm-2.5.1.tar.gz
[ejr@hobbes ejr]$ cd ~/src
[ejr@hobbes src]$ gunzip rpm-2.5.1.tar.gz
[ejr@hobbes src]$ tar -ixf rpm-2.5.1.tar
[ejr@hobbes src]$ cd rpm-2.5.1
[ejr@hobbes rpm-2.5.1]$
```

while, depending on how how fast your connection is.

7. `quit`

   Quit the `ftp` program after the transfer is complete.

8. `mv rpm-2.5.1.tar.gz ~/src/`
   `→ rpm-2.5.1.tar.gz`

   Move the archive file into the `src` subdirectory under your main directory. (Create the directory first, if necessary.) You could use any directory, but it's standard to use an `src` directory because many programs expect that they'll be installed from an `src` directory.

9. `cd ~/src`

   Change into the `src` directory.

10. `gunzip rpm-2.5.1.tar.gz`

    Unzip the source code archive with `gunzip`. You'll be left with a `.tar` file.

11. `tar -ixf rpm-2.5.1.tar`

    Untar the archive with `tar -ixf` plus the file name. With most programs, you'll get a new subdirectory that has the same name as the program (`rpm-2.5.1` in this case), with lots of files and sub-subdirectories in it.

12. `cd rpm-2.5.1`

    Change into your new directory, and get ready to install. Whew!

✔ Tip

- You can also use `lynx` to download your software, which might be easier if you used `lynx` to browse the Web and find the software.

Configuring software

After you've downloaded and uncompressed your new software, you'll have to configure and tweak it to conform to your system. In general, the changes you'll make will be things like:

- Adjusting path names (e.g., to install it into `/home/yourid/bin` rather than into `/usr/local/bin`, where you likely cannot install software).
- Specifying what kind of UNIX system you're working on.
- Inserting your e-mail address and similar data.
- Choosing one of two or three system-specific settings. What to choose for each system is clearly marked in the files you'll be using.

If you're installing a program that will be compiled, your steps will closely resemble these. If you're installing a script, the steps will likely differ somewhat, but go ahead and read through these steps because the principles of what to change are the same for scripts and programs.

Precisely what changes you'll have to make (in programs or scripts) are almost always documented in the `README` file that comes with the software, in the `Makefile` (in the case of programs), or in the actual `.pl` or `.sh` files that you'll run (in the case of scripts). (See **Code Listing 14.2.**) So be sure to read these files! The steps in this section assume that you're starting in the main directory of uncompressed and untarred files that you downloaded.

To configure software:

1. `more README*`

   To begin, type `more README*` at the shell prompt to see the README file one screen at a time. This file should give you installation instructions as well as information about what details you need to provide. **Code Listing 14.2** shows part of rpm's README file.

2. `ls configure`

   Type `ls configure` to see if there's a file named `configure` in the current directory.

   - If you have a `configure` file, just continue to step 3.
   - If you don't have a `configure` file, skip ahead to step 4.

3. `./configure`

   Usually you can just enter `./configure` to run `configure` and let the configuration

Code Listing 14.2 Checking out the instructions is essential.

```
[ejr@hobbes rpm-2.5.1]$ more README*
::::::::::::::
README
::::::::::::::
This is RPM, the Red Hat Package Manager.

The latest releases are always available at:

        ftp://ftp.redhat.com/pub/redhat/code/rpm

Additional RPM documentation (papers, slides, HOWTOs) can also be
found at the same site.

There is a mailing list for discussion of RPM issues, rpm-list@redhat.com.
To subscribe, send a message to rpm-list-request@redhat.com with the word
"subscribe" in the subject line.

RPM was written and is maintained by:

    Erik Troan <ewt@redhat.com>
    Marc Ewing <marc@redhat.com>

See the CREDITS file for a list of folks who have helped us out
tremendously.  RPM is Copyright (c) 1997 by Red Hat Software, Inc.,
--More--(89%)
```

happen by itself (**Code Listing 14.3**), though you may have a little more to do. `configure` makes a special `Makefile`, just for you, which makes the next steps much easier.

4. `cp Makefile Makefile.bak`

   Make a backup copy of the `Makefile` before you start editing it, so you can eas-

Code Listing 14.3 The ./configure program goes on and on.

```
[ejr@hobbes rpm-2.5.1]$ ./configure
loading cache ./config.cache
checking host system type... i486-unknown-linux
checking target system type... i486-unknown-linux
checking build system type... i486-unknown-linux
checking for gcc... (cached) gcc
checking whether the C compiler (gcc  ) works... yes
checking whether the C compiler (gcc  ) is a cross-compiler... no
checking whether we are using GNU C... (cached) yes
checking whether gcc accepts -g... (cached) yes
checking how to run the C preprocessor... (cached) gcc -E
checking whether gcc needs -traditional... (cached) no
checking for a BSD compatible install... (cached) /usr/bin/install -c
checking what additional CFLAGS are needed to link statically... -static
checking POSIX chmod...... yes
checking for mkdir... (cached) /bin/mkdir
checking if /bin/mkdir supports -p... yes
checking for AIX... no
checking for minix/config.h... (cached) no
checking for POSIXized ISC... no
checking for mawk... (cached) gawk
checking whether ln -s works... (cached) yes
checking whether make sets ${MAKE}... (cached) yes
checking for ranlib... (cached) ranlib
checking for ar... (cached) ar
checking GNU gzip...... yes
checking for bzip2...... no
configure: warning: RPM will not work without GNU gzip.
checking old version of patch... patch later then 2.2 found

creating ./config.status
creating Makefile
[ejr@hobbes rpm-2.5.1]$ cp Makefile Makefile.bak
[ejr@hobbes rpm-2.5.1]$
```

ily recover from any mistakes. If you didn't use `configure`, the `Makefile` was one of the files you untarred in the previous section. Otherwise, the `Makefile` was just created by `configure`.

You'll nearly always have a `Makefile`, but you should also make a backup of any other files you're going to edit. (And remember, the `README` file will tell you what to do for the specific software you're using.)

5. `vi Makefile`

   Use the text editor of your choice to edit the `Makefile`, reading the instructions in it and checking the accuracy of things like directory and path names, program names, and similar settings. If you don't know what something is or does, ignore it for now. Even if `configure` automatically set up the `Makefile` for you, you should still glance through it to make sure that it's putting stuff into the correct directories and that it doesn't expect any additional information from you.

   Figure 14.2 shows the `Makefile` for `rpm`. All that we changed was the base directory.

6. Save the file and close out of the editor.

   There! You've configured your software!

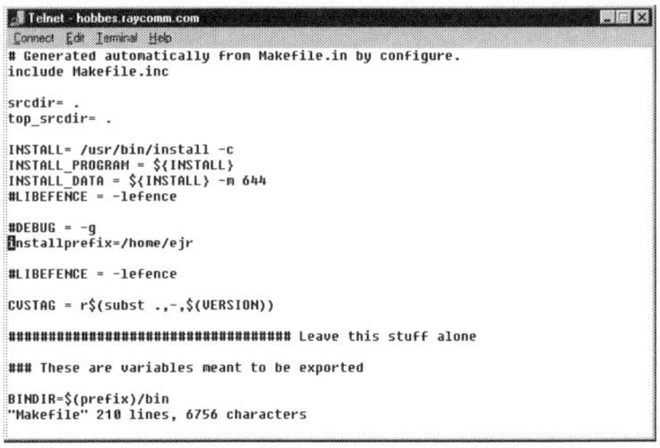

Figure 14.2 Fortunately, many programs require minimal changes.

✔ Tips

- Exactly what steps you'll have to take will depend on the software. Scripts will come as plain text files and you might not have to do anything besides download them. Most of the time, however, you'll have to tweak scripts as well as programs (although the scripts won't need to be compiled).
- A good rule of thumb is to make minimal changes to the `Makefile`. Doing more than is required often causes the program not to compile or gives you a bazillion error messages. If this happens, just go to your backup `Makefile`, make a new copy, and try again making only the necessary modifications. Better to make too few changes than to take the time and effort to make too many.
- Pay particular attention to the paths to programs and files as you're editing scripts and other setup files—a little error in a path can be hard to spot and completely prevent the new software from working.

Compiling and installing with make install

Your final step is to get the software installed on the UNIX system. With some programs, all you'll have to do is put the files in the directory where you want them to live (often `~/bin` for programs or scripts, or sometimes `cgi-bin` for scripts or programs for Web use). With others, though, you'll have to compile first, then install.

You can compile and install using `make install`, which reads the `Makefile` (to see how to set everything up) and takes care of compiling and installing for you (**Code Listing 14.4**). Again, be sure to read the instructions carefully before you start and follow them exactly.

Code Listing 14.4 make and make install both deliver incredible quantities of junk (but hopefully no error message) to your screen.

```
[ejr@hobbes rpm-2.5.1]$ make
for d in popt  lib build tools po; do \
       (cd $d; make) \
         || case "" in *k*) fail=yes;; *) exit 1;; esac;\
done && test -z "$fail"
make[1]: Entering directory '/home/ejr/src/rpm-2.5.1/popt'
gcc -g -O2  -DHAVE_UNISTD_H=1 -DHAVE_ALLOCA_H=1 -DHAVE_MMAP=1 -DHAVE_STRERROR=1
   -c popt.c -o popt.o
ar rv libpopt.a popt.o
a - popt.o
ranlib libpopt.a
make[1]: Leaving directory '/home/ejr/src/rpm-2.5.1/popt'
make[1]: Entering directory '/home/ejr/src/rpm-2.5.1/lib'
gcc -I/home/ejr/src/rpm-2.5.1 -I/home/ejr/src/rpm-2.5.1 -g -O2  -DHAVE_CONFIG_H
I/home/ejr/src/rpm-2.5.1/lib -I/home/ejr/src/rpm-2.5.1/misc   -c header.c -o hea
er.o

gcc -o rpm2cpio -L/home/ejr/src/rpm-2.5.1/lib -L/home/ejr/src/rpm-2.5.1/build -L
home/ejr/src/rpm-2.5.1/misc -L/home/ejr/src/rpm-2.5.1/popt rpm2cpio.o -lrpmbuild
-lpopt -lrpm  -ldb  -L/usr/local/lib  -lz
[ejr@hobbes rpm-2.5.1]$
```

To compile and install using make install:

1. `make`

   For starters, type `make` at the shell prompt (in the main directory containing your program setup files) to set up all of the variables you specified in the previous section. **Code Listing 14.4** shows what `make` displays on the screen.

   If you see error messages that aren't accompanied by a reassuring "Will continue to use something else" message, you may need to return to editing the `Makefile`. When you `make` successfully, without nasty error messages, you're ready to move ahead to step 2.

2. `make install`

   Type `make install` to finish the process.

3. `./rpm`

   Try out the new software! (Of course, replace `rpm` with the name of the software you installed.)

   We had to look around a little for the software. Based on the `Makefile`, we expected to find it in `~/bin`; however, it was still in the directory from which we installed it. No problem, though. We're specifying `./rpm` to run the program from a directory that's not in the path, as we discussed in Chapter 9.

   Whoops! We've encountered a small problem. The `rpm` program expected to see an `rpmrc` file (with setup data) in a specific place where we (as average users on the system) couldn't put it (**Code Listing 14.5**). Hmmm. What to do, what to do?

4. `./rpm --rcfile ./lib-rpmrc`

   We looked at the error message and found the information the system was looking for. We encountered this problem because we installed the program as a normal user, not as a system administrator; these issues come up fairly frequently. By reading the rpm man page and looking around for a file that sounds and looks like an rc file, we came up with a workaround. At the shell prompt again, we typed in the rpm command, followed by a flag to specify a nonstandard rc file, then the name of the file (**Code Listing 14.6**).

Zowie! It works!

5. `cd ; rm -Rf ~/src/rpm*`.

   After you're sure that everything works right, either tar and gzip the complete

Code Listing 14.5 Type make install to finish the installation process.

```
[ejr@hobbes rpm-2.5.1]$ make install
for d in popt  lib build tools po; do \
       (cd $d; make) \
         || case "" in *k*) fail=yes;; *) exit 1;; esac;\
done && test -z "$fail"
make[1]: Entering directory '/home/ejr/src/rpm-2.5.1/popt'
make[1]: 'libpopt.a' is up to date.
make[1]: Leaving directory '/home/ejr/src/rpm-2.5.1/popt'
make[1]: Entering directory '/home/ejr/src/rpm-2.5.1/lib'
make[1]: Nothing to be done for 'all'.
make[1]: Leaving directory '/home/ejr/src/rpm-2.5.1/lib'
make[1]: Entering directory '/home/ejr/src/rpm-2.5.1/build'
make[1]: Nothing to be done for 'all'.
make[1]: Leaving directory '/home/ejr/src/rpm-2.5.1/build'
make[1]: Entering directory '/home/ejr/src/rpm-2.5.1/tools'
make[1]: Nothing to be done for 'all'.
make[1]: Leaving directory '/home/ejr/src/rpm-2.5.1/tools'
make[1]: Entering directory '/home/ejr/src/rpm-2.5.1/po'
make[1]: Nothing to be done for 'all'.
make[1]: Leaving directory '/home/ejr/src/rpm-2.5.1/po'

/usr/bin/install -c -m 755 -d /home/ejr//usr/local/share/locale/$l/LC_MESSAG
S; \
    /usr/bin/install -c -m 644 $n /home/ejr//usr/local/share/locale/$l/LC_MESSAG
S/rpm.mo; \
done
make[1]: Leaving directory '/home/ejr/src/rpm-2.5.1/po'
[ejr@hobbes rpm-2.5.1]$
```

source tree (in case you need to reinstall). Or, if space is tight, save the `Makefile` and any other files you edited, and remove the rest. (If space is tight and you didn't make any substantive changes to get everything to compile, just `rm` it all.)

✔ Tips

- Be patient, and puzzle your way through if you encounter unexpected errors or if something just doesn't go right. Reading the `Makefile` and source code is your best bet for solving problems.
- In this example, instead of using the `-rcfile` workaround, we could have grepped our way through the files for references to the `rpmrc` file, then changed the references to that file to point to the correct path, then used `make clean`, `make`, and `make install` to get it all the way right.
- After a failed attempt, type `make clean` to clear out the garbage before you try again.
- Sometimes stuff just isn't worth the trouble. Compiling and installing new software can be fairly difficult, and sometimes the problems you encounter aren't easily resolved. In writing this chapter, for example, we had a great program to install, but had to spend about four hours tweaking and fixing it to get it to compile. (That's about three hours and 15 minutes longer than we'd planned on.) This can happen to anyone, so don't get discouraged, but feel free to seek out help or simply find another program that does essentially the same thing—there's enough software out there that technical difficulties in one place shouldn't be any kind of serious obstacle.

Code Listing 14.6 It works! We didn't do anything with it, but it works.

```
[ejr@hobbes rpm-2.5.1]$ ./rpm
Unable to open /usr/local/lib/rpmrc for reading: No such file or directory.
[ejr@hobbes rpm-2.5.1]$

[ejr@hobbes rpm-2.5.1]$ ./rpm --rcfile ./lib-rpmrc
RPM version 2.5
Copyright (C) 1998 - Red Hat Software
This may be freely redistributed under the terms of the GNU Public License

usage: rpm {--help}
       rpm {--version}
       rpm {--initdb}   [--dbpath <dir>]
       rpm {--install -i} [-v] [--hash -h] [--percent] [--force] [--test]
                        [--replacepkgs] [--replacefiles] [--root <dir>]
                        [--excludedocs] [--includedocs] [--noscripts]
                        [--rcfile <file>] [--ignorearch] [--dbpath <dir>]
                        [--prefix <dir>] [--ignoreos] [--nodeps] [--allfiles]
                        [--ftpproxy <host>] [--ftpport <port>] [--justdb]
                        [--noorder] [--relocate oldpath=newpath]
                        [--badreloc] file1.rpm ... fileN.rpm
       rpm {--upgrade -U} [-v] [--hash -h] [--percent] [--force] [--test]
                        [--oldpackage] [--root <dir>] [--noscripts]
                        [--excludedocs] [--includedocs] [--rcfile <file>]
                        [--ignorearch]  [--dbpath <dir>] [--prefix <dir>]
                        [--ftpproxy <host>] [--ftpport <port>]
                        [--ignoreos] [--nodeps] [--allfiles] [--justdb]
                        [--noorder] [--relocate oldpath=newpath]
                        [--badreloc] file1.rpm ... fileN.rpm
       rpm {--query -q} [-afpg] [-i] [-l] [-s] [-d] [-c] [-v] [-R]
                        [--scripts] [--root <dir>] [--rcfile <file>]
                        [--whatprovides] [--whatrequires] [--requires]
                        [--ftpuseport] [--ftpproxy <host>] [--ftpport <port>]
                        [--provides] [--dump] [--dbpath <dir>] [--changelog]
                        [targets]
       rpm {--verify -V -y} [-afpg] [--root <dir>] [--rcfile <file>]
                        [--dbpath <dir>] [--nodeps] [--nofiles] [--noscripts]
                        [--nomd5] [targets]
       rpm {--setperms} [-afpg] [target]
       rpm {--setugids} [-afpg] [target]
       rpm {--erase -e} [--root <dir>] [--noscripts] [--rcfile <file>]
                        [--dbpath <dir>] [--nodeps] [--allmatches]
                        [--justdb] package1 ... packageN
       rpm {-b|t}[plciba] [-v] [--short-circuit] [--clean] [--rcfile  <file>]
```

(continued on next page)

Code Listing 14.6 (continued)

```
                        [--sign] [--test] [--timecheck <s>] [--buildos <os>]
                        [--buildarch <arch>] [--rmsource] specfile
        rpm {--rmsource} [--rcfile <file>] [-v] specfile
        rpm {--rebuild} [--rcfile <file>] [-v] source1.rpm ... sourceN.rpm
        rpm {--recompile} [--rcfile <file>] [-v] source1.rpm ... sourceN.rpm
        rpm {--resign} [--rcfile <file>] package1 package2 ... packageN
        rpm {--addsign} [--rcfile <file>] package1 package2 ... packageN
        rpm {--checksig -K} [--nopgp] [--nomd5] [--rcfile <file>]
                           package1 ... packageN
        rpm {--rebuilddb} [--rcfile <file>] [--dbpath <dir>]
        rpm {--querytags}
[ejr@hobbes rpm-2.5.1]$
```

15

USING HANDY UTILITIES

Just when you thought UNIX was great...it gets better! UNIX gives you a plethora of handy-dandy *utilities*—small programs—that can make your life a bit easier. For example, you might want to use the calendar, calculator, or interactive spell checker. None of these utilities is likely to be essential to your day-to-day UNIX doings; however, they are handy to have and use. Ask your system administrator about which utilities you have available or venture to Chapter 1 to explore your system and find out what's there. In this chapter, we'll look at a few of the most useful ones.

Chapter contents

Calendaring with cal

One of the handiest UNIX utilities is `cal`, which—logically—is a calendar. Find out what today's date is, what day of the week December 31st is, or what the calendar year looks like. As **Code Listing 15.1** shows, all you have to do is type `cal` and any specific options you want.

To use the calendar utility:

1. `cal`

   Type `cal` at the shell prompt to see the current month's calendar, as shown in **Code Listing 15.1**. Then, start playing with options, as shown in the next few steps.

2. `cal -j`

   Use `cal -j` to see the Julian calendar, which shows each day numbered from the beginning of the year.

3. `cal 1999 | more`

   Pipe `cal 1999` to `more` to see the whole year's calendar.

4. `cal 12 1941`

   Type `cal` plus specific dates to view dates for a particular year.

✔ Tips

- Note that `cal` is Y2K compliant. If you ask for `cal 98`, you'll get the calendar for the year 98. That is, 1900 years ago.

- Put `cal` into your startup configuration files to get a reminder of the date whenever you log in. Check out Chapter 8 for details.

Code Listing 15.1 Just type cal to see the current month's calendar, or check out other calendar options with flags.

```
[ejr@hobbes ch15]$ cal
    August 1998
Su Mo Tu We Th Fr Sa
                   1
 2  3  4  5  6  7  8
 9 10 11 12 13 14 15
16 17 18 19 20 21 22
23 24 25 26 27 28 29
30 31
[ejr@hobbes ch15]$ cal -j
       August 1998
Sun Mon Tue Wed Thu Fri Sat
                        213
214 215 216 217 218 219 220
221 222 223 224 225 226 227
228 229 230 231 232 233 234
235 236 237 238 239 240 241
242 243
[ejr@hobbes ch15]$ cal 1999 | more
                               1999

       January               February                 March
Su Mo Tu We Th Fr Sa   Su Mo Tu We Th Fr Sa   Su Mo Tu We Th Fr Sa
                1  2       1  2  3  4  5  6       1  2  3  4  5  6
 3  4  5  6  7  8  9    7  8  9 10 11 12 13    7  8  9 10 11 12 13
10 11 12 13 14 15 16   14 15 16 17 18 19 20   14 15 16 17 18 19 20
17 18 19 20 21 22 23   21 22 23 24 25 26 27   21 22 23 24 25 26 27
24 25 26 27 28 29 30   28                     28 29 30 31
31
        April                   May                   June
Su Mo Tu We Th Fr Sa   Su Mo Tu We Th Fr Sa   Su Mo Tu We Th Fr Sa
             1  2  3                      1          1  2  3  4  5
 4  5  6  7  8  9 10    2  3  4  5  6  7  8    6  7  8  9 10 11 12
11 12 13 14 15 16 17    9 10 11 12 13 14 15   13 14 15 16 17 18 19
18 19 20 21 22 23 24   16 17 18 19 20 21 22   20 21 22 23 24 25 26
25 26 27 28 29 30      23 24 25 26 27 28 29   27 28 29 30
                       30 31
        July                  August               September
Su Mo Tu We Th Fr Sa   Su Mo Tu We Th Fr Sa   Su Mo Tu We Th Fr Sa
             1  2  3    1  2  3  4  5  6  7             1  2  3  4
 4  5  6  7  8  9 10    8  9 10 11 12 13 14    5  6  7  8  9 10 11
11 12 13 14 15 16 17   15 16 17 18 19 20 21   12 13 14 15 16 17 18
18 19 20 21 22 23 24   22 23 24 25 26 27 28   19 20 21 22 23 24 25
```

(continued on next page)

Code Listing 15.1 (continued)

```
25 26 27 28 29 30 31  29 30 31              26 27 28 29 30

       October               November              December
Su Mo Tu We Th Fr Sa  Su Mo Tu We Th Fr Sa  Su Mo Tu We Th Fr Sa
                1  2      1  2  3  4  5  6         1  2  3  4
 3  4  5  6  7  8  9   7  8  9 10 11 12 13   5  6  7  8  9 10 11
10 11 12 13 14 15 16  14 15 16 17 18 19 20  12 13 14 15 16 17 18
17 18 19 20 21 22 23  21 22 23 24 25 26 27  19 20 21 22 23 24 25
24 25 26 27 28 29 30  28 29 30              26 27 28 29 30 31
31

[ejr@hobbes ch15]$ cal 12 1941
   December 1941
Su Mo Tu We Th Fr Sa
    1  2  3  4  5  6
 7  8  9 10 11 12 13
14 15 16 17 18 19 20
21 22 23 24 25 26 27
28 29 30 31

[ejr@hobbes ch15]$
```

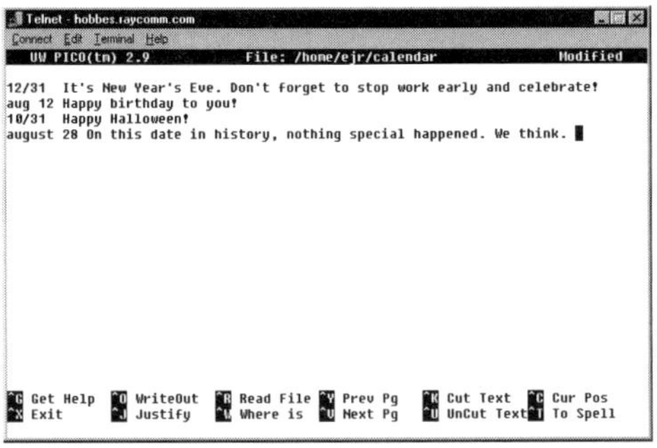

Figure 15.1 Setting reminders is as easy as entering a date and typing the reminder.

Code Listing 15.2 The system presents you with the reminder on command.

```
xmission> calendar
august 28 On this date in history, nothing
  → special happened. We think.
xmission>
```

✔ Tips

- You can put `calendar` in your startup configuration files so you see reminders as soon as you log in. See Chapter 8 for details about configuration files.
- Some UNIX systems automatically mail you your daily reminders at midnight, but even if yours doesn't, you can set it up on your own—see *Scheduling regularly occurring jobs with* ***`crontab`***, in Chapter 9.
- If you want `calendar` but it's not available on your system, see Chapter 14 for the basics of how to install it yourself.

Setting up calendar reminders

If you're like us, you need help remembering birthdays, anniversaries, and national holidays (otherwise we work right through them!). By typing in `calendar` whenever you log in, you can get reminders of important dates, as shown in **Figure 15.1**. This command checks a file that you've set up beforehand and tells you whether there are any reminders for today. Here, we'll show you how to set up calendar reminders.

To set up calendar reminders:

1. `pico -w ~/calendar`

   At the shell prompt, start your favorite editor and edit the file called `calendar` in your home directory.

2. `12/31  It's New Year's Eve. Don't → forget to stop work at midnight → and celebrate!`

   Specify the date and the reminder (**Figure 15.1**). You can use practically any month-day format, such as `12/31`, `aug 12`, or `July 4`.

3. `aug 12 Happy birthday to you!`

   Continue adding dates and reminders. You should also enter a reminder for the current day's date so you can test it out.

4. Save and close the file.

   Refer to Chapter 4 if you need a quick review of saving and closing files.

5. `calendar`

   Type `calendar` to test out the reminder for the current day, as shown in **Code Listing 15.2**.

Calculating with bc

UNIX even offers a handy calculator utility that lets you...er, um...calculate things. Just use bc, as shown in **Code Listing 15.3**.

To calculate with bc:

1. bc

   At the shell prompt, type bc. You'll find yourself at a blank line, waiting for math to do.

2. 6*5

   Enter the numbers, operators, expressions, or whatever you want to calculate. Use + to add, - to subtract, * to multiply, and / to divide. The answer appears on the next line (**Code Listing 15.3**).

3. Ctrl D

   Quit bc when you're done.

✔ Tips

- You can tell bc to calculate expressions within a file with bc bcfile. (Of course, replace bcfile with the real file name.) Then, bc waits for more to do from the command line.
- Type man bc for more details about bc's capabilities.

Code Listing 15.3 Using the bc utility, you can calculate and calculate and calculate....

```
xmission> bc
6*5
30
xmission>
```

Figure 15.2 ispell lets you interactively spell-check your files.

Table 15.1

ispell menu items	
ITEM	DESCRIPTION
Spacebar	Accept your spelling, but don't add it to the dictionary.
r	Replace with a word that you'll specify (after you type r).
A	Accept the word for the rest of the current session.
i	Insert the word into your dictionary.
u	Insert the word (as all lowercase) into your dictionary.
q	Quit `ispell`, saving all changes.
x	Exit `ispell` without saving any changes.
0-n	Replace highlighted word with a suggested word.

Checking spelling with ispell

Back in Chapter 6, we showed you how to spell-check your files by using `spell` and piping the output to `more`. UNIX also offers you `ispell`, which gives you an interactive way of spell-checking files, similar to the spell-checking capabilities of many word processing programs (**Figure 15.2**).

To check spelling with ispell:

1. `ispell gudspeler`

   At the shell prompt, type `ispell` followed by the name of the file you want to spell-check. You'll be greeted with your first (allegedly) misspelled word, the sentence the misspelling appears in, suggested words to replace the misspelled word with, and (probably) a menu at the bottom of the screen, as shown in **Figure 15.2**. The key menu items are listed in **Table 15.1**.

2. Complete your spell-check using `ispell`'s menu items.

3. `q`

   Press `q` to exit `ispell`, saving all of your changes.

✔ Tips

- Try one (or more) of these flags with the `ispell` command:
- `-b` creates a backup file.
- `-S` sorts guesses by likely correctness.
- `-B` reports run-together words as spelling errors.
- `-M` makes sure the menu appears at the bottom of the screen, assuming it doesn't appear automatically.

Keeping a record of your session with script

Occasionally, you may need to keep a record of a UNIX session—for example, if you're using UNIX as part of a class assignment or need a session record to submit to your untrusting boss. You can do this using `script`, which keeps a record of every command you type from the shell prompt (**Code Listing 15.4**). You might think of typing `script` as pressing a Record button on a UNIX tape recorder.

Code Listing 15.4 Using script is a great way to keep records.

```
[ejr@hobbes ch15]$ more covermybutt
Script started on Fri Aug 28 14:30:16 1998
[ejr@hobbes ch15]$ pwd
/home/ejr/ch15
[ejr@hobbes ch15]$ who
root     tty1     Aug 28 14:18
ejr      ttyp0    Aug 28 14:20 (calvin.raycomm.com)
ejr      ttyp1    Aug 28 14:28 (calvin.raycomm.com)
[ejr@hobbes ch15]$ ps ax
  PID TTY STAT TIME COMMAND
    1  ?  S    0:02 init [3]
    2  ?  SW   0:00 (kflushd)
    3  ?  SW<  0:00 (kswapd)
   48  ?  S    0:00 /sbin/kerneld
  229  ?  S    0:00 syslogd
  238  ?  S    0:00 klogd
  260  ?  S    0:00 crond
  272  ?  S    0:00 inetd
  283  ?  S    0:00 lpd
  298  ?  S    0:00 sendmail: accepting connections on port 25

  310  ?  S    0:00 gpm -t ms
  321  ?  S    0:00 httpd

  355  ?  S    0:00 nmbd -D
  368   1 S    0:00 /bin/login -- root
  369   2 S    0:00 /sbin/mingetty tty2
  370   3 S    0:00 /sbin/mingetty tty3
  371   4 S    0:00 /sbin/mingetty tty4
```

To record your session with script:

1. `script covermybutt`

   At the shell prompt, type `script` to start recording your actions. You can save the transcript to a specified file name, as in `script covermybutt`. If you don't specify a file, UNIX will save the transcript in the current directory as `typescript`.

2. Do your thing. See you in a couple of hours.

3. Ctrl D

Code Listing 15.4 (continued)

```
  372   5 S    0:00 /sbin/mingetty tty5
  373   6 S    0:00 /sbin/mingetty tty6
  375  ?  S    0:00 update (bdflush)
  381   1 S    0:00 -bash
  402  ?  S    0:00 in.telnetd
  436  ?  S    0:00 in.telnetd
  249  ?  S    0:00 /usr/sbin/atd
  327  ?  S    0:00 httpd
  328  ?  S    0:00 httpd
  329  ?  S    0:00 httpd
  330  ?  S    0:00 httpd
  331  ?  S    0:00 httpd
  332  ?  S    0:00 httpd
  333  ?  S    0:00 httpd
  334  ?  S    0:00 httpd
  335  ?  S    0:00 httpd

  403  p0 S    0:00 /bin/login -h calvin raycomm.com -p
  404  p0 S    0:00 -bash
  437  p1 S    0:00 /bin/login -h calvin raycomm.com -p
  438  p1 S    0:00 -bash
  449  p1 S    0:00 ispell gudspeler
  450  p0 S    0:00 script covermybutt
  451  p0 S    0:00 script covermybutt
  452  p3 S    0:00 bash -i
  455  p3 R    0:00 ps ax
[ejr@hobbes ch15]$ exit

Script done on Fri Aug 28 14:30:44 1998
[ejr@hobbes ch15]$
```

When you're done, type Ctrl D to stop recording the session.

4. `more covermybutt`

   Use `more` or the editor of your choice to view the script. **Code Listing 15.4** shows a sample transcript.

✔ Tips

- Screen-based programs, like `vi`, `pico`, `pine`, `elm`, or `lynx`, tend to wreak havoc with the output of `script`. You can still read the content, but the formatting is often out of whack, as shown in **Figure 15.3**.
- You would use `script` if you want to record both what you did and what happened ("geez, I typed `rm unbackedupdata`, then `ls`, and sure enough, the `ls` listing showed that I was in big trouble"). On the other hand, if you just want the list of commands you typed with no indication of what happened, check out `history`, from Chapter 3 ("geez, I typed `rm` → `unbackedupdata`, then I typed `ls`, then I logged out and cried").

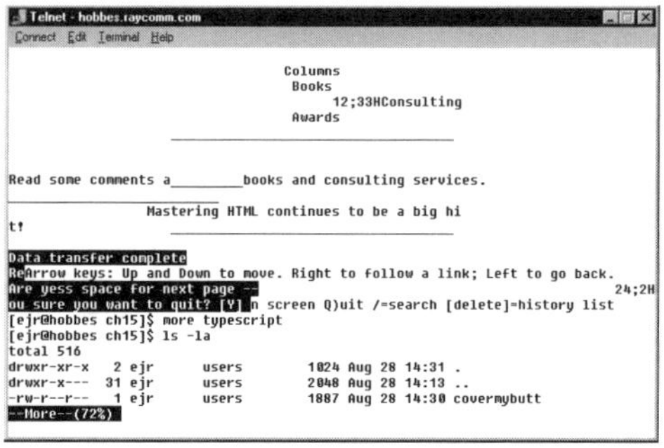

Figure 15.3 Some programs give you oddly formatted script output and strange beeps when you view the script.

Sensational UNIX Tricks

16

Throughout this book, we've given you UNIX building blocks—individual UNIX commands, scripting techniques, and other insights that you can use individually or combine with each other. In this chapter, we'll show you some clever things to do with UNIX. You might consider this an "advanced" chapter, but most of the things we'll show you here are simply combinations of things you've already learned about in earlier chapters.

Chapter contents

- Sorting and filing mail
- Searching and replacing throughout multiple documents
- Generating reports
- Using input to customize your environment
- Using ROT13 encoding
- Embedding ROT13 encoding in shell scripts

Sorting and filing mail with procmail

Let's see...two messages from the boss...17 messages from the string collector's discussion group...oh, hey, a message from mom...and....

One of the handiest things you can do to make your UNIX life easier is to use `procmail` (a mail filtering program) to automatically sort and file your incoming mail. Gone are the days of having 427 new e-mail messages clogging up your inbox. You can set your account to sort messages into separate folders, making it much easier to sift through your messages. Plus, you can automatically toss messages from people you don't want to hear from. Hmmm. Now this has potential!

In this section, we'll show you how to filter incoming messages using the `pine` e-mail program. If you're using `elm`, you can still use these instructions, but you'll have to adjust the information accordingly. As **Figures 16.1** through **16.4** show, you need to do four things to set up your system to filter mail with `procmail`:

- Specify settings for `procmail` (**Figure 16.1**). For example, incoming mail normally gets plunked directly into your inbox; however, `procmail` filters mail before it even gets to your inbox, so you need to tell `procmail` where your mail folders are, among other things.
- Set up a mail folder (**Figure 16.2**). You need to specify a new folder (or folders) for incoming messages to go to.
- Specify how you want messages filtered (**Figure 16.3**). For example, you could filter them by the sender's name or by specific information within the Subject line. This process, by the way, is technically called "writing a recipe."

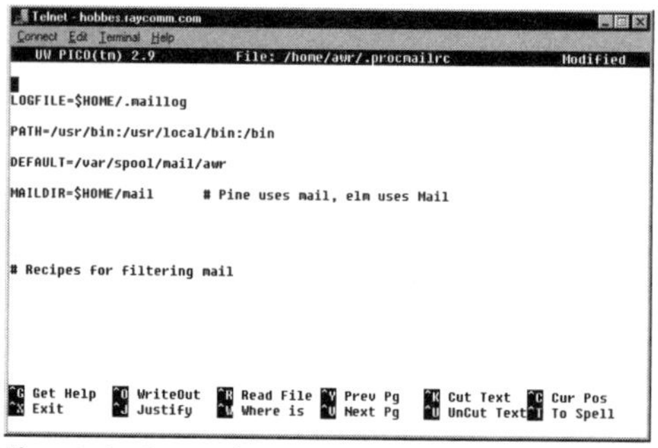

Figure 16.1 Set up the .procmailrc file to give procmail the information it needs about your environment.

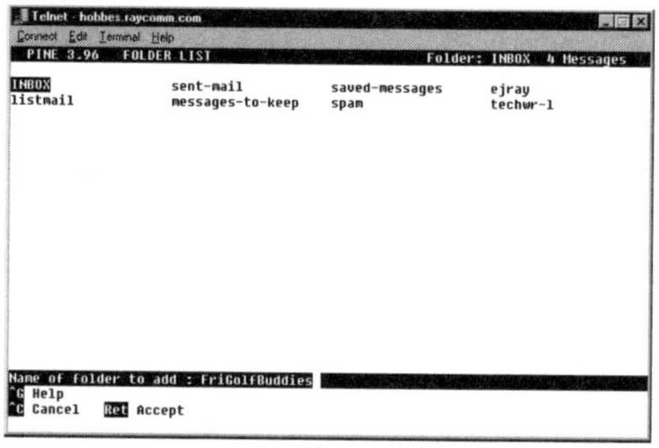

Figure 16.2 Specify a new folder (or folders) for incoming messages to go into.

Figure 16.3 Define "recipes" for filtering messages.

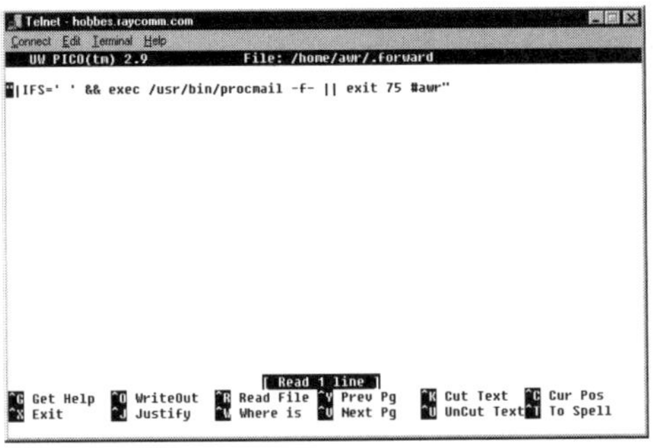

Figure 16.4 Create a .forward file that sends your incoming mail to procmail for processing.

- Tell `procmail` to do its thing (**Figure 16.4**). Essentially, you create a `.forward` file that sends your incoming mail to `procmail` for processing before you ever see it.

To specify settings for procmail:

1. `pico ~/.procmailrc`

   To begin, access your editor and create a `.procmailrc` file in your home directory.

2. `LOGFILE=$HOME/.maillog`

   Give `procmail` a place to log all of its activities, so it can tell you what it's done: "I threw away 7 messages from your boss...filed 3 messages from Joe in the GolfBuddies folder...." In this example, we tell `procmail` to keep a log file called `.maillog` in our home directory (**Figure 16.1**).

3. `PATH=/usr/local/bin:/usr/bin:/bin`

   Specify the path for your executable programs. It's a good idea to do this now, just in case you eventually use `procmail` to more extensively filter or auto-respond to messages.

4. `DEFAULT=/var/spool/mail/yourid`

   Specify the location for your incoming mail. Remember, the filter gets the mail before it ever reaches the inbox, so you need to tell `procmail` where your inbox is. Check with your system administrator to confirm the `DEFAULT`. (`/var/spool/mail/yourid` is typically, but not always, the location.)

5. `MAILDIR=$HOME/mail`

   Specify where `procmail` should find your mail program and all the folders and information it creates. If you're using `pine`, type this line exactly as shown. If you're using `elm`, use `Mail` instead of `mail`.

To set up a mail folder:

1. `pine`

   At the shell prompt, start `pine`.

2. `m`

   Make sure you're at the mail menu.

3. `l`

   Go to the folder list. Just use `pine`'s menu.

4. `a`

   Type `a` to add a new folder.

5. `FriGolfBuddies`

   Enter a folder name and press Enter. Be as descriptive as possible (**Figure 16.2**).

   Repeat steps 4 and 5 for as many folders as you think you're going to need. Remember you can always add more later if you want to.

6. `q`

   Quit `pine`.

To specify how messages should be filtered (or to "write a recipe"):

1. `pico ~/.procmailrc`

   In `pico`, access your `.procmailrc` file.

2. Move to the end of the file, below the setup information.

3. `:0:`

   Start a new recipe with `:0:, as shown in Figure 16.3`. (Don't ask why to use `:0:`. That's just the way it is.)

4. `* ^TOGolfBuddies`

   Set the criteria for `procmail` to filter with. Here,

   - `*` tells `procmail` to search through all incoming messages.
   - `^TO` tells `procmail` to examine the `TO` line (and, actually, the `CC` line, too).
   - `GolfBuddies` is the text to match in the `TO` line (as in TO: GolfBuddies@

nowhere.nowhen.com) . Of course, you'd put in the actual name of the list to look for (or the alias for your mailing list, or whatever), rather than GolfBuddies.

5. `$MAILDIR/FriGolfBuddies`

   Specify where the filtered mail should go—in this case, it would go in the `FriGolfBuddies` folder, but you might filter messages from mailing lists into a `listmail` folder.

6. Save and close the file.

To turn on procmail filtering:

1. `pico ~/.forward`

   Use your favorite editor to create a `.forward` file in your home directory.

2. `"|IFS=' ' && exec /usr/bin/procmail → -f- || exit 75 #yourid"`

   Enter the text exactly as shown, but substitute your userid for `yourid` above (**Figure 16.4**). If `procmail` is not located at `/usr/bin`, type in the actual location. `/usr/local/bin` would be another likely directory.

3. Save and close the file.

   That's it! Now all you have to do is wait for incoming messages and see if they get filtered as you intended.

✓ Tip

- After you set up your new `.forward` and `procmail` processing, be patient. Sometimes `procmail` only processes mail on a specific schedule (hourly, for example), so testing it will be a little time-consuming.

Use procmail to toss spam messages

For example, the following recipe:

```
:0:
* !^TO.*awr@.*raycomm.com
$MAILDIR/spam
```

filters messages that aren't explicitly addressed to a userid with `awr` before the `@` and `raycomm.com` at the end into a special folder called `spam`. Put the spam filter at the end of your list of rules so all of the messages originating from your mailing lists and other important messages are filed first. After testing this and making sure that you like it and it doesn't pitch valuable messages, you could change the last line to `/dev/null` to just throw the garbage away.

For a more complex and sophisticated spam solution, try the process outlined at `www.best.com/~ariel/nospam/`.

Searching and replacing throughout multiple documents with sed

Back in Chapter 6, we talked about `sed` and how to use it to search and replace throughout files, one file at a time. Although we're sure you're still coming down off of the power rush from doing that, we'll now show you how to combine `sed` with shell scripts and loops. In doing this, you can take your search-and-replace criteria and apply them to multiple documents. For example, you can search through all of the `.html` documents in a directory and make the same change to all of them. In this example (**Figure 16.5**), we strip out all of the `<BLINK>` tags, which are offensive to some HTML purists.

Before you get started, you might have a look at Chapter 6 for a review of `sed` basics and Chapter 10 for a review of scripts and loops.

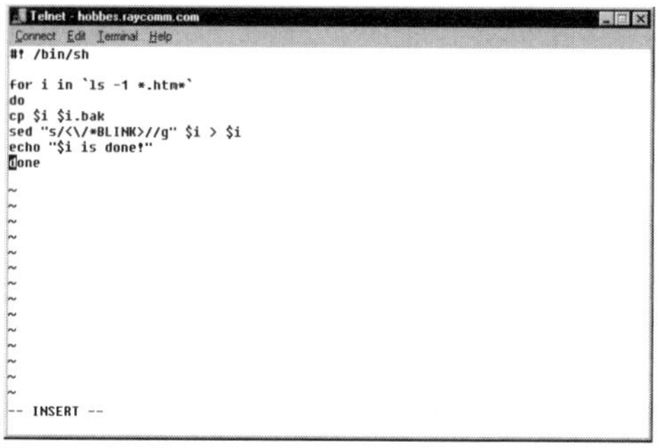

Figure 16.5 Create a script to search and replace in multiple documents.

To search and replace throughout multiple documents:

1. `vi thestinkinblinkintag`

   Use the editor of your choice to create a new script. Name the file whatever you want.

2. `#! /bin/sh`

   Start the shell script with the name of the program that should run the script.

3. ``for i in `ls -l *.htm*` ``

   Start a loop. In this case, the loop will process all of the `.htm` or `.html` documents in the current directory.

4. `do`

   Indicate the beginning of the loop content.

5. `cp $i $i.bak`

   Make a backup copy of each file before you change it. Remember, Murphy is watching you.

Code Listing 16.1 You can even use sed to strip out bad HTML tags, as shown here.

```
[ejr@hobbes scripting]$ more
  → thestinkinblinkintag
#! /bin/sh

for i in `ls -1 *.htm*`
do
cp $i $i.bak
sed "s/<\/*BLINK>//g" $i > $i
echo "$i is done!"
done

 [ejr@hobbes scripting]$ chmod u+x
  → thestinkinblinkintag
[ejr@hobbes scripting]$ ./thestinkinblinkintag
above.htm is done!
file1.htm is done!
file2.htm is done!
html.htm is done!
temp.htm is done!
[ejr@hobbes scripting]$
```

6. `sed "s/<\/*BLINK>//g" $i > $i`

   Specify your search criteria and replacement text. A lot is happening in this line, but don't panic. From the left, this command contains `sed` followed by

   - `"`, which starts the command.
   - `s/`, which tells `sed` to search for something.
   - `<`, which is the first character to be searched for.
   - `\/`, which allows you to search for the `/`. (The `\` escapes the `/` so the `/` can be used in the search.)
   - `*`, which specifies none or one of the previous character (`/`), which takes care of both the opening and closing tags (with and without a `/` at the beginning).
   - `BLINK>`, which indicates the rest of the text to search for. Note that this only searches for capital letters. You'll want to add a line if your HTML document might use lowercase tags.
   - `//`, which ends the search section and the replace section (there's nothing in the replace section because the tag will be replaced with nothing).
   - `g`, which tells `sed` to make the change in all occurrences (globally), not just in the first occurrence on each line.
   - `"`, which closes the command.
   - `$i` is replaced with each file name in turn as the loop runs.
   - `> $i` indicates that the output is redirected back to the same file name.

   (See **Code Listing 16.1.**)

7. `echo "$i is done."`

   Optionally, print a status message onscreen, which can be reassuring if there are a lot of files to process.

8. `done`

   Indicate the end of the loop.

9. Save and close out of your script.

10. Try it out.

    Remember to make your script executable with `chmod u+x` and the file name, then run it with `./thestinking → blinkintag`. In our example, we'll see the "success reports" for each of the HTML documents processed (**Code Listing 16.1**).

✔ Tip

- You could perform any number of other operations on the files within the loop, if you wanted. For example, you could strip out other codes, replace a former Webmaster's address with your own, or automatically insert comments and last-update dates.

Code Listing 16.2 Use awk to generate quick reports.

```
[ejr@hobbes /home]$ ls -la | awk '{print $9 "
→ owned by "  $3 } END { print NR " Total
→ Files" }'
 owned by
. owned by root
.. owned by root
admin owned by admin
anyone owned by anyone
asr owned by asr
awr owned by awr
bash owned by bash
csh owned by csh
deb owned by deb
debray owned by debray
ejr owned by ejr
ejray owned by ejray
ftp owned by root
httpd owned by httpd
lost+found owned by root
merrilee owned by merrilee
oldstuff owned by 1000
pcguest owned by pcguest
raycomm owned by pcguest
samba owned by root
shared owned by root
22 Total Files
[ejr@hobbes /home]$
```

Generating reports with awk

Back in Chapter 6, we showed you how to edit delimited files with awk, which is cool because it lets you extract specific pieces of information, such as names and phone numbers, from delimited files. As shown in **Code Listing 16.2**, you can also use awk to generate reports. We start with the information from an `ls -la` command, then use awk to generate a report about who owns what.

To generate reports with awk:

◆ `ls -la | awk '{print $9 " owned → by "  $3 } END { print NR " Total → Files" }'`

Whew! In general, pipe `ls -la` to the long-winded awk command. (Yes, this is the origin of awkward.) awk then prints the ninth field ($9), the words "owned by," then the third field ($3), and at the end of the output, the total number of records processed (`print NR " Total Files"`). **Code Listing 16.2** shows the printed report.

✔ Tip

- Remember that you could embed awk scripts in a shell script, as with the previous `sed` example, if it's something you'll use frequently.

Using input to customize your environment

Way back in Chapter 8, we talked about setting up your environment variables by customizing the configuration files that run upon login. You can further customize your environment variables by requiring input whenever a startup script runs. For example, you can set your configuration files (which are actually scripts) so that they request that you specify the default editor for the session (**Code Listing 16.3**).

To use input to customize your environment:

1. `vi .bash_profile`

   Use your favorite editor to edit your script, and move to the end of the file.

2. `echo -e "Which editor do you want as → the default? (vi or pico)"`

   Using `echo -e`, specify the text that will prompt you to input information (**Figure 16.6**).

3. `read choice`

   On the next line, add `read` followed by the name of the variable to read in. We chose `choice` because we're using this input to set the preferred `EDITOR` environment variable.

4. `if [ $choice = "vi" ]`

   Start an if statement—in this case, one that tests for the `vi` option.

5. `then EDITOR=/usr/bin/vi ; export → EDITOR ; echo "You chose vi!"`

   Here, the `then` clause sets the `EDITOR` environment variable to `vi`, exports the environment variable, and announces your choice.

Code Listing 16.3 When the system asks your preferences, you know you're on top.

```
[ejr@hobbes ejr]$ su - ejr
Password:
Which editor do you want as the default?
  → (vi or pico)
vi
You chose vi!
[ejr@hobbes ejr]$
```

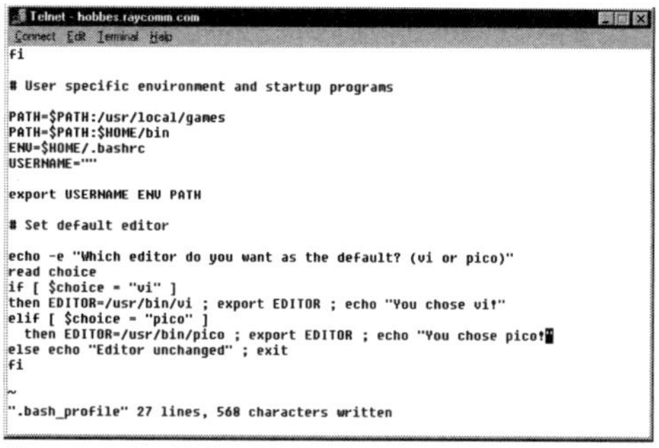

Figure 16.6 Add the mini-script to your .bash_profile or .profile configuration file, right at the end.

6. `elif [ $choice = "pico" ]`

   Check for your other option with `elif` (else if). This statement covers the `pico` option.

7. `then EDITOR=/usr/bin/pico ; export → EDITOR ; echo "You chose pico!"`

   This `then` clause sets the `EDITOR` environment variable to `pico`, exports the environment variable, and announces your choice.

8. `else echo "Editor unchanged"`

   Set up an else statement, which will be used if neither option was entered at the `read` prompt. In this example, if neither `vi` nor `pico` was entered, it'll just say that the editor was unchanged.

9. `fi`

   End the if statement.

10. Save and exit.

11. `su - yourid`

    At the shell prompt, type `su -` followed by your userid to log in again and test the revised login script (**Code Listing 16.3**).

✔ Tip

- This technique is very useful for setting the `TERM`(inal) environment variable if you access the system from different remote locations with different capabilities.

Using ROT13 encoding with sed

In Usenet newsgroups (among other places), text is often encoded with something called *ROT13*, which is an abbreviation for "rotate (the alphabet by) 13." That is, A becomes N, B becomes O, and so forth. If text is encoded, people have to take extra steps to decode the message. For example, if a message includes an offensive joke, people who don't want to see the joke won't have to. Similarly, if the message is a movie review, people who don't want to know the ending won't have the surprise spoiled. Instead, the message encoded with ROT13 might look like this:

```
Tbbq sbe lbh--lbh svtherq vg bhg! Naq ab,
gurer'f ab chapuyvar. Ubcr lbh rawblrq
gur obbx! Qrobenu naq Revp
```

A great way to use ROT13 encoding (and decoding) is with `sed`, which will let you easily manipulate text.

To use ROT13 encoding with sed:

1. `vi script.sed`

   Use the editor of your choice to create a file called `script.sed`. Because the command we're using will be reused, we'll use a `sed` script instead of just typing everything in at the shell prompt.

2. `y/abcdefghijklmnopqrstuvwxyzABCDEFG`
   `→ HIJKLMNOPQRSTUVWXYZ/`

   Start with a `y` at the beginning of the command. `y` is the `sed` command to translate characters (capital to lowercase or whatever you specify).

   After `y`, type a slash (`/`), the original characters to look for (all lowercase and uppercase characters), and another slash (**Code Listing 16.4**).

Code Listing 16.4 A spiffy sed command can ROT13 encode and decode messages.

```
[ejr@hobbes creative]$ sed -f script.sed
  → limerick
Bhe snibevgr yvzrevpx
1.
Gurer bapr jnf n zna sebz Anaghpxrg,
Jub pneevrq uvf yhapu va n ohpxrg,
Fnvq ur jvgu n fvtu,
Nf ur ngr n jubyr cvr,
Vs V whfg unq n qbahg V'q qhax vg.
[ejr@hobbes creative]$ sed -f script.sed
  → limerick | sed -f script.sed
Our favorite limerick
1.
There once was a man from Nantucket,
Who carried his lunch in a bucket,
Said he with a sigh,
As he ate a whole pie,
If I just had a donut I'd dunk it.
[ejr@hobbes creative]$
```

3. ```
   y/abcdefghijklmnopqrstuvwxyzABCDEF
   → GHIJKLMNOPQRSTUVWXYZ/nopqrstuvwxy
   → zabcdefghijklmNOPQRSTUVWXYZABCDEF
   → GHIJKLM/
   ```
   After the second slash, add the translation characters (the lowercase alphabet, starting with n and continuing around to m, then uppercase from N to M), followed by a slash to conclude the replace string.

4. Save the script and exit the editor.

5. `sed -f script.sed limerick | more`

   Test the ROT13 encoding by applying it to a file. Here we apply it to the `limerick` file, then pipe the output to `more` for your inspection. You'll see that all you get is gibberish. To test it more thoroughly, use `sed -f script.sed limerick | sed -f script.sed | more` to run it through the processor twice. You should end up with normal text at the end of this pipeline.

✔ Tips

- Text is rotated by 13 simply because there are 26 letters in the alphabet, so you can use the same program to encode or decode. If you rotate by a different number, you'll need to have separate programs to encode and decode.
- Check out the next section to see how to make this lengthy process into a shell script and make it even easier to reuse over and over.
   ```

Embedding ROT13 encoding in a shell script

If you completed the steps in the previous section, you might have noticed that you did a lot of typing. And, goodness, if you made it through steps 3 and 5, your fingers are probably on strike right about now. If you plan to encode or decode with ROT13 frequently, consider embedding the `sed` commands in a shell script to avoid retyping them each time you encode or decode text, as shown in **Figure 16.7**. You might refer back to Chapter 10 for details on shell scripts before you get started here.

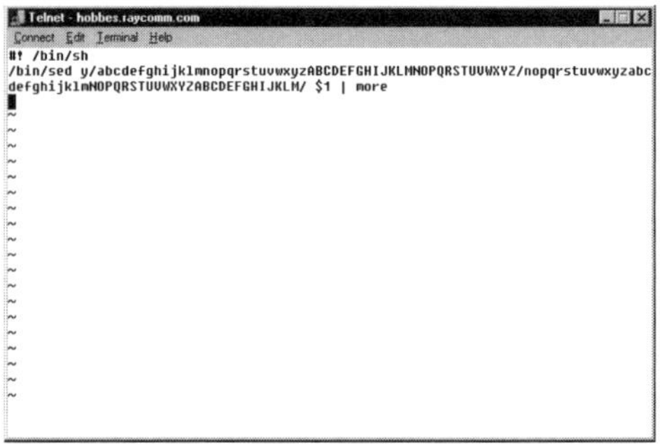

Figure 16.7 A brief shell script makes ROT13 as easy as, well, EBG13.

To create a ROT13 shell script:

1. `vi rot13`

   Start a new shell script to process your commands.

2. `#! /bin/sh`

   Add the obligatory shell specification, as shown in **Figure 16.7**.

3. `/bin/sed y/abcdefghijklmnopqrstuvw`
   `→ xyzABCDEFGHIJKLMNOPQRSTUVWXYZ/nop`
   `→ qrstuvwxyzabcdefghijklmNOPQRSTUVW`
   `→ XYZABCDEFGHIJKLM/`

   Specify the `sed` program (using the full path to make the program a little more flexible) and the command that encodes and decodes ROT13 text. It's better to make the shell script self-contained, so instead of referencing an external file with the `sed` script, we'll just put it in the command line here.

4. `/bin/sed y/abcdefghijklmnopqrstuvw`
   `→ xyzABCDEFGHIJKLMNOPQRSTUVWXYZ/nop`
   `→ qrstuvwxyzabcdefghijklmNOPQRSTUVW`
   `→ XYZABCDEFGHIJKLM/ $1`

   Here, we added `$1` to pass the file name from the command line (as in `rot13 thisfile`) to `sed`.

5. `/bin/sed y/abcdefghijklmnopqrstuvw`
   `→ xyzABCDEFGHIJKLMNOPQRSTUVWXYZ/nop`
   `→ qrstuvwxyzabcdefghijklmNOPQRSTUVW`
   `→ XYZABCDEFGHIJKLM/ $1 | more`

   Next, pipe the output to `more` so to see the file one screen at a time.

6. Save and exit out of the file.

7. `chmod u+x rot13`

   Make the shell script executable, so you can just enter the name `rot13` rather than `sh rot13`.

8. `./rot13 limerick`

   Test the script. Because we developed this script in a directory that's not in the path, we have to execute the script with `./rot13`. If you develop the script in a

Code Listing 16.5 If you want to get really fancy with the script, you can bring together some of the handiest bits of other chapters to make a masterpiece.

```
[ejr@hobbes creative]$ more rot13
#! /bin/sh

#     If the first item (after the script name) on the command
#     line is save or s, and the second item is a readable file
#     then do the first case.
if [ \( "$1" = "save" -o "$1" = "s" \) -a \( -r "$2" \) ]
then

#     This case saves the ROT13 output under the same filename with
#     a rot13 extension.
/bin/sed y/abcdefghijklmnopqrstuvwxyzABCDEFGHIJKLMNOPQRSTUVWXYZ/nopqrstuvwxyzabcdefghijklmNOPQRSTU
  → VWXYZABCDEFGHIJKLM/ $2 > $2.rot13
else

#     This case pipes the ROT13 output to
  → more, because a save
#     wasn't specified.
/bin/sed y/abcdefghijklmnopqrstuvwxyzABCDEFGHIJKLMNOPQRSTUVWXYZ/nopqrstuvwxyzabcdefghijklmNOPQRSTU
  → VWXYZABCDEFGHIJKLM/ $1 | more

fi

[ejr@hobbes creative]$
```

directory in your path, you should just be able to type `rot13`.

✔ Tip

- You can also build in an option to redirect the output of the script to a file and save it for later. Basically, all you do is create an if-then statement and give yourself the option of automatically redirecting the output to a file name, as **Code Listing 16.5** shows. Check out Chapter 10 for more information about scripts and if-then statements.

A

UNIX Reference

Table A.a

Summary of Appendix Tables

Table Number	Description
Table A.1	Getting started with UNIX
Table A.2	Using directories and files
Table A.3	Working with your shell
Table A.4	Creating and editing files
Table A.5	Controlling file ownership and permissions
Table A.6	Manipulating files
Table A.7	Getting information about your system
Table A.8	Configuring your UNIX environment
Table A.9	Running scripts and programs
Table A.10	Writing basic scripts
Table A.11	Sending and reading e-mail
Table A.12	Accessing the Internet
Table A.13	Working with encoded and compressed files
Table A.14	Installing software
Table A.15	Using handy utilities

In this appendix, you'll find a fairly thorough reference on UNIX commands and flags as well as examples and descriptions of each. We organized this appendix to parallel the book, so that you can easily reference key commands and related flags without being overwhelmed with long lists of commands..

Table A.a summarizes what you'll find in this appendix.**Tables A.1–A.15** contain commands and flags that relate to the topics covered by the similarly numbered chapter. In addition to the commands and flags discussed in the chapters, you'll also find related commands and options that you might find useful in your UNIX adventures, reference information that will jog your memory, and ideas to help you get off and running on additional projects. If you're looking for a thorough command flag reference, check out Appendix C.

Table A.1

Getting Started with UNIX: Survival Skills

Command	Description
`apropos` *keyword*	Find appropriate `man` pages for *keyword*.
`cat` *file*	Display file contents onscreen or provide `file` contents to standard output.
`cat` *file1 file2*	Display *file1* and *file2*.
`cd`	Return to your home directory from anywhere in the UNIX system.
`cd ..`	Move up one level in the directory tree.
`cd /etc`	Change to the `/etc` directory relative to the system root.
`cd ~/subdir`	Use a tilde (~) as a handy shortcut for your home directory.
`cd Projects`	Move to the `Projects` directory relative to the current directory.
`col -b`	Filter backspaces out of input. Use to make `man` pages editable without odd formatting.
Ctrl D	Close your current process (usually a shell) and your UNIX session if you close the login shell.
`exit`	Close your current shell and your UNIX session if you're in the login shell.
`less` *file*	Use to view *file* screen by screen.
`logout`	Close your UNIX session.
`ls`	List files and directories.
`ls /`	List the files and directories in the root directory.
`ls` */directory*	List the files and directories in *directory*.
`ls -a`	List all files and directories, including hidden ones.
`ls -c`	List files and directories by modification date.
`ls -l`	List files and directories in long format, with extra information.
`man 5` *command*	View the specified section (5) of the `man` pages for command. Sometimes used as `man -s 5` *command*.
`man` *command*	View the manual (help) pages for *command*.
`man -k` *keyword*	Find appropriate `man` pages for *keyword*.
`more` *filetoview*	View *filetoview* screen by screen.
`passwd`	Change your password.
`pwd`	Display the path and name of the directory you are currently in.
`stty sane`	Try to fix unexpected, sudden, and strange display problems.
`su -` *yourid*	Re-log in without having to log out.

Table A.2

Using Directories and Files

COMMAND	DESCRIPTION
`cp` *existingfile newfile*	Copy *existingfile* to a file named *newfile*.
`cp -i` *existingfile* `oldfile`	Copy `existingfile` to a file named *newfile*, prompting you before overwriting existing files.
`cp -r /Projects /shared/Projects`	Copy the directory `/Projects` to the new name `/shared/Projects`, specifying recursive copy.
`find . -name lostfile -print`	Find a file in the current directory or subdirectories named `lostfile`.
`find /home -name pending* -print`	Find all files with names starting with "pending" in the home directory or subdirectories.
`find /home/shared -mtime -3 -print`	Find all files in the `shared` directory that were modified within the last three days.
`find ~/ -name '*.backup' -exec compress {} \;`	Compress all files in the current directory with names containing "backup," without confirmation.
`find ~/ -name '*.backup' -ok rm {} \;`	Find and remove, with confirmation, all files in the current directory whose names end with ".backup".
`ln /home/a/* /home/b/*`	Hard link all of the files in the `a` directory to the files in the `b` directory.
`ln` *afile alink*	Link *afile* and *alink*, making the same file essentially exist in two different directories.
`ln -s /home/deb/Projects /home/helper/Project`	Create a soft link from `/home/deb/Projects` to `/home/helper/Project`.
`mkdir` *Newdirectory*	Make a new directory named *Newdirectory*.
`mv` *existingfile newfile*	Rename *existingfile* to *newfile*.
`mv -i` *oldfile newfile*	Rename *oldfile* to *newfile*, requiring the system to prompt you before overwriting (destroying) existing files.
`rm` *badfile*	Remove *badfile*.
`rm -i *`	Delete interactively, with prompting before deletion. Good for files with problematic names that UNIX thinks are command flags.
`rm -i` *badfile*	Remove *badfile* interactively.
`rm -ir dan*`	Interactively remove all the directories or files that start with "dan" in the current directory and all of the files and subdirectories in the subdirectories starting with "dan".
`rmdir` *Yourdirectory*	Remove the empty directory *Yourdirectory*.
`touch` *newfile*	Create a file named *newfile* with no content.
`touch -t` *123123592001 oldfile*	Update file date for *oldfile* to December 31, 23 hours, and 59 minutes in 2001.
`which` *command*	Find out the full path to *command*. This is valuable for seeing which of multiple commands with the same name would be executed.

Table A.3

Working with Your Shell

Command	Description
`!10`	Rerun command 10 from the history list in `csh`.
`bash`	Start a `bash` sub-shell or run a `bash` script.
`chsh`	Change your shell.
`csh`	Start a `csh` (C) sub-shell or run a `csh` shell script.
`echo $SHELL`	Display the value of the `$SHELL` environment variable.
`exit`	Leave the current shell and return to the previous one, or log out of the login shell.
`history`	View a numbered list of previous commands.
`ksh`	Start a `ksh` (Korn) sub-shell or run a `ksh` shell script.
`r 2`	Repeat a specific command in `ksh` from the history output(in this case command 2).
`set -o emacs`	Enable command completion with `emacs` commands in the `ksh` shell.
`set -o vi`	Enable command completion with `vi` commands in the `ksh` shell.
`sh`	Start a `sh` (Bourne) sub-shell or run a `sh` shell script.
`stty erase '^?'`	Make [Del] erase characters to the left of the cursor.
`stty erase '^H'`	Make [Ctrl][H] erase characters to the left of the cursor. Type `stty erase` then press [Ctrl][V] [Ctrl][H].
`stty erase Backspace`	Make [Backspace] erase characters to the left of the cursor.
`su - yourid`	Start a new login shell as `yourid`.
`su user`	Switch user to `user`.
`tcsh`	Start a `tcsh` sub-shell or run a `tcsh` shell script.

UNIX REFERENCE

Table A.4

Creating and Editing Files

Command	Description
ed	Choose a line-oriented text editor.
joe	Choose a fairly friendly editor.
pico	Choose for menu-oriented, user-friendly text editing.
pico *filename*	Open and edit *filename* in pico.
pico -w *filename*	Disable word wrapping for *filename* in pico. This is particularly useful for configuration files.
vi	Choose for text editing with lots of power but little ease of use.
vi *filename*	Open and edit *filename* in vi.

Table A.5

Controlling File Ownership and Permissions

Command	Description
chgrp	Change the group association of files or directories.
chgrp *groupname filename*	Change the group association of *filename* to *groupname*.
chgrp -R *group directory*	Recursively change the group association of *directory* and all subdirectories and files within it to *group*.
chmod	Change the permissions for a file.
chmod a-w *file*	Remove write permission for *file* for all (everyone).
chmod g+w *file*	Add write permission for *file* for the current group.
chmod -R go-rwx *	Revoke all permissions from everyone except the user for all files in the current directory and all subdirectories and their contents.
chmod u=rwx,g=rx,o=r *file*	Set the permissions on *file* to user read, write, and execute, group read and write, and others read.
chmod ugo= *	Revoke all permissions for everything in the current directory from everyone.
chown	Change the ownership of files or directories.
chown -R user *Directory*	Recursively change the ownership of *Directory* and all contents to user.
chown user *file*	Change the ownership of *file* to user.
umask *022*	Specify the default permissions for all created files.

Table A.6

Manipulating Files

Command	Description
awk	Manipulate a file as a database.
awk /CA/'{ print $2 $1 $7 }' *file*	Select (and display) three fields in each record in *file* that contains "CA".
awk '{ print $1 }' *file*	Select (and display) the first field in each record in *file*.
awk -f script.awk *file*	Run an awk command from a script called script.awk on *file*.
awk -F, '{ print $1 }' *file* > *newfile*	Select the first field in each record in *file*, specifying that a "," separates fields, and redirect the output to *newfile*.
awk -F: '{ print $2 " " $1 " in " $7 }' *file*	Select (and display) several fields and some text for each record in *file*, using a colon (:) as a field delimiter.
basename	Remove the path from a file name, leaving only the name proper. Good to use in scripts to display just a file name.
cmp *newfile oldfile*	Compare *newfile* to *oldfile*.
crypt	Encrypt or decrypt a password-protected file.
csplit	Divide files based on line number or other characteristics.
diff -b *newfile oldfile*	Find differences (ignoring blank lines) between *newfile* and *oldfile*.
diff *Directory Newdirectory*	Find differences between *Directory* and *Newdirectory*.
diff -i *newfile oldfile*	Find differences (except in case) between *newfile* and *oldfile*.
diff -ibw *file1 file2*	Find all differences between *file1* and *file2* except those involving blank lines, spaces, tabs, or lowercase/uppercase letters.
diff *newfile oldfile*	Find the differences between *newfile* and *oldfile*.
diff -w *newfile oldfile*	Find differences (ignoring spaces and blank lines) between *newfile* and *oldfile*.
fold -n 60 *file*	Reformat *file* so no lines exceed a specified length (60 characters here).
grep *expression file*	Find *expression* in *file* and view the lines containing *expression*.
grep -c *expression file*	Count how many times *expression* appears in *file*.
grep -i *expression file*	Find all lines containing *expression* in *file*, using any capitalization (case insensitive).
grep -n *expression file*	Display each found line and a line number.
grep *Nantucket$ limerick**	Find the lines in the *limerick* files that end with "Nantucket".
grep -v *expression file*	Find all lines in *file* that do not contain *expression*.
grep ^[A-Z,a-z] *limerick*	Find all the lines in *limerick* that start with any letter, but not with a number or symbol.
grep ^[A-Z] *limerick*	Find all the lines in *limerick* that start with a capital letter.
grep *^Nantucket limerick**	Find all the lines in the *limerick* files that start with "Nantucket".
grep -5 *word[1234] file*	Find *word1*, *word2*, *word3*, or *word4* in *file* and view the surrounding five lines as well as the lines containing the words.
head -20 *file*	View the first 20 lines of *file*.
head *file*	View the first 10 lines of *file*.

UNIX Reference

Table A.6 (continued)

Manipulating Files (continued)

Command	Description
sdiff *newfile oldfile*	View the differences between *newfile* and *oldfile*.
sdiff -s *newfile oldfile*	View the differences between *newfile* and *oldfile*, without showing identical lines.
sed	Make changes throughout a file according to command line input or a sed script.
sed /old/new/g *file.htm* > *file.htm*	Search through *file.htm* and replace every occurrence of "old" with "new".
sed -f script.sed *file* > *file*	Run the commands in script.sed, apply them to *file*, and replace *file* with the manipulated content.
sort *file* | uniq	Sort *file* and send it to uniq to eliminate duplicates.
sort *file* > *sortedfile*	Sort the lines in *file* alphabetically and present the sorted results in *sortedfile*.
sort *file1* | tee *sorted* | mail *boss@raycomm.com* -	Sort *file1* and, with tee, send it both to the file sorted and to standard output, where it gets mailed to the boss.
sort *file1 file2* | uniq -d	Sort *file1* and *file2* together and find all the lines that are duplicated.
sort *file1 file2 file3* > *bigfile*	Sort and combine the contents of *file1*, *file2*, and *file3* and put the sorted output in *bigfile*.
sort -n *file*	Sort *file* numerically.
sort -t, +2 *file*	Sort on the third (really) field in the comma-delimited *file*.
sort -t, *file*	Sort fields in the comma-delimited *file*; the character following -t (,) indicates the delimiter.
spell *file*	Check the spelling of all words in *file*. Returns a list of possibly misspelled words.
tail -15 *file*	View the last 15 lines of *file*.
tail *file*	View the last 10 lines of *file*.
uniq	Use with sorted files to eliminate duplicate lines.
wc -b *file*	Count the bytes in *file*.
wc *file*	Count the lines, words, and bytes in *file*.
wc -l *file*	Count the lines in *file*.
wc -w *file*	Count the words in *file*.

Table A.7

Getting Information About the System

Command	Description
`df`	See what hard drives are installed, what file systems are mounted where, and how much space is used and available.
`df /usr/local/src`	Find out where `/usr/local/src` is mounted and how much space is available on it.
`df -k /home`	View the file system for `/home` with the usage reported in 1K, not 512 byte, blocks.
`du`	Get information about disk usage in the current directory as well as in all subdirectories.
`du /home`	Get information about disk usage in the `/home` directory.
`du -k`	Get information about disk usage, measured in 1K blocks.
`file /usr/bin/pico`	Find out the file type of `/usr/bin/pico`.
`finger`	See who else is logged into the system and get a little information about them.
`finger @stc.org`	Find out who is logged into the `stc.org` system.
`finger ejr`	Get information about user `ejr` on your system.
`finger ejray@xmission.com`	Get information about user `ejray@xmission.com`
`id`	Find out the numeric value of your userid and what groups (by name and numeric userid value) you belong to.
`id otheruser`	Check someone else's status to find out what groups they're in.
`quota`	Find out if you're over quota.
`quota -v`	View your current quota settings and space usage.
`uname`	Use to find out what kind of UNIX system you're using.
`uname -a`	Print all system information, including the UNIX system type, hostname, version, and hardware.
`uname -sr`	Find both the system type and release level.
`w`	Get information about other users on the system and what they're doing.
`who`	Get information about the other users on the system.
`whoami`	Find out what userid you're currently logged in as.

Table A.8

Configuring Your UNIX Environment

Command	Description
`alias ourterm="longhonking` → `command -w -many -flags` → `arguments"`	Create the alias `ourterm` to substitute for the command `longhonkingcommand -w` → `-many -flags arguments`.
`export` *`VARIABLE`*	Use in `bash` and `ksh` to make the value of *`VARIABLE`* available to other scripts.
`set`	Find out what environment variables are set and their current values in `bash` and `ksh`.
`set` *`VARIABLE`*`="long value"`	Use in `csh` to set the value of *`VARIABLE`* with spaces or special characters in it.
`set` *`VARIABLE`*`=`*`value`*	Use in `csh` to set *`VARIABLE`* to *`value`*.
`setenv`	Use in `csh` to find out what environment variables are set and their current values.
`setenv` *`VARIABLE value`*	Use in `csh` to make the *`VARIABLE`* available to other scripts in the current shell.
`VARIABLE``="long value"`	Use in `bash` and `ksh` to set the value of *`VARIABLE`* with spaces or special characters in it.
`VARIABLE``=`*`value`*	Use in `bash` and `ksh` to set the *`VARIABLE`* to *`value`*.

Table A.9

Running Scripts and Programs

Command	Description
`at 01:01 1 Jan 2000`	Schedule a job or jobs to run at 01:01 on January 1, 2000.
`at 01/01/99`	Schedule a job to run on 1/1/99.
`at 3:42am`	Schedule a job to run at 3:42 A.M..
`at noon tomorrow`	Schedule a job to run at noon tomorrow.
`at now + 3 weeks`	Schedule a job to run in three weeks.
`at teatime`	Schedule a job to run at 4 P.M..
`atq`	Review jobs in the `at` queue.
`atrm 3`	Remove the specified queued job (3, in this case).
`batch`	Schedule jobs to run when system load permits.
`bg`	Run the most recently suspended or controlled job in the background.
`bg 2`	Run job 2 in the background.
`crontab -e`	Edit your `crontab` in the default editor to schedule regular processes or jobs.
Ctrl Z	Suspend a running job, program, or process.
`fg`	Run the most recently suspended or controlled job in the foreground.
`fg 1`	Run job 1 in the foreground.
`jobs`	See a list of the currently controlled jobs.
`kill %ftp`	Kill a job by name or job number.
`kill 16217`	Kill process number 16217.
`kill -9 16217`	Kill process 16217; the -9 flag lets you kill processes that a regular kill won't touch.
`nice`	Run a job "nicely"—slower and with less of an impact on the system and other users. Bigger numbers are nicer, up to 19. 10 is the default.
`nice -n 19 slowscript`	Run `slowscript` nicely with a priority of 19.
`ps`	View the list of current processes that you're running.
`ps a`	View all processes, including those from other users.
`ps f`	View processes and their interrelationships (the forest view).
`ps x`	View the processes that the system itself is running (also called daemons).
`time` *`script`*	Time how long it takes (in real time and system time) to run *`script`*.
`top`	Monitor system load and processes in real time.

Table A.10

Writing Basic Scripts

COMMAND	DESCRIPTION
`case ... in ... esac`	Use in a shell script to perform separate actions for a variety of cases.
`clear`	Clear the screen.
`continue`	Use in a shell script to skip the rest of the commands in the loop and restart at the beginning of the loop.
`echo`	Display a statement or the value of an environment variable onscreen.
`echo "Your shell is $SHELL"`	Display "Your shell is $SHELL" onscreen.
`echo -e "\tA Tab Stop"`	Move one tab stop to the right and print "A Tab Stop" on the screen.
`for ... do ... done`	Use in a shell script with conditions and commands to specify a loop to occur repeatedly.
`getopts`	Use in a shell script to read flags from the command line.
`if ... then ... else ... fi`	Use in a script (with conditions and commands) to set a conditional process.
`read variable`	Use in a script to get input (the variable) from the terminal.
`sh -x` *`script`*	Execute *`script`* and require the script to display each command line as it is executed.
`sleep 4h5m25s`	Pause for 4 hours, 5 minutes, and 25 seconds here.
`sleep 5s`	Pause for 5 seconds.
`test`	Use in a script to check to see if a given statement is true.
`test` *`expression`*	See if *expression* is true or false—usually used with conditional statements.
`while ... do ... done`	Use in a shell script to perform a loop only while the condition is true.

Table A.11

Sending and Reading E-mail

COMMAND	DESCRIPTION
`elm`	Start the `elm` mail program and read, respond to, or send e-mail.
`elm unixvqs@raycomm.com`	Start a new `elm` mail message to `unixvqs@raycomm.com`.
`elm unixvqs@raycomm.com,info@raycomm.com`	Start a new `elm` mail message to `unixvqs@raycomm.com` and `info@raycomm.com`.
`mail`	Sstart the `mail` program. (Use `pine` or `elm` rather than `mail` if possible.)
`mail unixvqs@raycomm.com <` *`file`*	Send *`file`* to `unixvqs@raycomm.com`.
`mail unixvqs@raycomm.com -s "For you!" <` *`file`*	Send *`file`* to `unixvqs@raycomm.com` with the subject "For you!".
`mail unixvqs@raycomm.com`	Start a simple mail message to `unixvqs@raycomm.com`.
`mail unixvqs@raycomm.com,info@raycomm.com`	Start a simple mail message to `unixvqs@raycomm.com` and `info@raycomm.com`.
`pine`	Start the `pine` mail program and read, respond to, or send e-mail, or to read Usenet newsgroups.
`pine unixvqs@raycomm.com,info@raycomm.com`	Start a `pine` mail message to `unixvqs@raycomm.com` and `info@raycomm.com`.
`pine user@raycomm.com`	Start a `pine` mail message to `user@raycomm.com`.
`vacation`	Initialize `vacation` and edit the message template.
`vacation -I`	Start `vacation` and tell it to respond to incoming messages.
`vacation -j`	Start `vacation` and automatically respond to all messages.

Table A.12

Accessing the Internet

Command	Description
`archie`	Start the local `archie` client. Telnet to an `archie` server if you encounter problems.
`ftp ftp.raycomm.com`	Transfer files to or from `ftp.raycomm.com` using the ftp protocol.
`irc wazoo irc.netcom.com`	Connect to the irc server at `irc.netcom.com` and use the nickname `wazoo`.
`lynx -dump http://url.com > newname.txt`	Get a spiffy plain text file named `newname.txt` out of an HTML document from `http://url.com`.
`lynx`	Start the `lynx` Web browser.
`lynx http://www.yahoo.com/`	Start the `lynx` Web browser on `http://www.yahoo.com/`.
`mesg n`	Refuse `talk` and `write` messages.
`mesg y`	Accept `talk` and `write` messages.
`nn`	Read Usenet News.
`nslookup www.raycomm.com nameserver.some.net`	Look up the name `www.raycomm.com` from the name server `nameserver.some.net`.
`nslookup www.raycomm.com`	Look up the IP number for the host `www.raycomm.com`.
`ping www.raycomm.com`	Test the connection to the host `www.raycomm.com`.
`rn`	Read Usenet News.
`talk deb`	Talk interactively with the owner of the ID `deb`.
`talk id@whereever.com`	Talk interactively with a user `id` the system `whereever.com`.
`telnet somewhere.com`	Connect to and use a computer on the Internet named `somewhere.com`.
`tin`	Read Usenet News.
`tin comp.unix.userfriendly`	Read Usenet News from the `comp.unix.userfriendly` group.
`tn3270 library.wherever.edu`	Connect to a host computer named `library.wherever.edu` that uses an IBM-mainframe-type operating system, like many library card catalogs.
`traceroute www.yahoo.com`	Identify the computers and other devices between you and the host `www.yahoo.com`.
`traceroute -n` *`hostname`*	Check the path to *`hostname`* without resolving the intervening hostnames for faster results.
`trn`	Read Usenet News.
`trn comp.unix.shell`	Read Usenet News from the `comp.unix.shell` group.
`wall`	Send a `write`-type message to all users on the system.
`write` *`otherid`*	Send a message to the user *`otherid`* on the same system.

Table A.13

Working with Encoded and Compressed Files

Command	Description
compress -c file.tar > file.tar.Z	Compress file.tar under the same name with a .Z ending while retaining the original file.
compress file.tar	Compress file.tar. The named file will be replaced with a file of same name ending with .Z.
gunzip archive.tar.gz	Uncompress (un-gzip) archive.tar. Including .gz on the end of the file name is optional.
gzip archive.tar	Gzip (compress) archive.tar. The zipped file will replace the unzipped version and will have a new .gz extension
gzip -c filetogzip > compressed.gz	Gzip filetogzip and keep a copy of the original, unzipped file.
gzip -d	Uncompress (un-gzip) a file. Including .gz on the end of the file name is optional.
tar -cf newfile.tar Directory	Create a new tar archive containing all of the files and directories in Directory.
tar -v	Add the -v flag to tar for a verbose description of what is happening.
tar -xf archive.tar "*file*"	Extract the files with names containing "file" from the tar archive.
tar -xf archive.tar	Extract the contents of archive.tar.
uncompress archive.tar.Z	Uncompress archive.tar.Z, resulting in a file of the same name but without the .Z ending.
uncompress -c archive.tar.Z > archive.tar	Uncompress archive.tar.Z and retain the original file.
unzip zipped	Unzip zipped without specifying the extension.
uudecode file.uue	Uudecode file.uue.
uuencode afile.jpg a.jpg > tosend.uue	Uuencode afile.jpg and a.jpg and save the encoded output as tosend.uue.
uuencode -m	Use uuencode with the -m flag to specify base64 encoding, if your version of uuencode supports it.
zcat archive.gz | more	Uncompress (on the fly without deleting the original) archive.gz to read the contents.
zip zipped file	Create a new zip file named zipped from file.

Table A.14

Installing Software

Command	Description
make	Set up, link, and compile new programs.
make clean	Clear out the garbage from a messed-up installation before you try again.
make install	Complete installation of new programs.

Table A.15

Using Handy Utilities

Command	Description
bc	Use a calculator to add, subtract, multiply, divide, and more.
bc bcfile	Do the calculations specified in `bcfile`, then more from the command line.
cal	View the current month's calendar.
cal 12 1941	View the calendar for December 1941.
cal 1999	View the calendar for 1999.
cal -j	View the Julian calendar.
calendar	View reminders for the current date, read from the file `~/calendar`.
fortune	Display a fortune, saying, quotation, or whatever happens to come up.
ispell gudspeler	Interactively spell-check the `gudspeler` file.
procmail	Filters and sorts mail according to a "recipe." Run from the `.forward` file.
script	Record your actions in a file called `typescript` in the current directory.
script covermybutt	Record your actions in the file `covermybutt`.

B

What's What and What's Where

As you're using UNIX, you'll undoubtedly encounter files that look important or directories that look interesting, but it's often hard to know what files belong to which programs, and even harder to figure out what some directories are for. Therefore, we're trying to help out a little with the information in this appendix.

Table B.1 lists important UNIX files and directories.

Table B.1

Key Files in Your UNIX Environment

File Name	Description
.forward	Includes address(es) to forward mail to or redirects mail to a vacation program or to procmail.
.newsrc	Includes records of read, unread, and subscribed newsgroups for use by news readers.
.procmailrc	Includes configuration information for procmail.
.signature	Contains your signature, which is appended to your messages by e-mail programs and news readers.
/etc/bashrc	System-wide bash resource file shared by all bash users.
/etc/csh.cshrc	System-wide csh resource file.
/etc/group	System group records.
/etc/ksh.kshrc	System-wide configuration files for ksh users.
/etc/passwd	System passwords and user records.
/etc/profile	System-wide configuration file used by bash and ksh.
~/.bash_profile	Primary personal configuration file for bash users.
~/.cshrc	Resource file for csh users.
~/.kshrc	Configuration file for ksh users.
~/.login	Configuration file for csh users.
~/.profile	Primary configuration file for ksh users; used by bash if .bash_profile isn't available.
~/calendar	Includes data for calendar to use to issue reminders.
~/mail	Mail directory used by pine.
~/Mail	Mail directory used by system mailer and elm.
Makefile	Includes configuration information used by make to compile and install new software.
README	Includes important information, usually distributed with a new program or script, about installation or usage.

Table B.2 lists the contents of common UNIX directories. In practice, the contents of these directories (and their existence) varies greatly by system, but the configuration described here is fairly standard.

Table B.2

Common UNIX Directories and Their Contents

DIRECTORY	CONTENTS
/bin	Essential programs and commands for use by all users.
/boot	Files that the system boot loader uses.
/dev	Devices (CD-ROM, serial ports, etc.) and special files.
/etc	System configuration files and global settings.
/etc/skel	Template configuration files for individual users.
/etc/X11	Configuration files and information for the X Window System.
/home	Home directories for users.
/lib	Essential shared libraries and kernel modules.
/mnt	Mount point for temporarily mounted file systems.
/opt	Directory for add-on application software packages.
/proc	Location of kernel and process information (virtual file system).
/root	Home directory for the root user/system administrator.
/sbin	Essential programs and commands for system boot.
/tmp	Temporary files.
/usr/bin	Commands and programs that are less central to basic UNIX system functionality than those in /bin but were installed with the system.
/usr/include	Standard include files and header files for C programs.
/usr/lib	Libraries for programming and for installed packages.
/usr/local	Most files and data that were developed or customized on the system.
/usr/local/bin	Locally developed or installed programs.
/usr/local/man	Manual (help) pages for local programs.
/usr/local/src	Source code for locally developed or installed programs.
/usr/sbin	Additional nonessential standard system binaries.
/usr/share	Shared (system-independent) data files.
/usr/share/dict	Word lists.
/usr/share/man	Manual (help) pages for standard programs.
/usr/share/misc	Miscellaneous shared system-independent data.
/usr/src	Source code for standard programs.
/usr/X11R6	X Window System, Version 11 Release 6.
/usr/X386	X Window System, Version 11 Release 5, on x86 platforms.
/var	Changeable data, including system logs, temporary data from programs, and user mail storage.
/var/account	Accounting logs, if applicable.
/var/cache	Application-specific cache data.
/var/cache/fonts	Locally generated fonts.
/var/cache/man	Formatted versions of manual pages.

(continued on next page)

Table B.2 (continued)

Common UNIX Directories and Their Contents (continued)	
/var/crash	Information stored from system crashes, if applicable.
/var/games	Variable game data.
/var/lock	Lock files created by various programs.
/var/log	Log files and directories.
/var/mail	User mailbox files.
/var/run	Run-time variable files.
/var/spool	General application spool data.
/var/spool/cron	Contains cron and at job schedules.
/var/spool/lpd	Line-printer daemon print queues.
/var/state	Variable state information for the system.
/var/state/editorname	Editor backup files and state information.
/var/state/misc	Miscellaneous variable data.
/var/tmp	Temporary files that the system keeps through reboots.
/var/yp	Database files that the Network Information Service (NIS) uses.

C

COMMAND FLAGS

This appendix provides a list of many (but still not all) UNIX commands and programs as well as the related command-line flags.

In general, flags offer a thorough selection of options for programs that operate exclusively from command line input, as well as an overview of the functionality for many other programs. Please keep in mind, however, that command flags only touch the surface of the capabilities of interactive programs (like `pico`, `vi`, `lynx`, or `pine`) or particularly complex programs that rely on special expressions (such as `grep`) or that use multiple files or sources for information (such as `procmail`).

Table C.1 should provide you with a brief reminder and starting point for learning more about these UNIX commands. While the flags we've included here work on our system, they will likely vary somewhat on different systems or with different shells. Check your local `man` pages for specifics.

Note that multiple equivalent commands or flags all appear on the same line, separated by commas. Additionally, multiple flags (unless contradictory) can be used with all commands. The [ ] brackets indicate that one of the options enclosed may be used.

Table C.1

Commands and Flags

COMMAND/FLAG	DESCRIPTION
`alias`	Use to create command aliases.
`-t`	Specifies tracking command paths
`-x`	Exports aliases for use by scripts.
`archie`	Use to query Archie-style anonymous ftp databases
`-c`	Searches with case sensitivity.
`-e`	Searches for exact strings.
`-r` *regexp*	Searches with a regular expression.
`-s`	Searches without case sensitivity.
`-o`*name*	Searches and puts results in the file `name`
`-l`	Provides results for processing by other programs.
`-t`	Sorts results by date.
`-m`*hits*	Specifies maximum number of hits to retrieve.
`-N` *level*	Sets Archie niceness to *level*. Default is 0, maximum is 35765.
`-h` *hostname*	Specifies *hostname* to query.
`-L`	Lists known Archie servers
`-V`	Provides feedback as search progresses.
`at`	Use to schedule, examine, or delete jobs for queued execution.
`-V`	Displays version information.
`-q` *queue*	Specifies queue to use (as a letter). Higher letters are nicer.
`-m` *address*	Specifies mail notification to user when job has completed.
`-f` *file*	Reads job from *file*.
`-l`	Lists queues, just like `atq`.
`-d`	Deletes scheduled jobs, just like `atrm`.
`atq`	Use to show queues of scheduled jobs.
`-q` *queue*	Specifies queue to use (as a letter).
`-v`	Displays completed but not deleted jobs or scheduled time for unexecuted jobs.
`atrm`	Use to remove a job from the queue
`-q` *queue*	Specifies queue to use (as a letter).
`awk`	Use to manipulate files as databases.
`-F`*fieldseparator*	Specifies field separator.
`-v` *variable=value*	Sets *variable* to *value*.
`-f` *program* `-file`	Specifies file or files containing `awk` program source.
`--help`	Prints help information
`--version`	Prints version information.
`--`	Specifies end of option list.
`bash`	Use the efficient, user-friendly shell `bash`.
`-c` *string*	Reads commands from *string*.
`-i`	Makes the shell interactive, as opposed to non-interactive as in a shell script.
`-s`	Specifies that additional options, beyond those given, should be read from standard input.
`-, --`	Indicates the end of options and stops further option processing.

Table C.1 (continued)

Commands and Flags (continued)

COMMAND/FLAG	DESCRIPTION
-norc	Specifies not to read ~/.bashrc.
-noprofile	Specifies not to read system-wide or individual configuration files.
-rcfile *file*	Specifies alternative configuration file.
-version	Displays bash version number.
-quiet	Specifies not to display informative messages when starting (default setting).
-login	Specifies to start bash as a login shell.
-nobraceexpansion	Specifies not to interpret or complete statements within curly braces.
-nolineediting	Specifies not to allow command line editing if shell is interactive.
-posix	Specifies Posix compliance which helps make anything more portable from system to system.
batch	Use to schedule jobs for low system loads.
bg	Use to move a job to the background.
cal	Use to display a calendar
-j	Displays Julian dates with days numbered through the year from January 1.
-y	Displays the current year's calendar.
month year	Specifies month (1 to 12) and year (1 to 9999).
cat	Use to send text to standard output, usually the screen.
-b, --number-nonblank	Specifies to number all nonblank output lines.
-n, --number	Specifies to number all output lines.
-s, --squeeze-blank	Specifies to replace adjacent blank lines with a single blank line.
-v, --show-nonprinting	Specifies to display control characters with "^" preceding them.
-A, --show-all	Specifies to show all control characters.
-E, --show-ends	Specifies to display a "$" at the end of each line.
-T, --show-tabs	Specifies to display tab characters as "^I".
--help	Displays a help message.
--version	Displays the version number.
cd	Use to change the working directory.
chgrp	Use to change the group ownership of files.
-c, --changes	Specifies to list files whose ownership actually changes.
-f, --silent, --quiet	Suppresses error messages for files that cannot be changed.
-v, --verbose	Specifies to describe changed ownership.
-R, --recursive	Specifies to recursively change ownership of directories and contents.
--help	Displays help message.
--version	Displays version information.
chmod	Use to change the access permissions of files.
-c, --changes	Specifies to list files whose permissions actually change.
-f, --silent, --quiet	Suppresses error messages.
-v, --verbose	Specifies to describe changed permissions.
-R, --recursive	Specifies to recursively change permissions of directories and contents.
--help	Displays help message.
--version	Displays version information.

(continued on next page)

Table C.1 (continued)

Commands and Flags (continued)

Command/Flag	Description
chown	Use to change the user and group ownership of files.
`-c, --changes`	Specifies to list files whose ownership actually changes.
`-f, --silent, --quiet`	Suppresses error messages for files that cannot be changed.
`-v, --verbose`	Specifies to describe changed ownership.
`-R, --recursive`	Specifies to recursively change ownership of directories and contents.
`--help`	Displays help message.
`--version`	Displays version information.
chsh	Use to change your login shell.
`-s, --shell`	Specifies the new login shell.
`-l, --list-shells`	Displays the shells in `/etc/shells`.
`-u, --help`	Prints a help message.
`--version`	Prints version information.
cmp	Use to compare two files.
`-l`	Displays the byte number (which starting byte in the file) in decimal and the differing bytes in octal for each difference.
`-s`	Displays nothing for differing files except exit status.
compress	Use to compress and expand archives.
`-c`	Specifies that `compress/uncompress` write to standard output (usually your screen) and leave files unchanged.
`-r`	Specifies to recursively process directories.
`-V`	Displays version information.
cp	Use to copy files or directories.
`-a, --archive`	Specifies to preserve file structure and attributes.
`-b, --backup`	Specifies to make backups of files before overwriting.
`-d, --no-dereference`	Specifies to copy symbolic links as symbolic links rather than the files that they point to.
`-f, --force`	Specifies to overwrite all existing destination files.
`-i, --interactive`	Requires prompting before overwriting.
`-l, --link`	Specifies to make hard links instead of copies of files.
`-P, --parents`	Completes destination file names by appending the source file name to the target directory name.
`-p, --preserve`	Specifies to preserve the original file characteristics, including permissions and ownership.
`-r`	Specifies to copy directories recursively.
`-s, --symbolic-link`	Specifies to make symbolic links instead of copies of files.
`-u, --update`	Specifies not to overwrite newer files.
`-v, --verbose`	Displays file names before copying.
`-x, --one-file-system`	Restricts action to a single file system.
`-R, --recursive`	Specifies to copy directories recursively.
`--help`	Prints a help message.
`--version`	Prints version information.
`-S, --suffix` *backup-suffix*	Specifies a suffix for backup files.

Table C.1 (continued)

Commands and Flags (continued)

COMMAND/FLAG	DESCRIPTION
-V, --version-control {*numbered,existing,simple*}	Specifies version control as numbered, existing, or simple, to allow controlled and regulated backups with cp.
crontab	Use to maintain crontab files.
-l	Displays current crontab.
-r	Removes current crontab.
-e	Opens crontab in default editor.
df	Use to display information about free disk space
-a, --all	Specifies that all file systems, including special ones (e.g. CDROM, MSDOS), should be processed.
-i, --inodes	Displays inode (disk element) usage information.
-k, --kilobytes	Displays sizes in 1K blocks instead of 512-byte blocks.
-P, --portability	Uses Posix standard output format.
-T, --print-type	Displays type of each file system.
-t, --type=*fstype*	Displays only named file system types.
-x, --exclude-type=*fstype*	Displays only non-named file system types.
--help	Prints help information.
--version	Prints version information.
diff	Use to display differences between text files.
-b	Specifies to ignore trailing blanks (spaces and tabs) and consider other blanks equivalent.
-i	Specifies case-insensitive comparisons.
-t	Specifies to display tab characters in output.
-w	Specifies to ignore all blanks and consider groups of blanks equivalent.
-c	Specifies a listing of differences with three lines of context.
-C *number*	Specifies a listing of differences with *number* lines of context.
-e	Specifies output of a script for the ed editor to re-create the second file from the first.
-f	Specifies output of a script to create the first file from the second. This does not work with ed.
-h	Specifies fast and not necessarily complete comparison.
-n	Specifies output of a script to create the first file from the second along with a total of changed lines for each command.
-D *string*	Outputs combined version of first and second files with C controls to compile as the first or the second file.
-l	Specifies directory output in long format.
-r	Specifies that diff should recursively process subdirectories common to both given directories
-s	Outputs names of identical (not different) files.
-S *name*	Begins comparison within a directory with the specified file name.
du	Use to display disk usage information.
-a, --all	Displays information for all files.
-b, --bytes	Displays sizes in bytes.
-c, --total	Displays totals for all arguments.

(continued on next page)

COMMAND FLAGS

Table C.1 (continued)

Commands and Flags (continued)

Command/Flag	Description
`-k, --kilobytes`	Displays sizes in kilobytes.
`-l, --count-links`	Displays sizes of all files, including linked files counted elsewhere.
`-s, --summarize`	Displays only totals for each argument.
`-x, --one-file-system`	Specifies not to process directories on other file systems.
`-L, --dereference`	Displays space used by linked file or directory, not just space used by link.
`-S, --separate-dirs`	Counts directories separately.
`--help`	Prints help information.
`--version`	Prints version information.
`elm`	Use to send and receive mail.
`-a`	Specifies arrow cursor.
`-c`	Expands specified aliases and exits.
`-d` *level*	Specifies debugging output.
`-f alternative-folder`	Specifies folder to read instead of incoming mail folder.
`-h, -?`	Displays help message.
`-i` *file*	Read named file into message editor.
`-m`	Disables menu.
`-s` *subj*	Specifies subject for mail messages.
`-v`	Displays version information.
`-z`	Specifies not to start `elm` if no mail is present.
`fg`	Use to move a job to the foreground.
`file`	Use to determine file type.
`--version`	Prints version information.
`-m` *list*	Specifies alternative list of files with magic numbers (helping to indicate file type).
`-z`	Attempts to look into compressed files.
`-b`	Specifies brief output mode.
`-c`	Checks magic file.
`-f` *file*	Specifies to read names of the files to be examined from *file*.
`-L`	Specifies to follow symbolic links.
`find`	Use to find files in the UNIX system.
`-daystart`	Specifies to measure all times starting today, not 24 hours ago.
`-depth`	Specifies to process directory contents before the directory.
`-follow`	Specifies to follow symbolic links.
`-help, --help`	Prints a help message.
`-maxdepth` *levels*	Specifies how many *levels* below starting directory level to descend.
`-mindepth` *levels*	Specifies how many *levels* below starting directory level to start processing.
`-mount, -xdev`	Specifies not to descend directories on other file systems.
`-noleaf`	Specifies not to optimize for UNIX systems, which is needed for CD-ROM directories, for example.
`--version`	Prints version information.
`-amin` *n*	Finds files accessed *n* minutes ago.

Table C.1 (continued)

Commands and Flags (continued)

Command/Flag	Description
-anewer *file*	Finds files accessed more recently than they were modified.
-atime *n*	Finds files accessed *n* days ago.
-cmin *n*	Finds files whose status was changed *n* minutes ago.
-cnewer *file*	Finds files whose status was changed more recently than the file was modified.
-ctime *n*	Finds files whose status was changed *n* days ago.
-empty	Finds files that are empty.
-fstype *type*	Finds files on file systems of specified type.
-gid n	Finds files with numeric group ID of *n*.
-group *gname*	Finds files with group name of *gname* or corresponding group ID.
-ilname *pattern*	Finds files that are symbolic links with pattern text in the name.
-iname *pattern*	Finds files with *pattern* in the name, case-insensitive.
-inum *n*	Finds files with inode number *n*.
-ipath *pattern*	Finds files with regular expression *pattern* in the path, case insensitive.
-iregex *pattern*	Finds files with regular expression *pattern* in name, case insensitive.
-links *n*	Finds files with *n* links.
-lname *pattern*	Finds files that are symbolic links with *pattern* in the name.
-mmin *n*	Finds files last modified *n* minutes ago.
-mtime *n*	Finds files last modified *n* days ago.
-name *pattern*	Finds files with name of *pattern*.
-newer *file*	Finds files modified more recently than *file*.
-nouser	Finds files with no user name corresponding to the numeric userid.
-nogroup	Finds files with no group name corresponding to the numeric group ID.
-path *pattern*	Finds files with paths matching *pattern*.
-regex *pattern*	Finds files with regular expression *pattern* in name, case sensitive.
-size *n[bckw]*	Finds files using *n* blocks, bytes, kilobytes, or words, respectively, of space.
-type *type*	Finds files of type *type*, where b is block (buffered) special, c is character (unbuffered) special, d is directory, p is named pipe (FIFO), f is regular file, l is symbolic link, or s is socket.
-uid *n*	Finds files with numeric userid of *n*.
-used *n*	Finds files last accessed *n* days after status changed.
-user *uname*	Finds files owned by userid or numerid user ID.
-exec *command* ;	Executes *command.*
-fprint *file*	Prints full file name into *file*.
-ok *command* ;	Executes *command* with confirmation.
-print	Prints results to standard output.
finger	Use to display information about users.
-s	Displays the login name, real name, terminal name and write status, idle time, login time, office location, and office phone number.
-l	Specifies multiple-line format with information from -s option plus user's home directory, home phone number, login shell, mail status, and the contents of the .plan, .project, and .forward files.
-p	Prevents -l from displaying contents of .plan and .project files.

(continued on next page)

Table C.1 (continued)

Commands and Flags (continued)	
COMMAND/FLAG	DESCRIPTION
-m	Disables matching user names.
ftp	Use to put files in or get files from ftp (file transfer protocol) archives.
-v	Specifies verbose output of responses and statistics.
-n	Restricts automatic login.
-i	Turns off interactive prompting during multiple file transfers.
-d	Enables debugging output.
-g	Disables wildcards ("globbing").
grep	Use to display lines matching a given pattern.
-n	Displays matches with *n* lines before and after matching lines.
-A n, --after-context=*n*	Displays matches with *n* lines after matching lines.
-B *n*, --before-context=*n*	Displays matches with *n* lines before matching lines.
-C, --context	Displays matches with two lines of surrounding context.
--version	Displays version information.
-c, --count	Displays count of matches for each file.
-e pattern, --regexp=*pattern*	Specifies pattern explicitly.
-f file, --file=file	Reads patterns from *file*.
-h, --no-filename	Specifies not to display file names in output.
-i, --ignore-case	Searches without regard to case.
-L, --files-without-match	Prints name of first non-matching file.
-l, --files-with-matches	Prints name of first matching file.
-n, --line-number	Displays output line numbers.
-q, --quiet	Suppresses output and stops scanning on first match.
-s, --silent	Suppresses error messages.
-v, --revert-match	Inverts matching to select opposite files.
-w, --word-regexp	Finds only matches for whole words.
-x, --line-regexp	Finds only matches for the whole line.
gzip	Use to compress (gzip) or expand files.
-a –ascii	Specifies to convert ends of lines in ASCII text mode to conform to UNIX conventions.
-c --stdout --to-stdout	Sends output to standard output while maintaining original files unchanged.
-d --decompress –uncompress	Uncompresses files.
-f –force	Forces compression or decompression.
-h –help	Displays help message.
-l –list	Lists information about compressed files.
--verbose	Displays additional information about archive files.
-L –license	Displays the gzip license.
-n --no-name	Specifies not to save the original file name and time.
-N –name	Specifies to always save the original file name and time stamp information when compressing.
-q –quiet	Suppresses all warnings.
-r –recursive	Specifies to descend subdirectories.

COMMAND FLAGS

Table C.1 (continued)

Commands and Flags (continued)

COMMAND/FLAG	DESCRIPTION
-S .suf --suffix *.suf*	Specifies alternative suffixes.
-t -test	Tests compressed file integrity.
-v -verbose	Displays name and percentage reductions for each file processed.
-V -version	Displays version information.
head	Use to output the first part of files.
-c [*b*,*k*,*m*], --bytes *N*	Displays first *N* bytes of file, in b (512-byte blocks), k (1-kilobyte blocks), or m (1-megabyte blocks).
-n N, --lines *N*	Displays first *N* lines of a file.
-q, --quiet, --silent	Specifies not to display file names.
-v, --verbose	Displays file name.
--help	Displays help message.
--version	Displays version information.
id	Use to display real and effective userids and group IDs.
-g, --group	Displays only group ID.
-G, --groups	Displays only supplementary groups.
--help	Displays help message.
-n, --name	Displays user or group name, not number.
-r, --real	Displays real, not effective, userid or group ID.
-u, --user	Displays only userid.
--version	Displays version information.
jobs	Use to display list of jobs under control.
-l	Displays additional information (long listing) for jobs.
-p	Displays job process IDs.
-n	Displays jobs that have stopped or exited since notification.
kill	Use to terminate a process.
-s	Specifies kill signal to send.
-p	Specifies to print process ID but not send kill signal.
-l	Displays a list of signal names.
less	Use to page through files; similar to more.
-?, --help	Displays a command summary.
-a	Specifies to start searches below visible display.
-b*n*	Specifies number of buffers for each file.
-B	Specifies automatic buffer allocation.
-c	Specifies not to scroll, but rather to paint each screen from the top.
-C	Specifies not to scroll, but rather to clear and display new text.
-d	Suppresses error messages for dumb terminals.
-e	Specifies to automatically exit if you move down after hitting the end of the file.
-E	Specifies to automatically exit when you hit the end of the file.
-f	Forces all files to be opened.
-g	Specifies to highlight only last found string.
-G	Specifies no highlighting of found strings.

(continued on next page)

COMMAND FLAGS

Table C.1 (continued)

Commands and Flags (continued)	
COMMAND/FLAG	DESCRIPTION
-h*n*	Specifies maximum number (*n*) of lines to scroll backward.
-i	Specifies case-insensitive searches except when search string contains capital letters.
-I	Specifies case-insensitive searches always.
-j*n*	Specifies a line on the screen where a target line should be located.
-k *filename*	Specifies to open and interpret *filename* as a lesskey file.
-m	Specifies verbose prompting , displaying percentage into the file viewed.
-M	Specifies even more verbose prompting.
-n	Suppresses line numbers.
-N	Specifies line number for each displayed line.
-o*filename*	Tells less to copy input to *filename* as it is viewed.
-O*filename*	Tells less to copy input to *filename* as it is viewed and overwrite without confirmation.
-p*pattern*	Specifies to start display at first occurrence of *pattern*.
-q	Specifies quiet operation and only rings bell on certain errors.
-Q	Specifies totally quiet operation and never rings bell.
-r	Specifies to display control characters directly, even if display problems result.
-s	Compresses consecutive blank lines into a single blank line.
-S	Specifies that long lines should be chopped off, not wrapped.
-u	Specifies that backspaces and carriage returns should be sent to the terminal.
-U	Specifies that backspaces, tabs, and carriage returns should be treated as control characters.
-V, --version	Displays the version number.
-w	Specifies that blank lines, not tilde (~) represent lines after the end of the file.
-x*n*	Sets tab stops every *n* columns.
-X	Disables termcap initialization strings.
-y*n*	Specifies maximum number of lines to scroll.
-*n*	Specifies the scrolling window size as *n*.
-"	Specifies file name quoting character.
--	Indicates end of options.
ln	Use to make links between files
-b, --backup	Backs up files before removing them.
-f, --force	Overwrites destination files.
-i, --interactive	Prompts before overwriting files.
-n, --no-dereference	Attempts to replace symbolic links.
-s, --symbolic	Specifies to make symbolic links when possible.
-v, --verbose	Specifies to display file names before linking.
--help	Prints a help message.
--version	Prints version information.
-S, --suffix backup-suffix	Specifies suffix for backup files.
-V, --version-control {*numbered,existing,simple*}	Specifies version control as numbered, existing, or simple, as with cp.

Table C.1 (continued)

Commands and Flags (continued)

COMMAND/FLAG	DESCRIPTION
`ls`	Use to list directory contents
`-a, --all`	Lists all files
`-b, --escape`	Quotes nongraphic characters using backslash sequences.
`-c, --time=ctime, --time=status`	Sorts according to status change time, not modification time.
`-d, --directory`	Lists directory names, not contents.
`-f`	Does not sort directory contents
`--full-time`	Provides full, not abbreviated time listings.
`-g`	Does nothing; for backwards compatibility.
`-i, --inode`	Displays index number of each file.
`-k, --kilobytes`	Displays file sizes in kilobytes.
`-l, --format=long, --format=verbose`	Displays file name, file permissions, number of hard links, owner, group, size in bytes, and time.
`-m, --format=commas`	Displays names separated by commas.
`-n, --numeric-uid-gid`	Displays numeric userid and group ID.
`-p, -F`	Displays extra character for each file name to show the file type.
`-q, --hide-control-chars`	Displays question marks rather than nongraphic characters.
`-r, --reverse`	Sorts names in reverse order.
`-s, --size`	Displays file sizes in 1K blocks.
`-t, --sort=time`	Sorts directory contents by modification time, newest first.
`-u, --time=atime, --time=access, --time=use`	Sorts names by last access time instead of the modification time.
`-x, --format=across, --format=horizontal`	Displays names in columns, sorted horizontally.
`-A, --almost-all`	Lists all names except for "." and "..".
`-B, --ignore-backups`	Does not display names that end with "~".
`-C, --format=vertical`	Displays names in columns, sorted vertically.
`-G, --no-group`	Does not display group information.
`-L, --dereference`	Lists names of symbolic links instead of the link contents.
`-N, --literal`	Does not quote names.
`-Q, --quote-name`	Quotes names in double quotes and non-graphic characters in C syntax.
`-R, --recursive`	Displays the contents of all directories recursively.
`-S, --sort=size`	Sorts names by file size, largest first.
`-U, --sort=none`	Does not sort names.
`-X, --sort=extension`	Sorts names alphabetically by file extension.
`-1, --format=single-column`	Lists one file per line.
`-w, --width` *n*	Sets display to *n* columns wide.
`-T, --tabsize` *n*	Sets tabs to *n* columns wide.
`-I, --ignore pattern`	Does not display names matching *pattern*.
`--color, --colour, --color=yes, --colour=yes`	Displays the names in color depending on the type of file and terminal characteristics.
`--color=tty, --colour=tty`	Displays names in color only if standard output is a terminal.
`--color=no, --colour=no`	Disables color display of names.

(continued on next page)

Table C.1 (continued)

Commands and Flags (continued)

COMMAND/FLAG	DESCRIPTION
--help	Displays help message.
--version	Displays version information.
lynx	Use to browse the World Wide Web
-	Specifies to take arguments from standard input.
-anonymous	Specifes anonymous account.
-assume_charset=ID:MIMEname	Specifies default character set.
-assume_local_charset=ID:MIMEname	Specifies character set for local files.
-assume_unrec_charset=ID:MIMEname	Specifies character set to use if remote character set is not recognizable.
-auth=ID:PASSWD	Specifies authorization ID and password for protected documents.
-base	Specifies HTML BASE tag to use when dumping source code.
-blink	Specifies high-intensity background colors for color mode if possible.
-book	Specifies bookmark page as initial file.
-buried_*news*	Specifies automatic conversion of embedded URLs to links in Netnews.
-cache=*n*	Specifies to cache *n* documents in memory.
-case	Specifies case-sensitive searching within pages.
-cfg=*file*	Specifies alternative lynx configuration file.
-child	Specifies no save to disk and quick exit with ← in first document.
-color	Specifies color mode, if possible.
-cookies	Toggles handling of cookies.
-core	Toggles core dumps on crashes.
-crawl -traversal	Specifies to output each browsed page to a file.
-dump	Specifies to dump formatted output of specified page to standard output.
-editor=*editor*	Enables editing with specified editor.
-emacskeys	Enables emacs-style key movement.
-enable_scrollback	Toggles scrollback when supported by communication programs.
-error_file=*FILE*	Specifies where to save error code.
-force_*html*	Specifies that the start document be considered HTML.
-force_*secure*	Toggles security flag for SSL cookies.
-from	Toggles use of From headers.
-ftp	Specifies no ftp access.
-get_*data*	Retrieves form data from standard input and dumps results.
-head	Requests MIME headers.
-help	Displays help message.
-hiddenlinks=[*merge,listonly,ignore*]	Specifies handling of hidden links.
-historical	Toggles use of > or --> as comment terminator.
-homepage=*URL*	Sets home page URL for session.
-image_*links*	Toggles display of links for all images.
-index=*URL*	Sets the default index file to the specified URL.
-ismap	Toggles presentation of links for client-side image maps.
-link=*NUMBER*	Specifies starting number for files crawled.
-localhost	Specifies only browsing on local host.

Table C.1 (continued)

Commands and Flags (continued)

COMMAND/FLAG	DESCRIPTION
-locexec	Enables local program execution from local files
-mime_*header*	Displays MIME header with document source.
-minimal	Toggles minimal or valid comment parsing.
-newschunksize=*n*	Specifies *n* articles in chunked news listings.
-newsmaxchunk=*n*	Specifies maximum number of news articles before chunking.
-nobrowse	Disables directory browsing.
-nocc	Disables prompts for user copies of sent mail.
-nocolor	Disables color mode.
-noexec	Disables local program execution.
-nofilereferer	Disables Referrer headers for file URLs.
-nolist	Disables link listings in formatted text output (dumps).
-nolog	Disables mailing error messages to document owners.
-nopause	Disables pauses on status messages.
-noprint	Disables printing.
-noredir	Disables automatic redirection.
-noreferer	Disables Referrer headers for all URLs.
-nosocks	Disables SOCKS proxy use.
-nostatus	Disables retrieval status messages.
-number_links	Numbers links.
-pauth=*ID:PASSWD*	Sets ID and password for a protected proxy server.
-popup	Toggles handling of single-choice SELECT options as popup windows or as lists of radio buttons.
-post_*data*	Sends form data from standard input with POST dump results.
-preparsed	Specifies that HTML source be preparsed and reformatted when viewed.
-print	Enables printing.
-pseudo_*inlines*	Toggles pseudo-ALT text for inline images with no ALT string.
-raw	Toggles default setting of 8-bit character translations or CJK mode for the initial character set.
-realm	Specifies access only to URLs in initial domain.
-reload	Specifies to empty proxy server cache and reload document.
-resubmit_*posts*	Toggles forced resubmissions of forms when the documents they returned are revisited.
-rlogin	Disables rlogin commands.
-selective	Restricts directory browsing to those specified with .www_*browsable*.
-show_*cursor*	Specifies cursor to be shown at start of current link.
-source	Sends output as HTML source to standard output.
-telnet	Disables telnet commands.
-term=*TERM*	Specifies terminal type for lynx.
-tlog	Toggles lynx tracing log.
-trace	Enables WWW trace mode.
-traversal	Follows links from start file.
-underscore	Toggles use of underline in dumps.

(continued on next page)

COMMAND FLAGS

Table C.1 (continued)

Commands and Flags (continued)	
COMMAND/FLAG	DESCRIPTION
-useragent=*Name*	Specifies alternative lynx User-Agent header name.
-validate	Accepts only HTTP URLs for validation.
-version	Displays version information.
-vikeys	Enables vi-like key movement.
-width=*n*	Specifies number of columns for dump formatting.
man	Use to display online manual pages.
-C config_*file*	Specifies the man.conf file to use
-M path	Specifies the directories to search for man pages.
-P pager	Specifies which pager (more or less) to use.
-S section_*list*	Specifies list of manual sections to search.
-a	Specifies to display all matching man pages, not just the default first one.
-c	Reformats the source man page before displaying it.
-d	Specifies not to display man page; rather, display debugging information.
-D	Displays and prints debugging info.
-f	Provides whatis information.
-h	Prints help message.
-k	Provides same information as apropos.
-K	Searches for string in all man pages.
-m *system*	Specifies alternate man pages for *system*.
-w, --path	Specifies not to display man pages; rather, print the path of the files.
-W	Specifies not to display man mages; rather, print the file names without additional information.
mail	Use to send and receive mail
-v	Specifies verbose mode and displays delivery details.
-i	Specifies to ignore interrupt signals.
-I	Specifies interactive mode even if input is not from a terminal.
-n	Disables mail.rc reading when starting.
-N	Disables initial display of message headers when reading mail.
-s *subject*	Specifies subject on command line.
-c *addresses*	Specifies addresses for carbon copies.
-b *addresses*	Specifies addresses for blind carbon copies.
-f *file*	Reads contents of file for processing and returns undeleted messages to this file.
mkdir	Use to make directories.
-m, --mode *mode*	Sets the mode of created directories as with chmod.
-p, --parents	Makes directories and any necessary parent directories.
--help	Displays help message.
--version	Displays version information.
more	Use to view files a screen at a time.
-num	Specifies number of lines onscreen.
-d	Specifies prompting and no bell on errors.

Table C.1 (continued)

Commands and Flags (continued)

COMMAND/FLAG	DESCRIPTION
`-l`	Specifies not to pause after a Ctrl L in the file.
`-f`	Specifies to count logical lines rather than screen lines.
`-p`	Specifies not to scroll, rather, to clear and display new text.
`-c`	Specifies not to scroll, but rather to paint each screen from the top.
`-s`	Specifies to squeeze multiple blank lines together.
`-u`	Specifies to suppress underlining.
`+/`	Specifies a string to find and start at for displaying the file.
`+num`	Specifies to start at line number *num*.
`mv`	Use to rename or move files.
`-b, --backup`	Specifies to make backups of files before removal.
`-f, --force`	Specifies to overwrite all existing destination files.
`-i, --interactive`	Requires prompting before overwriting.
`-v, --verbose`	Displays file names before moving.
`--help`	Prints a help message.
`--version`	Prints version information.
`-S, --suffix backup-suffix`	Specifies suffix for backup files.
`-V, --version-control {numbered,existing,simple}`	Specifies version control as numbered, existing, or simple.
`nice`	Use to run a program with a different priority.
`-n adjustment, -adjustment, --adjustment=adjustment`	Adds *adjustment* number to initial priority.
`--help`	Displays help message.
`--version`	Displays version information.
`passwd`	Use to set a password for the system.
`pico`	Use for user-friendly text editing.
`+n`	Starts `pico` with the cursor located *n* lines into the file.
`-d`	Specifies that the Delete key rubs out the character the cursor is on rather than the character to its left.
`-e`	Enables file name completion.
`-f`	Specifies to use function keys for commands.
`-j`	Specifies that goto commands to indicate directories are allowed.
`-k`	Specifies that "Cut Text" removes characters from the cursor position to the end of the line.
`-nn`	Enables mail notification every *n* seconds.
`-o` *dir*	Specifies operating directory.
`-rn`	Specifies column *n* for right margin of justify command.
`-t`	Sets tool mode for when `pico` is the default editor in other programs.
`-v`	Specifies view-only.
`-w`	Disables word wrap.
`-x`	Disables menu.
`-z`	Allows Ctrl Z suspension of `pico`.

(continued on next page)

Table C.1 (continued)

Commands and Flags (continued)

Command/Flag	Description
pine	Use to read news and e-mail.
-d debug-level	Displays diagnostic information at levels from 0 (none) to 9 (complete).
-f *folder*	Specifies to open *folder* instead of inbox.
-F *file*	Opens specified file with pine.
-h	Displays brief help message.
-i	Specifies to start in folder index.
-I *keystrokes*	Specifies initial set of keystrokes to execute on startup.
-k	Specifies to use function keys for commands.
-l	Specifies to expand all collections in folder-list display.
-n *number*	Specifies to start with given message number.
-o	Opens first folder as read-only.
-p *config-file*	Specifies configuration file to use instead of default personal configuration file.
-P *config-file*	Specifies configuration file to use instead of system-wide configuration file.
-r	Requires demo mode.
-z	Allows eventual suspension of pine process.
-conf	Outputs a new copy of system-wide configuration file.
-pinerc *file*	Outputs new pinerc configuration file.
-sort *order*	Specifies sort *order* in folders as arrival, subject, from, date, size, orderedsubj, or reverse.
ping	Use to see if a specific host is reachable.
-c *count*	Specifies number of responses to receive before stopping.
-d	Specifies SO_DEBUG option.
-f	Specifies flood ping (for system administrators only).
-i *wait*	Specifies how many seconds to wait between packets.
-l *preload*	Specifies initial flurry of packets before reverting to normal behavior; for system administrators only.
-n	Specifies not to look up domain names.
-p *pattern*	Specifies content for packets to diagnose data-dependent problems.
-q	Specifies quiet output with only initial and ending summary information displayed.
-r	Specifies to ignore routing and send directly to host on attached network.
-s *packetsize*	Specifies size of packet to send in bytes.
-v	Specifies verbose output and lists all received packets.
ps	Use to report process status (note that ps arguments work with or without a -, and warn you not to use - in the future).
-l	Specifies long format.
-u	Specifies user-oriented format with user name and start time.
-j	Specifies jobs format.
-s	Specifies signal format.
-v	Specifies vm (virtual machine) format.
-m	Displays memory information.
-f	Specifies "forest" tree format.

Table C.1 (continued)

Commands and Flags (continued)

Command/Flag	Description
-a	Displays processes of other users.
-x	Displays processes without controlling terminal (daemons).
-S	Displays add child CPU time and page faults.
-w	Specifies wide output and does not truncate command lines.
-h	Disables header display.
-r	Shows running processes only.
-n	Specifies numeric output for user and wchan fields.
-t*xx*	Specifies only processes with controlling tty xx.
-pids	Lists only specified processes.
--help	Displays help message.
--version	Displays version information.
pwd	Use to display name of current working directory.
--help	Displays help message.
--version	Displays version information.
quota	Use to display disk usage and limits.
-g	Displays group quotas for the executing user's group.
-v	Displays quotas on file systems where no storage is allocated.
-q	Displays only information for file systems over quota.
rm	Use to remove files.
-f, --force	Specifies to overwrite all existing destination files.
-i, --interactive	Requires prompting before overwriting.
-R, --recursive	Specifies to copy directories recursively.
-v, --verbose	Displays file names before moving.
--help	Displays a help message.
--version	Displays version information.
rmdir	Use to remove empty directories.
-p, --parents	Specifies to remove any parent directories listed, if they are empty after the specified files are removed.
--help	Displays a help message.
--version	Displays version information.
sed	Use for processing and editing files in batch mode.
-e	Specifies edit commands to follow as the next argument.
-f	Specifies edit commands to be taken from named file or files.
-n	Suppresses default output.
set	Use to set environment variable (bash, ksh).
setenv	Use to change or add an environment variable (csh).
sort	Use to sort text files by line.
-c	Checks to see if file is already sorted.
-m	Merges sorted files together.
-b	Ignores extra spaces at the beginning of each line.
-d	Sorts by ignoring everything but letters, digits, and blanks.

(continued on next page)

Table C.1 (continued)

Commands and Flags (continued)

Command/Flag	Description
-f	Sorts without case sensitivity.
-I	Ignores non-ASCII characters.
-M	Sorts by month, recognizing three-character month abbreviations.
-n	Sorts numerically.
-r	Reverses result order.
-o output-file	Sends output to specified file instead of standard output.
-t *separator*	Uses indicated character as field separator.
-u	Displays only one of the matching lines.
--help	Displays help information.
--version	Displays version information.
su *otherid*	Use to substitute *otherid* for current userid.
-c *command*, --command=*command*	Runs specified command as other user.
--help	Displays help information.
-, -l, --login	Specifies to start as login shell.
-m, -p, --preserve-environment	Specifies not to change environment variables from current settings.
-s, --shell *shell*	Uses the specified shell instead of the default.
--version	Displays program version.
stop	Use to stop job.
tail	Use to output the last part of a file.
-c [*b,k,m*] N, --bytes N	Displays last *N* bytes of file, in b (512-byte), k (1-kilobyte), or m (1-megabyte) blocks.
-f, --follow	Specifies to keep running and trying to read more from end of file.
-l, -n N, --lines *N*	Displays last *N* lines of file.
-q, --quiet, --silent	Specifies not to display file names.
-v, --verbose	Specifies to always display file names.
--help	Displays help message.
--version	Displays version information.
talk	Use to talk to another user.
tar	Use to create tar archives.
-A, --catenate, --concatenate	Specifies to append tar files to an archive.
-c, --create	Creates a new archive.
d, --diff, --compare	Identifies differences between archive and file system.
--delete	Removes files from the archive.
-r, --append	Appends files to the archive.
-t, --list	Lists contents of the archive.
-u, --update	Updates archive with newer files.
-x, --extract, --get	Extracts files from archives.
--atime-preserve	Specifies not to change access times.
-b, --block-size *N*	Specifies block size of Nx512 bytes.
-C, --directory *DIR*	Changes to specified directory.
--checkpoint	Displays directory names while processing.

Table C.1 (continued)

Commands and Flags (continued)

COMMAND/FLAG	DESCRIPTION
`-f, --file`	Uses specified file or device.
`--force-local`	Forces local archive file regardless of file name.
`-h, --dereference`	Processes linked files, not symbolic links.
`-i, --ignore-zeros`	Specifies to ignore zeros in archives (and not to interpret as EOF).
`-k, --keep-old-files`	Specifies that old files should be retained, not overwritten.
`-K, --starting-file` *`file`*	Starts at file *`file`* in the archive.
`-l, --one-file-system`	Specifies to remain in current file system.
`-m, --modification-time`	Specifies not to extract the file modification time.
`-M, --multi-volume`	Specifies to process as multi-volume archive.
`-N, --after-date` *`date`*`, --newer` *`date`*	Stores files newer than *date*.
`-o, --old-archive, --portability`	Specifies old archive format.
`-O, --to-stdout`	Specifies to extract files to standard output.
`-p, --same-permissions, --preserve-permissions`	Specifies to extract all permission data.
`-P, --absolute-paths`	Specifies to maintain absolute paths.
`--remove-files`	Specifies to remove files that have been added to archive.
`-s, --same-order, --preserve-order`	Specifies list of file names to match archive.
`--same-owner`	Specifies to extract files with same ownership.
`-T, --files-from` *`file`*	Retrieves names of files to extract or create from file *`file`*.
`--totals`	Displays total bytes of created files.
`-v, --verbose`	Displays verbose information about processed files.
`-V, --label` *`name`*	Creates archive with volume name of *name*.
`--version`	Displays version information.
`-w, --interactive, --confirmation`	Requires confirmation for actions.
`-W, --verify`	Verifies information in archive after creating archive.
`--exclude` *`file`*	Specifies to exclude *`file`* from archive.
`-X, --exclude-from` *`file`*	Specifies to exclude files listed in *`file`* from archive.
`-Z, --compress, --uncompress`	Specifies to compress or uncompress the archive.
`-z, --gzip, --ungzip`	Specifies to process the archive with `gzip`.
`--use-compress-program program`	Specifies name of compression program as *`program`*.
`tee`	Use to read from standard input and write to standard output and files.
`-a, --append`	Appends to specified files instead of overwriting.
`--help`	Prints help information.
`-i, --ignore-interrupts`	Specifies to ignore interrupt signals.
`--version`	Prints version information.
`telnet`	Use to connect to and use remote computers.
`-8`	Specifies 8-bit operation, which is not the telnet default.
`-E`	Disables the escape character.
`-L`	Specifies 8-bit operation on output.
`-a`	Attempts automatic login with the current user name.
`-d`	Enables debugging output.

(continued on next page)

Table C.1 (continued)

Commands and Flags (continued)	
COMMAND/FLAG	DESCRIPTION
`-r`	Specifies rlogin emulation.
`-e` *`character`*	Specifies the escape character to control command mode access.
`-l` *`user`*	Specifies the user for remote login.
`-n` *`tracefile`*	Starts tracing connection to *`tracefile`*.
`time`	Use to time a job.
`tin`	Use to read Usenet News.
`-c`	Creates or updates index for listed groups, marking all as read.
`-f` *`file`*	Specifies file to use for newsrc data.
`-h`	Displays help information.
`-H`	Displays introduction to `tin`.
`-I` *`dir`*	Specifies directory to hold newsgroup index files.
`-m` *`dir`*	Specifies mailbox directory to use.
`-M` *`user`*	Mails unread articles to *`user`*.
`-n`	Specifies to load only active, subscribed groups.
`-q`	Specifies startup without checking for new newsgroups.
`-P`	Purges all articles that do not exist. Time-consuming, particularly on a slow connection.
`-r`	Specifies remote news reading from nntpserver.
`-s` *`dir`*	Saves articles to directory specified.
`-S`	Saves unread articles for later reading with `-R` option.
`-u`	Creates and updates index files for all groups .
`-U`	Starts `tin` in background to update index files while reading news.
`-v`	Specifies verbose mode for some commands.
`-w`	Allows quick posting.
`-z`	Specifies to start `tin` only with new or unread news.
`-Z`	Checks for new or unread news.
`touch`	Use to change file times and create empty files.
`-a, --time=`*`atime`*`, --time=`*`access`*`, --time=`*`use`*	Changes access time only.
`-c, --no-create`	Specifies not to create files that do not already exist.
`-d, --date` *`time`*	Updates files with given (not current) time.
`-m, --time=`*`mtime`*`, --time=`*`modify`*	Changes modification time only.
`-r, --reference` *`file`*	Updates files with time of reference file.
`-t MMDDhhmm[[CC]YY][.ss]`	Specifies time argument for setting time.
`--help`	Displays help message.
`--version`	Displays version information.
`traceroute`	Use to identify the route packets take to a network host.
`-f`	Specifies initial time-to-live used in the first probe.
`-F`	Specifies "don't fragment" setting for probes.
`-d`	Enables socket level debugging.
`-g`	Specifies a source route gateway.

Table C.1 (continued)

Commands and Flags (continued)

COMMAND/FLAG	DESCRIPTION
-I	Specifies a network interface to use for probes.
-I	Specifies ICMP ECHO instead of UDP datagrams.
-m	Specifies maximum number of hops to use.
-n	Specifies not to look up domain names for addresses.
-p	Sets base UDP port number for probes.
-r	Specifies to ignore routing and send directly to host on attached network.
-s	Specifies IP address as source for probe.
-v	Specifies verbose output and lists all received packets.
-w	Specifies the number of seconds to wait for a response to a probe.
umask	Use to set the file creation mask
unalias	Use to remove aliases from the list.
-a	Removes all alias definitions.
uname	Use to display system information.
-m, --machine	Displays the machine or hardware type.
-n, --nodename	Displays the node or hostname.
-r, --release	Displays the operating system release number.
-s, --sysname	Displays the operating system name.
-v	Displays the operating system version.
-a, --all	Displays all the above information.
--help	Displays help information.
--version	Displays version information.
uniq	Use to remove duplicate lines from a sorted list.
-u, --unique	Outputs only unique lines.
-d, --repeated	Outputs only duplicate lines.
-c, --count	Outputs number of occurences of each line followed by the text of each line.
-number, -f, --skip-fields=*number*	Specifies number of fields to ignore before checking for uniqueness.
+number, -s, --skip-chars=*number*	Specifies number of characters to skip before checking for uniqueness.
-w, --check-chars=*number*	Specifies number of characters to compare.
--help	Prints help information.
--version	Prints version information.
unzip	Use to manipulate and extract compressed files in a zip file.
-f	Specifies to extract only files newer than those on disk.
-l	Lists archive files in short format.
-p	Extracts files to standard output.
-t	Tests archive files for accuracy and completeness.
-T	Sets the timestamp to the same as the newest file in the archive.
-u	Updates existing files from the archive and creates new files as needed.
-v	Displays verbose or diagnostic version information.
-z	Displays archive comments.
-j	Junks paths and puts all files in the current directory.
-n	Specifies never to overwrite existing files.

(continued on next page)

Table C.1 (continued)

Commands and Flags (continued)

Command/Flag	Description
-o	Overwrites existing files without prompting.
-P *password*	Requires password to decrypt zip file entries.
-q	Performs operations quietly, without displaying most status information.
-qq	Performs operations even more quietly.
uudecode	Use to decode a file created by uuencode.
-o *file*	Directs output to *file*.
uuencode	Use to encode a binary file.
-m	Specifies MIME (Base 64) encoding.
vacation	Use to reply to mail automatically.
-I	Initializes .vacation.db file and starts vacation.
-a *alias*	Specifies alias for vacation user, so that mail sent to that alias generates a reply.
-j	Specifies to always reply, regardless of To or Cc: addressing.
-tN	Specifies the number of days between repeat replies to the same sender.
-r	Specifies to use the "Reply-To:" header if available.
-?	Displays a short help message.
vi	Use for powerful text editing.
-, -s	Specifies no interactive feedback.
-l	Specifies LISP program editing setup.
-L	Lists names of files saved after crashes.
-R	Forces read-only mode.
-r *filename*	Recovers *filename* edit file saved after a crash.
-t *tag*	Starts editor with cursor at tag position.
-V	Specifies verbose output with input echoed to standard error.
-x	Specifies encryption option like that of ex and prompts for a key.
-w*n*	Specifies default window size.
-X	Specifies encryption option like that of ex and prompts for a key, assuming all text is encrypted.
+command, -c *command*	Starts editor and executes specified command.
w	Use to show who is logged on and what they are doing.
-h	Disables header.
-u	Ignores username for current process and CPU times.
-s	Specifies short format, omitting login, JCPU, and PCPU times.
-f	Toggles display of remotehostname.
-V	Displays version information.
wc	Use to count the number of bytes, words, and lines in a file.
-c, --bytes, --chars	Displays only byte counts.
-w, --words	Displays only word counts.
-l, --lines	Displays only newline counts.
--help	Displays help message.
--version	Displays version information.

Table C.1 (continued)

Commands and Flags (continued)

COMMAND/FLAG	DESCRIPTION
who	Use to display information about who is logged onto the system.
-m	Specifies "me", as in "who am I?".
-q, --count	Displays login names and total number of logged on users.
-i, -u, --idle	Displays idle time.
-H, --heading	Displays column headings.
-w, -T, --mesg, --writable	Displays user message status.
--help	Displays a help message.
--version	Displays version information.
write	Use to send a message to another user.
zip	Use to create a zip-format file archive.
-A	Accommodates a self-extracting executable archive.
-b *path*	Specifies a path for the temporary files.
-c	Provides one-line comments for each file in the archive.
-d	Deletes entries from an archive.
-D	Specifies not to create entries in the zip archive for directories.
-e	Encrypts the contents of the zip archive using a password.
-f	Freshens an existing entry in the archive if the new file has been modified more recently than the version in the zip archive.
-F	Fixes the zip archive.
-g	Appends to the specified archive.
-h	Displays help information.
-i *files*	Includes only specified files.
-j	Junks pathname and stores only file name.
-J	Junks prepended data (for self-extracting archives) from the archive.
-l	Translates UNIX text files to MS-DOS text files.
-ll	Translates MS-DOS text files to UNIX text files.
-L	Displays the zip license.
-m	Moves specified files into the archive and deletes originals.
-n *suffixes*	Specifies not to compress files with the given suffixes.
-o	Sets the modification time of the zip archive to that of oldest of the files in the archive.
-q	Specifies quiet mode to eliminate messages and prompts.
-r	Includes files and directories recursively.
-t *mmddyy*	Ignores files modified before the given date.
-T	Tests the new archive and reverts to the old archive if errors are found.
-u	Updates an existing entry in the archive only if the existing file has been changed more recently than the copy in the archive.
-v	Specifies verbose mode to print diagnostic and version information.
-x *files*	Excludes the specified files.
-z	Requires a multi-line comment for the entire archive.
-@	Gets a list of input files from standard input.

INDEX

D

E

F

INDEX

G

H

I

J

K

L

INDEX

M

N

O

P

INDEX

S

T

INDEX

U

V

INDEX

Showme (see process).

df -k /user10 (Room on your disk)

rm -r file directory/name.

ls -la | more

Q: to get out of "top"